The Victorian Experience:
The Poets

THE VICTORIAN EXPERIENCE:

The Poets

Edited by
RICHARD A. LEVINE

OHIO UNIVERSITY PRESS

Library of Congress Cataloging in Publication Data
Main entry under title:

The Victorian experience, the poets.

Includes bibliographical references.
Contents: Introduction / Richard A. Levine —
The persistence of Tennyson / Jerome H. Buckley —
Browning's irony / Clyde de L. Ryals — [etc.]
1. English poetry—19th century—History and
criticism—Addresses, essays, lectures.
I. Levine, Richard A.
PR593.V48   821'.8'09   81-4020
ISBN 0-8214-0447-4   AACR2
ISBN 0-8214-0748-1   AACR2

© Copyright 1982 Ohio University Press
Printed in the United States of America
All rights reserved.

Contents

INTRODUCTION

RICHARD A. LEVINE

This book and one on the essayists are companion volumes to *The Victorian Experience: The Novelists.* As with the *Novelists,* the charge to the critics was to discuss their writer from the vantage point of their familiarity with the author's work and times, and in the process to comment on a number of basic questions such as why they teach the writer, what their involvement with the writer is, and what their response to the writer is after years of study. These are important concerns in an age of increasingly specialized studies where we run the risk of sometimes losing sight of the whole writer and of our chosen mission of teaching. Once again, happily, the essays are more than personal testaments and are qualitatively very different from critical introductions to major authors. I gave the critics only the most broad and general guidelines and urged them to develop their essays as their imaginations and interests dictated.

As I wrote in the opening chapter of the novelists volume, the thesis of *The Victorian Experience* grows out of a Victorian critic's concern with the artistic engagement and the sometimes confused, often precarious state of literary studies in our own time. It was Walter Pater who said, "Not the fruit of experience, but experience itself, is the end." Pater was distinguishing between one's direct engagement with the artistic work (experience) and the intellectual process by which one attempts to recapture and make some rational sense of that engagement (the fruit of experience). If one might quarrel with Pater's sense of the "end," one cannot argue with Pater's chronology here:

the experience clearly must precede the fruit of the experience. That some readers, for example, try to interpose the intellectualizing process between themselves and the literary work is a violation not merely of Pater's notion, but—more importantly—of the integrity of the engagement itself. Upon reflection, most of us would acknowledge that our initial responses to works which moved or touched or excited us (and not only in positive or favorable ways) were not, properly speaking, intellectual. Certainly a portion of that initial response might well be intellectual, but the totality of our response comes much closer to Pater's sense of the fundamentally dynamic and individual quality of perception:

> the whole scope of observation is dwarfed into the narrow chamber of the individual mind. Experience, already reduced to a group of impressions, is ringed round for each of us by that thick wall of personality through which no real voice has ever pierced on its way to us, or from us to that which we can only conjecture to be without. Every one of those impressions is the impression of the individual in his isolation, each mind keeping as a solitary prisoner its own dream of a world. Analysis goes a step further still, and assures us that those impressions of the individual mind to which, for each one of us, experience dwindles down, are in perpetual flight; that each of them is limited by time, and that as time is infinitely divisible, each of them is infinitely divisible also; all that is actual in it being a single moment, gone while we try to apprehend it, of which it may ever be more truly said that it has ceased to be than that it is.

And when Pater says that "he who experiences these impressions strongly, and drives directly at the discrimination and analysis of them," he is still articulating the same ordering of critical activity: experience followed by the fruit of experience; experience followed by discrimination and analysis of the experience.

For some teachers of literature, especially in our age of the rhetorician, Pater's priorities can be unnerving, although they should not be. Indeed, Pater might well be offering a necessary corrective to much that has gone wrong in the academy. Too often the intensity of textual analysis—especially when elevated almost to an end in itself—has blunted the reader's sense of experiencing the artistic work rather than having complemented and augmented it. Certainly if we have learned something in the last quarter-century of academic criticism, it is precisely that explication of the text can enrich the reader's experience of the work. It is the quality of the engagement of the reader and the literary work which is at the heart of all criticism and scholarship. It is this wedding of experience and the fruit of experience which gives new meaning to Carlyle's statement in *The Hero as Poet:* "We are all poets when we read a poem well."

The premise of this book is that we can go a step beyond Pater's concept of experience and the fruit of experience by adding as a third possibility a new kind of experience which grows out of the first two. This is not intuitive or impressionistic criticism, because the critic's response is predicated on a considerable amount of learning and thought. Even though I believe that Pater is right when he talks of the fruit of experience being secondary to the experience itself, I see the essays in this book combining the experience and the fruit of experience and in the process producing a different kind of experience as the critic attempts to isolate and develop his or her involvement with a writer. Put in another way, we assume that the critic has spent a great deal of time in learning and study, in close analysis, in scholarship and criticism. Now, in a crucially important moment, the critic embraces the subject and tries to capture the distillation of all those factors which have been forced to run together—the critic attempts to describe his or her experience of the writer: not a new kind of criticism, but perhaps one of the logical ends of criticism and scholarship.

I rehearse all of this for two reasons. First, of course, I wish to offer a context for the essays which follow. Second, however, the approach of *The Victorian Experience* met with objections which are important enough to require comment. Those few objections are symptomatic of an illness within the academic world of letters which threatens to become more serious if untreated—and if untreated, to become epidemic. Because the movement from epidemic to normative to endemic is not unknown to us, I believe there is reasonable cause for alarm. My quarrel with particular critics is not the result of conventional thrusts and parries of academic dueling, but rather the results of the critics' basic lack of sympathy for the kind of criticism which *The Victorian Experience* strives to demonstrate. It is precisely that lack of sympathy which speaks to a major problem facing literary studies in our time. I do not refer only to the French critical orbit. As with any new intellectual or ideological movement, literary or otherwise, there will be excesses. Nevertheless, in the hands of talented readers the continental mode of inquiry has produced illuminating commentary. However, the failing I refer to may have been enlarged by the rush to embrace the "new" criticism, for in that rush too many understood too little of the method and aims of the new approaches.

While one realizes that some modes of discourse are admittedly difficult because a new language is being developed or because the ideas they convey are particularly dense, one must at the same time insist upon a style as close as possible to the lucid and fluent style of the best writers among us and upon a subject matter and approach which ultimately broaden rather than narrow the literary experience. To applaud the opaque and the insignificant is to limit dangerously the audience and force of literary commentary. It is, in Gerald Graff's term, to turn literature against itself. Therefore, I worry about those who questioned the validity of critics' caring about their own involvement with writers and the wider consideration of the relationship between literature and life. In a paradoxical turn, such a position seems to frown not only on the clarity of critical prose, but upon the humanity of literary studies—perhaps, even, upon the humanity of literature itself. It is particularly ironic that such positions have found their way into the study of Victorian life and letters, into a time which witnessed the growth of realism and an acute relationship between belles-lettres and life.

It is toward the broadening and liberating possibilities of literature that the approach of *The Victorian Experience* is directed. In accepting the Nobel Prize in 1962, John Steinbeck said: "Literature was not promulgated by a pale and emasculated critical priesthood singing their litanies in empty churches—nor is it a game for the cloistered elect." Steinbeck concluded his speech with the following: "Having taken God-like power, we must seek in ourselves for the responsibility and the wisdom we once prayed some deity might have. Man himself has become our greatest hazard and our only hope. So that today, Saint John the Apostle may well be paraphrased: In the end is the *word,* and the word is *man,* and the word is *with* man." And if the future of literature is immense, it is so because the word is with men and women who will share it with others.

THE PERSISTENCE
OF TENNYSON

JEROME H. BUCKLEY

Before he had written scarcely any of his best
poetry, the young Keats predicted, "I think I
shall be among the English Poets after my death." Tennyson, who had
frequent misgivings about all poetic fame, could never, even at the
peak of his career, be so assured of his own ultimate place. Despite
such public acclaim as no other English poet before or since has ever
enjoyed (or suffered), the reaction against Tennyson had well begun
by the time of the fulsome funeral eulogies in 1892, and it continued
with growing intensity and then with settled conviction for at least the
next half century. As late as 1944 W. H. Auden, in an ill-considered
and inaccurate preface to a selection of Tennyson's verse, declared the
once revered ancient sage of Aldworth "undoubtedly the stupidest"
of English poets, though the one with "the finest ear, perhaps"—an
estimate hardly calculated to secure him an elevated position in the
poetic hierarchy.

My own experience as reader and teacher has unfolded against the
background of Tennyson's decisively changing reputation. Few would
now question his pre-eminence in Victorian poetry or indeed his high
rank—somewhere close to that of Keats—among all the major English poets. But when I was a student in the late 1930s, I was made
to feel that my confessed sympathy with Tennyson and his world was
either wilfully heterodox or simply unsophisticated, naive, and even
"Victorian." T. S. Eliot's sensitive appraisal in 1936 of Tennyson's
"abundance, variety, and complete competence"[1] should have prepared the way for a thorough revaluation. Yet the common critical
response remained that of the narrator in Faulkner's *Light in August,*

1

where the Reverend Gail Hightower, unable to pray, opens his dog-eared copy of Tennyson and surrenders to an inane mellifluous music: "Soon the fine galloping language, the gutless swooning full of sapless trees and dehydrated lusts begins to swim smooth and swift and peaceful. It is better than praying without having to bother to think aloud. It is like listening in a cathedral to a eunuch chanting in a language which he does not even need to not understand."

Whether or not the minister's seduction is being accomplished by *Idylls of the King,* as the woodland lusts might suggest, the *Idylls* surely fared worst of all in the widespread repudiation of Tennyson and, perhaps for that very reason, the sequence as a whole, the longest and most ambitious work of the poet's lifetime, has received the most sustained favorable attention in a general revival. Harold Nicolson, attempting in the 1920s to rescue from neglect some of the lyrical poetry, chose to exclude the *Idylls* from any consideration. Many years later, reviewing my *Tennyson* in 1961, he saw no reason to alter his decision. By that time, however, most other reviewers were willing to concede to the *Idylls* a considerable merit, though some regarded my reading of the poem as excessively indulgent. Since the early sixties I have seen a good many new interpretations, more enthusiastic as well as more discerning than mine, mostly by American scholars (the British for some reason remain rather distrustful of the poem): in recent years we have had a half-dozen full-length books devoted entirely to the *Idylls,* an elaborate variorum edition, and a score of intelligent articles. In the new climate of opinion one bold Tennysonian can declare the *Idylls* "surely the major ironic work of art of the century,"[2] and another can extol it as "one of the four or five indisputably great long poems in our language" and confidently adjudge its author "the greatest poet of the nineteenth century."[3] Now when Faulkner's prose begins to seem muddled and portentous, Tennyson's lordship of language is openly acknowledged, and his meanings assume new cogency.

If posterity's shifting regard cannot change the fixed canon of a poet's work, it can make it more accessible, recover forgotten or neglected verses, suggest fresh emphases, and find unsuspected vitality in the familiar by submitting it to new critical approaches or bringing new standards and values to bear upon it. In Tennyson we have such amplitude, such range of choice, that we may linger over titles that his contemporaries slighted or did not even know, and by the same token we may be less patient with other pieces, such as the domestic genre studies, which were once much admired. (Yet I must speak with some hesitation of the poems I have considered to be beyond recovery, for there are already signs of a reviving interest even in the usually dismissed "English Idyls."[4]) We are now likely to accord "The Vision of Sin," for example, or "The Two Voices" (despite the idyl near its end) more attention than the Victorians were ready to grant it. Thanks to Eliot's praise of its metrics, we do not ignore "The Hesperides," which Tennyson himself suppressed. Our continuing interest in the wasteland imagery of modernist literature lends "The Holy Grail" an increased immediacy and a "relevance" both literary and social. Our sense of Tennyson's early commitment to his craft was enhanced by our acquaintance with the exuberant *Devil and the Lady* and the boyish virtuosity of the other juvenilia first published by the poet's grandson in 1930 and 1931. And our analysis of his aesthetic sensibility and growth has been enormously aided by our access to the unpublished notebooks now at Harvard and the manuscripts no longer under restriction at Trinity College, Cambridge.

Among Tennyson's shorter poems, "Ulysses" has received the most extensive reinterpretation in our time.[5] From the beginning a popular piece, it was said to have convinced Prime Minister Peel that the poet well deserved a civil pension. But Peel's high opinion apparently rested on his acceptance of its heroic statement at face value. We must assume that neither he nor the countless admirers "Ulysses" attracted during its first hundred years had any notion of the complexity and ambiguity that recent critics have detected beneath its vigorous assertion. Far from being a ringing challenge to heroic hearts, "Ulysses," we now are told, expresses an unconscious death wish. Its rhythms, we are to understand, are weary rather than resolute; it is elegiac in tone, backward-looking instead of hopeful, nostalgic for a lost good. Some ask whether the poem is a dramatic monologue or a soliloquy or an inconsistent amalgam of the two. Some question the occasion, circumstances, and precise setting of the speech. Others impugn the integrity of Ulysses himself, as a restless man prepared to rationalize his retreat from social responsibility, to abandon his people, desert his aged wife, and speak condescendingly of his "most blameless" son. His conduct is alleged to be wholly selfish, and his values more remote from Tennyson's own than are those of the cautious and contemned

3

Telemachus. Even his sanity has been doubted, for the men he addresses, the veterans of his remembered travels, must all, according to the Homeric account, now be dead. A few scholars, on the other hand, point to Dante rather than Homer as the true source and then proceed to show that Dante regarded Ulysses' last voyage as an act of unseemly and self-damning curiosity rather than a "work of noble note." It is a modern dogma that we must trust the poem rather than the poet. But when I sense that the logic of the poem is being unduly distorted, I return for guidance to the poet's own declaration of purpose. " 'Ulysses,' " said Tennyson, "was written soon after Arthur Hallam's death, and gave my feeling about the need of going forward, and of braving the struggle of life perhaps more simply than anything in *In Memoriam.*"[6] Giving no less weight to this than to revisionist readings, I am inclined once more to accept "Ulysses" as a heroic affirmation. And I am encouraged to do so by another bit of extrinsic evidence, the fact that one of Tennyson's unpublished sonnets, written a year or two earlier, supplied the image of "life piled on life" in an incontestably assertive context. If "Ulysses" were really expressing a death wish, even an unconscious one, it seems odd that the sonnet as one of its immediate verbal sources should extol "the sharp desire of knowledge" and the will to go forever forward:

> I thank thee, God, that thou hast made me live:
> I reck not for the sorrow or the strife:
> One only joy I know, the joy of life.[7]

Though in many ways patently more complex than "Ulysses," *In Memoriam* has inspired a less contentious and, I think, more revealing critical scholarship. Its place in the Tennyson canon has never been seriously threatened, and its central argument, though often questioned, has seldom been ingeniously subverted. Of all Tennyson's major poems. *In Memoriam* spoke most directly, for over fifty years, to the hopes and misgivings of the Victorians, and even during the period of most hostile reaction, its lyric cry commanded a reluctant respect. Indeed it seems to me a measure of its enduring quality that it has remained visible above all the tides of taste and that it has offered new perspectives to each passing generation. At any rate, it is the Victorian poem to which I most frequently return both as an achievement in itself and also as an anticipation of my twentieth-century concern with art and the role of the artist, alienation, autobiography, and the subjective impulse.

* * *

Published in 1850, *In Memoriam* is in more than one sense the central poem of the nineteenth century. If science is the intellectual watchword of the age, *In Memoriam* asks the most urgent questions of the new science as it clashes, or seems to clash, not just with the old faith but with any code of human and humane values. (We may, by the way, be struck by the high incidence of questioning in the rhetorical pattern of the whole, where we find about eighty interrogative sentences or phrases in the one hundred and thirty-one sections.) Do the stars run blindly in a world of meaningless chance? Is the individual human life, "Fore-shorten'd in the tract of time," at all significant in the context of a geology which postulates an ageless uniformitarian change, drawing down the aeonian hills? Does Nature, "red in tooth and claw," suggest that all the hardwon human ideals of truth and justice are merely hopeless delusions? Has the race itself any surer tenure than the extinct monsters, "seal'd within the iron hills" and now uncovered by the new paleontology? Above all, if Science can "prove we are," that is, can account for consciousness and conscience in mechanical terms, will Science or any other force really "matter" to us, provide us with any real incentive to go on living? Though Tennyson's formulation of such questions seems sometimes naive, his insight into the essentials of early-modern science is impressive and often profoundly moving. Some readers in our century have complained that the evolutionary speculations in *In Memoriam,* since they never approach the idea of transmutation, do adequately anticipate *The Origin of Species,* which appeared nine years later. But Tennyson is the poet, not the biologist, and as such he rightly chooses to probe the imaginative impact of current opinion, to "question" science, rather than to propound or even endorse scientific theory.

As for Darwin's great book, it seems just possible that Tennyson —in a properly poetic way—may have influenced its dominant metaphor. *In Memoriam* presents a personified Nature, "careless of the single life," bringing perhaps one of fifty seeds to bear, apparently "careful of the type," yet really in effect ruthlessly crying out, "A thousand types are gone; / I care for nothing, all shall go." Darwin writes, rather selfconsciously, as if his invoking of personification were an encroachment on the poet's territory, "It has been said that I speak of natural selection as an active power or Deity. . . . Every one knows what is meant and is implied by such metaphorical expressions; and that they are almost necessary for brevity.... *Nature,* if I may be allowed to personify the natural preservation or survival of the fittest, *cares nothing* for appearances, except insofar as they are useful to any being.... Man selects only for his own good; Nature only for that of the being which she tends."[8] We do know that Darwin read some of Tennyson's poetry with close attention, but whether or not actual "influence" on this passage is at all likely, the parallel in image and idiom suggests at least some broad cultural affinity between the scientist and the poet.

Nevertheless, though it addressed current issues in science, *In Memoriam* is not solely or even primarily a public document. I should like to consider it in more personal terms, terms which attract our regard on a quite different level. For it was as "central" to the poet as to the age, and the year of its publication was actually the middle year of his life. What Tennyson called "the voice of the human race speaking through him,"[9] which may be heard in some of the sections, gains its resonance from the depth of private experience. As in other great elegies, the subjective component is large; the poem is at least as much a meditation on the surviving self as it is a celebration of the dead friend. In the shadow of a death, which seems to mock the meaning and even the stability of the past, the poet reflects on the drives and conflicts of his own early life, until at length, recovering, he can suggest the direction of his mature work.

If we bear in mind the several planes of meaning in *In Memoriam,* we may interpret its inner action in current psychological terms, seeking not to give it a merely modern relevance, yet nonetheless reminding ourselves that some of its concerns may not be far removed from our own. Of the many questions the poem asks, the most personal is one that strikes at the very core of selfhood and all its fond illusions: "So runs my dream, but what am I?" The poet is describing what we should now call an "identity crisis," and a state of feeling all the more intense in that he is not selfconsciously exploiting that fashionable malady. The death of his friend has left him bewildered in an aimless youth and reluctant or unable to move onward to a purposeful maturity. The crisis occurs in what the identity psychologist Erik Erikson would recognize as the period of adjustment and delay between adolescence and "the onset of responsible adulthood."[10] The resolution of the poem depends on the recovery from the crisis and the acceptance of the mature responsibility, that is, on the poet's finding himself in his work and social role, the conviction that vocation will define identity. At the outset the poet has lost his sense of a living self. He is tempted "To dance with Death, to beat the ground." He seems "to fail from out [his] blood." His heart "beats . . . low"; he would willingly exchange places with the dead man and so give up "The life that almost dies in me." Indeed when he stands at the door of Hallam's house, it is he who partakes of death, "like a guilty thing" (the ghost in *Hamlet*), for the dead friend "is not here." As poet he calls upon the resources of language: how is he to explain himself to himself or to others when words at best but "half reveal / And half conceal the Soul within"? He fears radical derangement of personality and questions his own sanity; has the shock of grief, he wonders,

> stunned me from my power to think
> And all my knowledge of myself;
>
> And made me that delirious man
>   Whose fancy fuses old and new,
>   And flashes into false and true,
> And mingles all without a plan?

Here the loss of identity, of knowledge of the self, with the accompanying failure of the sense of time needed to maintain continuity and perspective, brings the poet close to the condition we now call schizophrenia, which makes no adequate distinction between the subjective and the objective and mingles at random the past and the present, the false and the true. But his very ability to describe such a state protects him from it.

Whereas many recent confessional poets, with the sanction of R. D. Laing's defense of the schizophrenic, cultivate the alienating subjectivity of madness, the poet of *In Memoriam* clings resolutely to the last shreds of sanity. He is thus eventually able to confront his "inner trouble," even his "spectral doubt," and to consider the general course of individuation, the process by which the separate self emerges. The new-born baby, he reflects,

> Has never thought that "this is I":
>
> But as he grows he gathers much,
>   And learns the use of "I," and "me,"
>   And finds "I am not what I see,
> And other than the things I touch."

> So rounds he to a separate mind
> From whence clear memory may begin,
> As through the frame that binds him in
> His isolation grows defined.

(The phrasing here curiously anticipates Erikson's account of "the battle for autonomy," an early stage in the acquisition of identity, when the infant learns to delineate his "worlds as 'I' and 'you' and 'me' and 'mine.' " And the speculation foreshadows the attention of Jacques Lacan to the *stade du miroir,* the phase at which the infant becomes conscious of his mirror-image.)[11] But the poet is not yet assured of the strength of his "separate mind." The self still seems reduced to a low light, a sick heart, slow "wheels of Being," a "sensuous frame, . . . racked with pangs." In despair he now asks his crucial question—"But what am I?"—which he answers with the metaphor of infancy and a serious pun (for the Latin *infans* means "not yet speaking"):

> An infant crying in the night:
> An infant crying for the light:
> And with no language but a cry.

As he regains clarity of perspective and confidence in more articulate language, he repudiates the tyranny of dream and the strange psychic displacement or transference it can bring; dreaming, he has found "a trouble" in Hallam's eye, but now

> I wake, and I discern the truth;
> It is the trouble of my youth
> That foolish sleep transfers to thee.

Hallam in life had been the source of stability, the sort of friend, according to the identity psychologist, whom a youth, alienated to a degree from father and family, may regard as a "new ancestor" and "genuine contemporary," a solid object of trust and fortitude.[12] Memory and willing idealization now evoke a sense of Hallam's heroic vitality strong enough to defy time and death and so to establish a persisting continuity with the poet's lost self.

Memory, however, must be cautiously examined. The poet would reject any force that tried to summon a ghostly presence from the dead, and he would repudiate any physical vision of Hallam as hallucination brought by "a wind / Of memory murmuring the past." The true spiritual vision, as in the intense ninety-fifth section, comes involuntarily to the soul within, calmly, in the moment of mystical insight, and the self is directly transformed, almost beyond description:

> And all at once it seemed at last
> The living soul was flashed on mine,
>
> And mine in this was wound, and whirled
>   About empyreal heights of thought,
>   And came on that which is, and caught
> The deep pulsations of the world. . . .
>
> Vague words! but ah, how hard to frame
>   In matter-moulded forms of speech,
>   Or even for intellect to reach
> Through memory that which I became.

Such intuitive experiences, not unlike Wordsworth's "spots of time," were, as we know, familiar to Tennyson at intervals all his life, eclipses of the self but also guarantees of the self's meaning, and at least in their aftereffect, quickeners of the self's identity, agents (the psychologist would say) of "the ego process" by which the individual maintains "a subjective sense of invigorating sameness" and a coherence of past and present.[13] None of the arguments for God or faith-in-life, the poet now confesses, begins to match the personal affirmation, "I have felt." Though words may be vague or inadequate, language is to remain his medium of self-expression and communication. At last, near the end of *In Memoriam*, he turns purposefully to his work in society, to the lessons of sorrow "under human skies" and a repudiation of profitless yearning for ontological certitude:

> I will not shut me from my kind,
>   And, lest I stiffen into stone,
>   I will not eat my heart alone,
> Nor feed with signs a passing wind: . . .
>
> What find I in the highest place,
>   But mine own phantom chanting hymns?
>   And on the depths of death there swims
> The reflex of a human face.

He has found his identity in the role that he must play. He has fought with death and conquered his fear, has come to see life and death as related parts of one whole, like morning star and evening star, twin aspects of a single planet.

In Erikson's psychological terms, we may say that the narrator by the end has achieved his "ego integrity" or "the ego's accrued assurance of its proclivity for order and meaning,"[14] the final mark of his maturity, the rejection of despair, and a spiritual realignment with his culture. In Tennyson's more aesthetic terms, the poet has come to see —or rather to "see in part"—

> That all, as in some piece of art,
> Is toil coöperant to an end.

The simile here is drawn appropriately from the poet's vocation as artist, and the implicit element of self-esteem which contributes to the sense of identity arises, as Erikson might explain, from the sense of skill and skillful performance in a social role, the awareness of a particular talent.

In Memoriam is not, of course, a case history, and it should not be reduced to such or abstracted in terms of a modern technical jargon. I wish simply to suggest that it accomplishes, along with much else, a serious plumbing of the soul within and that a later depth psychology may supply a provocative gloss on its intentions. It is clearly accessible to other readings, some more distinctly "Victorian." It may, for example, be related to what I have called "the pattern of conversion," the dialectic of the Everlasting No and the Everlasting Yea described in *Sartor Resartus,* the movement from self-absorbed denial toward a purposeful assent to work and society. But though the poem contains much private reference and a good deal of direct autobiography, Tennyson's actual career scarcely followed any single precise paradigm. The lonely lyrist, having had a sudden illumination (such as the epiphany of Section XCV) or even a more dramatic Carlylean "Baphometic Fire-Baptism," did not emerge irrevocably as the public bard. Yet there is in his work over the years from 1830 to 1850 a gradual maturing of attitude and concern, a slow resolution of early aesthetic conflicts, a deepening emphasis on social themes, and an increasing assurance of personal idiom.

My own "experience" of Tennyson has affirmed his status as a major poet—that is, as a poet ample in bulk and repeatedly, though not consistently, strong in performance, completing a remarkably full curve of development, responsive to a magnificent literary heritage, and faithful to his own rich endowment. To T. S. Eliot *In Memoriam* was "a long poem made by putting together lyrics, which have only the unity and continuity of a diary, the concentrated diary of a man confessing himself."[15] Though I should hesitate to call Tennyson, apart from the elegy, a confessional poet, I like to think of the whole Tennyson canon as one long poem made of many parts, some short, some of considerable length, diverse in tone, quality, and appeal, held together by a distinct sensibility and a variously modulated voice.

* * *

"What hope is here for modern rhyme?" asks the questioning elegist, overwhelmed by a sense of man's brief span in an apparently infinite and eternal universe, where all too soon even the best of poets and poetry must surely be forgotten. Nevertheless, from the beginning, Tennyson like Keats was very much aware of the masters of verse, against whose achievement, he hoped in more sanguine moods, his own might ultimately be measured. No earlier English poet, not even Keats, was more preoccupied, during his apprenticeship to his craft, with the essence of poetry and the vocation of the poet. In the early twentieth century, when "high modernism" was the dominant poetic mode, poetry itself frequently seemed the all-sufficient matter of poetry. More recently, at least among the "confessional" writers, the poet's own troubled and often alienated life has become his one recurrent theme. In Tennyson both subjects—that is to say art and self —serve as prelude to a broader social and intellectual concern.

Tennyson's earliest pieces pay the homage of respectful imitation to the poetic tradition, especially to Pope and Milton, Ben Jonson and Byron. His Cambridge prize poem, "Timbuctoo," warns that Discovery, the way of modern science, threatens the Spirit of Fable, the myth-making imagination of the artist. "Recollections of the Arabian Nights" and "The Hesperides" somewhat later celebrate with a rich sensuosity the flight into an exotic world of pure art, whereas "The Lotos-Eaters" and the allegorical fragment "Sense and Conscience" suggest the perils, as well as the seductions, of a sensuous aestheticism, and "The Vision of Sin" depicts a poet betrayed into cynicism and at last destroyed altogether by yielding to the life of sensations. "The Palace of Art," heavily revised between 1832 and 1842, presents the most elaborate and overt attack on the "crime" of the aesthetic Soul that withdraws from humanity into a complacent "Godlike isolation," for "he who shuts Love out in turn shall be / Shut out from Love." Yet the highly wrought description of the palace furnishings

11

testifies to the strong appeal of self-indulgent escape. "The Lady of Shalott," which on a primary level sketches the tale of Lancelot and Elaine, also intimates the dilemma of the alienated artist; the Lady, doomed to weave her "magic web with colours gay," able to observe reality only at the double remove of tower and mirror, pines for the living world outside her prison-studio, but perishes, "singing her last song," as soon as she enters it. Despite its protective title, "Supposed Confessions of a Second-rate Sensitive Mind" is more serious than ironic in depicting the ambivalence of the poetic temper, the reluctance or inability to make a firm conforming commitment. "Amphion," a comical salute to the ancient musician who could make all nature dance, places the blame for modern alienation on the present "brassy age," which has replaced the Muses by "withered Misses," prosy bluestockings suspicious of all true creative energy. "Will Waterproof's Lyrical Monologue," on the other hand, turns an easy colloquial irony on the poet himself, whose diffidence of outlook and play with language divert him from any grave subject matter; Will craves a mellow pint that he may pledge

> No vain libation to the Muse,
>   But may she still be kind,
> And whisper lovely words, and use
>   Her influence on the mind,
> To make me write my random rhymes,
>   Ere they be half-forgotten;
> Nor add and alter, many times,
>   Till all be ripe and rotten. . . .
>
> Half fearful that, with self at strife
>   I take myself to task;
> Lest of the fulness of my life
>   I leave an empty flask. . . .
>
> I hold it good, good things should pass:
>   With time I will not quarrel:
> It is but yonder empty glass
>   That makes me maudlin-moral.

"The Epic," an English idyl framing the stately "Morte d'Arthur," invokes a similar ironic self-portraiture, now to anticipate and disarm criticism; the poet Everard Hall has tried to burn up his epic since it has seemed to him old-fashioned, full of "faint Homeric echoes, nothing-worth," but he is soon persuaded, with little urging, to read aloud what has been retrieved from the fire, "mouthing out his hollow oes and aes, / Deep-chested music," precisely as, we know, Tennyson intoned his own verses. And "Edwin Morris" tellingly mocks another Tennysonian poet, whose style contains "A touch of something false, some self-conceit, / Or over-smoothness." In much of his work, then, before the writing of *In Memoriam* and coterminous with it, Tennyson appears as the distinctly self-conscious artist—defensive, self-critical, deeply aware of his medium and his aesthetic difference.

Of all these poems from the first half of his life, *The Princess* has been the most frequently slighted in the general revaluation of Tennyson and, I think, the most widely misunderstood. Yet it repays attention as a revealing index to his attitudes and resources. It is indeed, as the prologue designates it, a strange "medley" of farce and sober sentiment, satire and direct expository statement; and its intentions, as the conclusion admits, seem uncertain and confused, for it begins as a lively mock heroic and moves toward a solemn close. The Princess herself is an ambiguous figure. Her heroic posturing is patently absurd; yet the Prince as narrator considers her far less an object of ridicule than her father or bellicose brother, and he makes it quite clear that her defense of feminism is more to be respected than scorned. But whatever view we are expected to take of women's liberation, which gave (and should still give) the medley a topical relevance, late changes in the poem suggest the even greater importance of a secondary theme. The "weird seizures" of the Prince, added to the fourth edition, shift the focus from the Princess to the narrator himself, who now has the artist's gift or curse of second sight and the compulsion to distinguish appearance from reality, shadow from substance, in the very tale he is telling:

> The Princess with her monstrous woman-guard,
> The jest and earnest working side by side,
> The cataract and the tumult and the kings
> Were shadows; and the long fantastic night
> With all its doings had and had not been,
> And all things were and were not.

So obsessed with the problem of illusion, the Prince represents the poet, and the Princess becomes the imperious Muse, like the withdrawn Soul in "The Palace of Art," to be construed perhaps as the Jungian *anima*. [16] The union of Prince and Princess, the final harmony of the artist and his art, which completes the action, is foreshadowed by the mountain idyl, "Come down, O maid," which the Princess reads aloud. But it is to be regarded by both as the achievement, rather than the surrender, of identity. In aesthetic terms, the maid's descent from the heights to the valley implies not the domestication of the woman, but the humanization of the Muse.

* * *

The turn to humankind, announced at the end of *In Memoriam,* did not of course mean that after 1850 Tennyson lost all concern with poetry as itself a sufficient subject matter. Among his later pieces we find his memorable tributes to Milton, Lucretius, Catullus, and Virgil. From his last decade comes "Parnassus," raising the old question of poetic fame and deploring the "terrible Muses" of the nineteenth century, Astronomy and Geology. And to the same period belong "Merlin and the Gleam," a discreet review of his own poetic career, and his angry sonnet "Poets and their Bibliographies," rebuking the modern "Love of Letters, overdone," which has "swampt the sacred poets with themselves" by reprinting their discarded or suppressed verses. Nonetheless, art as subject is less conspicuous in his later work, and society correspondingly provides a more frequent and urgent theme. In the year of *In Memoriam* Tennyson became Poet Laureate, with some sense of obligation from time to time to write "occasional" poems on current affairs, such as his verses to welcome Alexandra and to salute Marie Alexandrovna or his odes to celebrate the Queen's golden jubilee and to mark the opening of various international exhibitions. But none of the Laureate pieces, not even, I should think, the resounding "Ode on the Death of the Duke of Wellington," now greatly attracts our attention. The social poetry that remains most compelling to us makes but small concession to the prejudices and complacencies of his time.

Maud, Tennyson's first extended work after accepting the post of Laureate, must have seemed distressingly and almost inexplicably radical to the serene and self-assured new generation of the 1850s, for the poem relates the disaffection of its hero to a predatory *laissez-faire* economy, the malpractices of a money-mad materialism in the "Wretchedest age, since Time began." As the original subtitle, "The Madness," suggests, the hero is often rather less than sane; yet there is method in his distraction, and Tennyson, we know from other sources, endorsed a good deal of his social indictment. Ralph W. Rader, though he may overstate the case, has shown that there is undoubtedly a considerable autobiographical component in *Maud,* probably a reflection of the poet's early love of Rosa Baring and its frustration by her snobbish family.[17] Yet the ranting hero is not simply Alfred Tennyson, exorcising a ghost from the past. In some respects he more closely resembles Tennyson's passionate brother Frederick. But in most ways he is rather the typical superfluous young man of much post-Romantic literature, both English and European, "at war with [himself] and a wretched race," unable or unwilling to conform to the moral crassness of a Philistine society. As such he has had his ready parallels in our own time. Unlike the alienated youths of the recent past, however, he ultimately seeks redemption by rushing off, "at one with [his] kind," on a battleship to a foreign war, less hypocritical, he fondly hopes, than the domestic war of trade. Our *post-factum* knowledge that the Crimean conflict was an international "blunder," for which no one properly reasoned why, scarcely renders the hasty denouement of the poem more convincing or acceptable. Yet the ending detracts but little from our sense of the dramatic energy with which the volatile hero is self-depicted.

The manner of *Maud,* as I have suggested elsewhere, may well owe something to Sydney Dobell's *Balder* and Alexander Smith's *A Life Drama,*[18] products of the febrile Spasmodic School, which enjoyed a considerable vogue in the fifties. Tennyson had certainly a far greater mastery of language and structure than any of the Spasmodics, but their tempestuous overstatement in lyrical drama could conceivably have furnished him the sanction for an increased exuberance of expression. *Maud,* at any rate, evinces a new freedom of style and a bolder metrical virtuosity. Unlike many of the early poems, it is not concerned with art and the role of the artist. Yet it is written with great aesthetic assurance, the skill of an accomplished librettist able to devise arias of operatic intensity. Tennyson is experimenting with his own new form, the "monodrama," in which, he explained, "different phases of passion in one person take the place of different characters."[19] *In Memoriam,* of course, delineated changing emotions, but with no such abrupt transitions, no such violence or variety of tempo, and with less effect of a detached judgment of the speaker. However personal it was in origin, *Maud* moves steadily toward an objective dramatic mode. An achievement in itself, it is also a vivid and necessary part of the one long poem that is Tennyson's continuing development.

Quickened interest in *Idylls of the King,* the writing of which preoccupied Tennyson immediately after *Maud* and at intervals for the last thirty-five years of his life, should induce us to look more carefully at some of his other late pieces less likely to win our approval but once conspicuous in the total context. *Enoch Arden,* for example, can scarcely be expected to recover the overwhelming appeal it made to its first readers, and we may wonder why a generation later so sophisticated a composer as Richard Strauss chose to set it as a tone-poem for speaker and piano.[20] Nonetheless, if we can for a moment forget Walter Bagehot's cogent objection to its ornateness and our own distaste for a certain domestic sentimentalism, we may recognize in the telling of the tale an undeniable narrative skill and a real sense of dramatic situation. The plays written after 1875 present similar problems of judgment. Though they won for a time a kind of *succès d'estime,* comparable perhaps to that of the theatrical ventures of the later T. S. Eliot, they no longer cry aloud for revival. Still, behind the outmoded Elizabethan structure and borrowed diction, the fatal imitation of Shakespeare, lie a fresh sense of scene and a genuine ability again and again, especially in *Becket* and *Queen Mary,* to set character in action. But most of us, I should think, will now be concerned, if at all, with such works simply as byproducts of the narrative and dramatic talent that shaped the *Idylls.*

Though adapted as "The Passing of Arthur" to close the *Idylls,* the "Morte d'Arthur" of 1834 differs distinctly from the eleven poems that precede it in the final sequence. It is marked by a stately subjectivity; Arthur sadly probes his own weariness and disillusion, and Tennyson, we may assume, grieving at the time of composition for the other Arthur who was his friend, identified with his mood. The other *Idylls* are more objective, less lyrical in intention and effect. In them the King is too recessive a figure to stand as the poet's surrogate. Even in "The Coming of Arthur" he remains largely in the background, while gossip and hearsay dispute his origins. Only in "The Holy Grail," when he describes his moments of mystical insight, does he seem to speak for the poet, and then only if we know Tennyson's claims to a like experience. Several recent commentators, somewhat in the mood of the revisionist critics of "Ulysses," have argued that Arthur, far from being "the blameless King," is in fact the villain of the piece, the cause of a general deceit and disillusion, insofar as he holds his all-too-human knights to an impossibly high standard of conduct, which none, except perhaps Galahad, can sustain.[21] *Idylls of the King* as a whole is indeed dramatic and impersonal in method. But Tennyson, I believe, nonetheless endorses Arthur's integrity, and he makes the poem, even in the long stretches where Arthur is not present, the vehicle of his deepest concern, designed to carry his mature vision of a society in peril. Unlike *Maud,* however, the *Idylls* suffers no immediate topicality; Arthur's "last weird battle in the west" is a timeless Armageddon rather than a mismanaged engagement in the Crimea. Whereas some of the Victorians thought the Arthurian setting merely the excuse for a fancy-dress masquerade, we can now appreciate the value of a deliberately distanced mythology and a free use of symbols remote from the demands of a circumstantial realism.

As the epilogue indicates, the *Idylls* shadows "Sense at war with Soul,/Ideal manhood closed in real man." The sequence from beginning to end deals in symbols and frequently hints at the allegorical; yet it is seldom precisely an allegory with one-to-one meanings in the manner of the old morality plays. Soul appears purely only in a few saintly characters—Galahad, the long-suffering Enid, the innocent young Gareth, and, of course, "the blameless King," who seems less the real man than the ideal manhood by which the motives of other men are to be measured. "The Holy Grail" presents several degrees of spirituality and a good deal of soul-sickness, insofar as a self-seeking religiosity makes the grail-quest, for most of Arthur's knights, a tragic dereliction of duty. Sense, discriminated and individualized, proves the strong antagonist, especially in the second two-thirds of the sequence. Here we have surely something more than the "dehydrated lusts" that Faulkner alleges: in the sensualism of the opportunistic Tristram, the violence of the frustrated Pelleas, the senile sexuality of Merlin aroused by the lubricious Vivien. Throughout the *Idylls* adulterous passion, even when as in the relationship of Lancelot and Guinevere it involves a measure of real love, becomes the token of social deceit, of the larger perfidious self-interest that eventually destroys the kingdom. If the trees are "sapless," they are simply symbols of the withered wasteland to which Camelot in its decadence returns.

The final arrangement of the *Idylls* "in Twelve Books" has prompted unfortunate comparison with twelve-book epic poems such

17

as *Paradise Lost* or *The Aeneid* and fruitless debate as to whether or not so loose a sequence can properly be considered epical. Had the *Idylls* been issued "in Twelve Cantos," we should have had a clearer understanding of the poet's method and intention. For the poem, like its medieval sources, is far closer in mode to romance than to epic; it deals in magic and illusion, deliberately violates clocked time, and freely mingles the probable and the symbolic, the fact and the dream. Merlin describes Camelot as a city "built to music," and the poem itself moves musically with recurrent images as leitmotifs. The older epic structure is consciously fragmented; a series of variations on the theme of moral stability and social decadence replaces a developing linear narrative. Tennyson was assuredly aware of the epic tradition and at one time perhaps determined to contribute to it. But as early as *The Princess* he saw the difficulties of making epic or even mock-epic materials credible to a self-conscious analytic Victorian world. The less presumptuous mode of romance in the *Idylls* allowed him to dispense with grand heroics, to place the King himself as hero at a distance, and to concentrate attention on the unheroic conduct of fallible human beings, involuntary representatives of the moral condition of their society. In my own experience as teacher, I have found that any one Idyll, unlike a single book of an epic, can be discussed and appraised as a self-contained unit but that each, nonetheless, gains power and interest from its place in the full context, the lighter early ones as foils to the darker late pieces, and the latter, written with a greater urgency, as grim counterparts to the first chronicles of innocence.

In the words of "Merlin and the Gleam," "Clouds and darkness/ Closed upon Camelot"; the *Idylls* ends with little hope, except that the new sun, mentioned in the last line, will bring a new year, and the heart-breaking cycle, without any promise of real progress or improvement, will begin all over again. The sequence as a whole, personal at least in implication, thus reinforces T. S. Eliot's image of Tennyson as "the saddest of all English poets, among the Great in Limbo."[22] And many of the most memorable lyrics and nostalgic and elegiac passages throughout the Tennyson canon seem to justify that designation: "Break, Break, Break," "Tears, Idle Tears," "Tithonus," the tribute to Catullus and his "hopeless woe," the salute to Virgil ("Thou majestic in thy sadness"), the plangent cries of *In Memoriam* and its description of April, anticipating and possibly suggesting Eliot's "cruellest month":

> Is it then regret for buried time
> That keenlier in sweet April wakes . . .?

But to overstress the sadness is to see Tennyson simply as Auden saw him, as the master of melancholia and of little else. It is to ignore his great range of mood and subject matter and, more damagingly, to exaggerate his direct emotional engagement, to underestimate his power of detachment, his aesthetic dispassion and cool craftsman's regard for shaped language and calculated metre.

When he applauds Goethe's singing "To one clear harp in divers tones," Tennyson suggests his own ideal of variety and something of his own achievement. If he had an acute awareness of life's transience and tragedy, he had also, as a good deal of his early work up through *The Princess* reveals, a sound sense of comedy and a capacity for a distanced appraisal of himself and others. Among the later poems, two companion dialect pieces represent different shades of irony: the "Northern Farmer—Old Style" exemplifies an earthy humor commingling with an amused sympathy, and the "Northern Farmer—New Style"—with its insistent gallop, "Proputty, proputty, proputty"—evinces a decided gift for satire. But Tennyson is not essentially a humorist, and his satire often, as in *Maud* and in both the early and the late "Locksley Hall" poems, tends to become shrill invective or heavy-handed sarcasm. Somewhere between the comic and the sad, he devised a gently ironic happy medium, a middle style, the true felicity of which has seldom been recognized and still less frequently recaptured. His letters in verse and rhymed greetings to F. D. Maurice, to Edward Lear, to Benjamin Jowett, to Mary Boyle; "The Daisy" (sent to his wife from Edinburgh); the last dedication to Emily ("June Bracken and Heather"); "In the Garden at Swainston" (remembering Sir John Simeon); and the gentle memorials for W. H. Brookfield and W. G. Ward, all in this middle style, are all testaments of friendship and affection and models of an urbane, Horatian grace. Polished but natural, warm or witty as the occasion demands, the idiom recurs throughout Tennyson's work. It appears even in *In Memoriam,* where the epilogue, addressed to Edmund Lushington, consciously relaxes the tension of the elegy and assigns its style to the man himself:

> And thou art worthy, full of power:
> As gentle; liberal-minded, great,

19

> Consistent; wearing all that weight
> Of learning lightly like a flower.

And it persists into the poems of the last decade, notably as in the dedication of "Tiresias" to Edward FitzGerald on the latter's seventy-fifth birthday:

> And so I send a birthday line
> Of greeting; and my son, who dipt
> In some forgotten book of mine
> With sallow scraps of manuscript,
> And dating many a year ago,
> Has hit on this, which you will take,
> My Fitz, and welcome, as I know,
> Less for its own than for the sake
> Of one recalling gracious times,
> When, in our younger London days,
> You found some merit in my rhymes,
> And I more pleasure in your praise.

The maker of such verses is hardly the loud-voiced bard of Max Beerbohm's caricature, declaiming *In Memoriam* to his Sovereign. But then, as less wilful biographers than Lytton Strachey have demonstrated, the Queen herself was scarcely the stiff matron who declined all but elegiac entertainment. Tennyson criticism of the past twenty years has had the task of discarding the bardic stereotype which was devised by the Edwardians and accepted with little question by the Georgian modernists and their American counterparts. Closer attention to Tennyson's language and the various levels of his rhetoric has done much to humanize the poet, to establish his personal identity and yet to widen and deepen our respect for his impersonal achievement. No artist, however timeless his vision, can or should wholly escape his place in time, for the artifact remains the most enduring witness to the taste and temper of an age. We have now begun to value Tennyson's artistry not only as a unique thing in itself, but also, and no longer apologetically, as a conscious and unconscious reflection of the culture that produced it, a vital part of our general Victorian experience.

NOTES

1. T. S. Eliot, *"In Memoriam,"* *Essays Ancient and Modern* (London, Faber and Faber, 1936), p. 175.

2. James R. Kincaid, *Tennyson's Major Poems: The Comic and Ironic Patterns* (New Haven, Yale University Press, 1975), p. 3.

3. John D. Rosenberg, *The Fall of Camelot* (Cambridge, Mass., Harvard University Press, 1973), p. 1, beginning a spirited defense and cogent analysis of the *Idylls.*

4. Cf. Christopher Ricks, *Tennyson* (New York, Macmillan, 1972), pp. 277–286, and A. Dwight Culler, *The Poetry of Tennyson* (New Haven, Yale University Press, 1977), pp. 106–128. Both Ricks and Culler are relatively unsympathetic to the *Idylls of the King.*

5. On "Ulysses" and Peel, see Hallam Tennyson, ed., *Alfred, Lord Tennyson: A Memoir,* 2 vols. (New York, Macmillan, 1897), I, 225. The revisionist criticisms of "Ulysses" appear with varying emphases in Paull F. Baum, *Tennyson Sixty Years After* (Chapel Hill, University of North Carolina Press, 1948), pp. 299–303; Robert Langbaum, *The Poetry of Experience* (New York, Random House, 1957), pp. 89–91; E. F. Chiasson's sharp attack on the "godless" adventurer, "Tennyson's *Ulysses,*" in John Killham, ed., *Critical Essays on the Poetry of Tennyson* (London, Routledge & Kegan Paul, 1960), pp. 164–173; Clyde de L. Ryals, "Point of View in Tennyson's *Ulysses,*" *Archiv,* CIC (1962), pp. 232–234, and Ryals, *Theme and Symbol in Tennyson's Poems to 1850* (Philadelphia, University of Pennsylvania Press, 1964), pp. 126–130.

6. *Memoir,* I, 196.

7. "Life," *Memoir,* I, 59, reprinted in Christopher Ricks, ed., *The Poems of Tennyson* (London, Longmans, 1969), pp. 296–297.

8. Charles Darwin, *The Origin of Species and The Descent of Man* (New York, Modern Library, n. d.), p. 65. Cf. my article, "Victorian England: the Self-conscious Society," Josef L. Altholz, ed., *The Mind and Art of Victorian England* (Minneapolis, University of Minnesota Press, 1976), p. 8. Since Darwin in *The Descent,* p. 492, quotes from the *Idylls,* it is reasonable to assume his familiarity with *In Memoriam,* especially those sections bearing on evolutionary science.

9. *Memoir,* I, 305.

10. Erik H. Erikson, ed., *The Challenge of Youth* (Garden City, N. Y., Doubleday, 1965), p. 10.

11. See Erikson, *Identity, Youth and Crisis* (New York, Norton, 1968), p. 108, and Jacques Lacan, *The Language of the Self* (Baltimore, Johns Hopkins University Press, 1968), pp. xiii, 160–161.

12. See Erikson, *Challenge of Youth,* p. 14.

13. Erikson, *Identity,* p. 19.

14. Erikson, *Childhood and Society* (New York, Norton, 1963), p. 268.

15. Eliot, p. 183.

16. Lionel Stevenson suggested a similar Jungian reading of Tennyson's early poems; see "The 'High-Born Maiden' Symbol in Tennyson,'" *PMLA,* LXVII (1952), 732–743. Culler, pp. 38–47, extends Stevenson's idea and speculates on Tennyson's symbol of "the immured maiden."

17. See Ralph W. Rader, *Tennyson's Maud: the Biographical Genesis* (Berkeley, University of California Press, 1963).

18. So, at any rate, I suggested in *The Victorian Temper* (Cambridge, Mass., Harvard University Press, 1951), pp. 63–65.

19. *Memoir,* I, 396. The genre of *Maud* is discussed in detail F. E. L. Priestley,

Language and Structure in Tennyson's Poetry (London, Deutsch, 1973), pp. 107–119, and by Culler, pp. 190–213.

20. On the performance of the Strauss *Enoch Arden* in 1897 ("a great success," because the narrator was a popular actor, even though "the work has only slight musical interest"), see George R. Marek, *Richard Strauss: the Life of a Non-hero* (New York, Simon and Schuster, 1967), p. 112.

21. On the ambiguity of Arthur's influence, see Stanley J. Solomon, "Tennyson's Paradoxical King," *Victorian Poetry,* I (1963), 258–271; on Arthur as the coercer of men's minds, see Clyde de L. Ryals, "The Moral Paradox of the Hero," *From the Great Deep* (Athens, Ohio, Ohio University Press, 1967), pp. 69–93.

22. Eliot, p. 189.

BROWNING'S IRONY

CLYDE DE L. RYALS

When one focuses intently on a literary figure, it is difficult not to overvalue him: one justifies one's work by insisting on the greatness of the subject of that work. Well aware of my own bias I nevertheless maintain that Robert Browning is the most daring English poet of the nineteenth century and that he came near to perfection of what he dared. His achievement, I believe, sets him among the most innovative poets in English.

Coming out of the closed world of the Enlightenment (and before that the medieval Christian system), the English Romantics of the period beginning around 1790 sought to synthesize into a harmonious union the disparate elements which confronted them. In *The Prelude,* Wordsworth tells of those counsels of head and heart which, working together, can alone make for right action; and Coleridge, especially in Chapter XIV of *Biographia Literaria,* speaks of the synthesis and reconciliation of opposites as the highest imaginative achievement: for the older Romantic generation the purpose of the imagination was to enclose the chaotic world in a harmonious sphere. Among the younger English Romantics only Keats addressed himself directly to "negative capability"—the acceptance of antinomies—but he was made uneasy by it and in the *Hyperion* fragments was surely working towards a means by which he hoped imaginative unity might be achieved. In sum, the English Romantics are visionary, allegorical, and mythical in their pursuit of a world where all discordant elements are harmonized into an ultimate unity.

It has long been a commonplace of Browning scholarship to trace the poet's literary lineage from the English Romantics, especially

23

Shelley. But once we question this bit of conventional wisdom we realize that almost no poet could be less like Shelley—or Wordsworth or Byron. For Browning does not offer a vision of the world redeemed, as does Shelley, or of the world devoid of values, as Byron so often does. On the contrary, with Browning it is not a question of either/or; rather, it is a matter of both/and. More than any of his immediate predecessors and contemporaries Browning is able to hold a view of the world in which the most contradictory statements to be made about it are alike true. In a word, Browning is an ironist—the supreme ironist among English poets of the nineteenth century.

Born in 1812, Browning came to manhood at a time when the great Romantics were either dead or moribund. For a while, if we can attribute to the poet some of the history of the speaker of *Pauline,* Browning shared the visionary hopes of Shelley but soon discovered that they were purely utopian and not to be realized. Further self-examination revealed to him something not to be gained from Shelley —namely, that in the phenomenal world truth is unattainable, although it surely exists. Three basic positions about the individual and truth—arrived at early—remained with the poet all his life: one cannot speak the truth because (1) language is inadequate to express it; (2) one's point of view—and ultimately there is no such thing as an overview—permits only certain perspectives on truth; and (3) one's sense of self, one's *amour propre,* necessitates special pleading. In short, man is limited by his speech, his angle of vision, and his need to justify himself. Or put another way, no matter how "objective" one wishes to be, to use the familiar terms of early nineteenth-century philosophical and literary discourse, one is always forced, by the very nature of reality itself, into "subjectivity." To the person who recognizes the validity of this proposition irony is the only stance possible.

The kind of irony Browning adopted was not the old rhetorical irony which had a polemical aim. It was instead more nearly like the romantic irony of the German writers of the end of the eighteenth century—the Schlegels, Novalis, Tieck—which had its home in philosophy and was metaphysical and aesthetic. As Friedrich Schlegel said in *Lyceum Fragment* No. 108, romantic irony "originates in the union of a sense of an art of living and a scientific intellect, in the meeting of accomplished natural philosophy and accomplished philosophy of art. It contains and incites a feeling of the insoluble conflict of the absolute and the relative. . . . " Like God, the ironist is both in and out of his creation—immanent and transcendent, subjective and objective. It is not without aesthetic implications that the Incarnation became the basic mythic pattern of Browning's poetry.

In what follows I shall sketch an account of Browning as an ironist. My valuations of his work will doubtless seem eccentric; in any case they are not the views generally accepted. I make no pretense at rendering a full and balanced account. I focus mainly on the early works (1) because they are still little known, (2) because those of the 1850s and sixties have already been copiously studied and evaluated, and (3) because I have already said, in *Browning's Later Poetry* (1975), almost all I have to say about this neglected last period in the poet's career.

From the beginning we find Browning attempting to break away from his Romantic inheritance. *Pauline* (1833), a lyric "confession," as its subtitle proclaims, is nevertheless, according to Browning's prefatory note to the 1868 edition, "dramatic in principle" and thus is the poet's first attempt to attain scope and diversity within an essentially lyric mode. The speaker of *Pauline* is realized by us dramatically in that we learn about him as much from how he tells of himself as from what he actually says. And although we are invited to sympathize with him, it is difficult to lend him our sympathy because of the emotional extravagances of his utterance. Hence the reason for many readers' difficulty with the poem: we are presented with a speaker who does not command our sympathy yet cannot be ignored. Browning had not yet learned how to individualize character to the extent that he could elicit our sympathetic interest in foolish or even despicable speakers.

Moreover, even though the speaker believes that he can bid farewell to Shelley (apostrophized as "Sun-Treader"), to Romantic ideals, and to the lyric mode, we discover that he retains a very Romantic notion of the poet's role. Pauline has convinced him that "a perfect bard was one / Who shadowed out the stages of all life" (883–84), which is to say that he is now willing to deal in verse with the general life instead of the personal emotion. But he retains the Romantic idea of the bard as priest and prophet (1019) who from his overview of life will disclose secrets about man and nature unrevealed to ordinary men.

It appears that the events narrated in *Pauline* are reflections of Browning's own experience, and because of that fact many readers

25

have understood the poem as the poet's own confession. Browning seems to have realized that this intended dramatic confession might be mistaken for his own, and to distance the poem from himself—and incidentally to cast in doubt the idea of the poet as bard—he enclosed it within a framework which signals us that *Pauline* should be read as something objective and distinct from the poet's own personality. The headnote in Latin, the motto in French, the affixed dates at the beginning and end, the long note in French signed by Pauline—all these invite us to read *Pauline* as a fictional edition.

Editing is of course a way of distancing experience. And the fiction of editing allowed the young Browning a technical means of distancing story from narration, of making the lyric and subjective more dramatic and impersonal. Moreover, the fiction of editing allowed the poet to be, like God, both immanent and transcendent, both in and out of his work.

In the last analysis, this rudimentary attempt at a fictional edition —what Pauline as editor speaks of in a note as a "sketch" of a new genre—permitted the young poet to find a solution to his Romantic desire, adumbrated in the confession, to arrive at the supreme point of view of the Absolute. "I cannot chain my soul," the speaker says;

> it will not rest
> In its clay prison; this most narrow sphere—
> It has strange powers, and feelings, and desires,
> Which I cannot account for, nor explain,
> But which I stifle not, being bound to trust
> *All* feelings equally—to hear *all* sides:
> Yet I cannot indulge them.... (593–99; italics added)

Obviously no life can indulge such a desire to view an object or an event from all sides, not sequentially, but simultaneously, to have in effect the last word. Only God, as Author and Judge, can assume this stance: "And what is that I hunger for but God?" asks the speaker. God is, Browning was to write in *Paracelsus,* "The PERFECT POET, / Who in his person acts his own creations" (II, 648–49). But might not other authors, imperfect poets, emulate the Divine if they also became judges? As editors, who in effect are judges, might they not have the final word? The fictional edition would then be a strategy in satisfying the Romantic urge to "be all, have, see, know, taste, feel, all" (278) while admitting all the time that such a desire, outside art, is utterly impossibly of fulfillment. Already, at age twenty-one, Robert Browning was well on his way towards a pronounced ironic view of life; it but remained for him to discover the forms which would best allow him to indulge it.

Paracelsus (1835), Browning's next work, seems to be cast in the form of a five-act play, but the poet specifically warns in the foreword that it is "a poem, not a drama." And certainly any effort to view it as a drama, as almost all Browning's critics do, must necessarily result in misvaluation. What we find is five important moments in the life of the protagonist in which he examines and reveals his inner life and is brought by his utterance at each moment to new insights allowing him to act. These moments of crisis are instants of lyrical intensity presented discontinuously; joining them together must be the work of the reader. As Browning said in the Preface, it is a "difficult form" which depends "on the intelligence and sympathy of the reader for its success—indeed were my scenes stars it must be his co-operating fancy which, supplying all chasms, shall connect the scattered lights into one constellation—a Lyre or a Crown." In effect, the five parts are—in spite of the fact that there are other characters who are not mere auditors, as in *Pauline*—like five monologues offered as a narrative of the protagonist's life. The pattern of the poem is ironic in that false attainment results from true aspiration in Scenes I and II and true attainment stems from false aspiration in Scenes IV and V.

Paracelsus is the first of Browning's many historical characters. If the enclosing of the confession in *Pauline* within a kind of fictional edition was a means of distancing and objectifying something of a personal experience, the turning to history and a historical character, plus the commentary on the historical context provided in the notes, was a further means of objectification of what certainly must have been some of the poet's own thoughts and aspirations. Born at the end of the fifteenth century, Paracelsus lived in an age of transition, in many respects resembling Browning's own. Humanism was emphasizing the importance of life in this world, science was providing a material explanation for phenomena formerly conceived as of supernatural origin, theology and religious practice were undergoing radical change—all alluded to in the several references to Erasmus, Paracelsus' own scientific research, and Martin Luther. In other words, Paracelsus lives in a time when self-definition is no longer a given, when the soul has become problematic. *Paracelsus,* more plainly than *Pauline,* is a poem in which, to quote the preface to the 1863 edition of *Sordello,* the poet's "stress lay on the incidents in the development of a soul."

Browning's hero fancies that he can realize his essential self only by knowing all that is to be known. Denying all help from friends or sages of earlier times, Paracelsus sets off on his quest for total knowledge. Failing in his quest, he encounters a young poet who too has sought an absolute—to "love infinitely, and be loved" (II, 420)—and hence has not put to use the talents he possesses. Because he could not reproduce "lovingly" in his art all the beauty and joy of the world, he has produced nothing. Aprile in his dying moments discovers that "God is the PERFECT POET" (II, 648) who alone can experience absolute love and beauty. But Paracelsus is unmindful of the vision vouchsafed to and related by Aprile, and abjuring the desire to know infinitely, he vows to seek infinite love. On this second quest he of course meets with no more success than on the first, and only in the last scene, in his dying hour, is he granted an understanding of the necessary limits on earthly love and knowledge.

In the last part, Paracelsus, like Aprile in Scene II, learns that his earlier quest had been ill-conceived because it had been founded on the idea of a static universe. Since "progress is / The law of life" (V, 741–42), both Paracelsus and Aprile had been deluded from the start. Aprile had wanted to record in art every aspect of reality; Paracelsus had wished to know the total creation; and each had despised his achievement because it had not attained completeness. Just before they died, each learned that the meaning, the "power" and "love," for which each had sought lies in the incompleteness of the process, learned in other words that failing to attain the goal each had sought was in part the way of attaining the power and love proper to human life. In their quests for the perfect they had overlooked the value of the imperfect in an evolving universe in which every new stage of advance modifies the past. Man's "half-reasons, faint aspirings, struggles / Dimly for truth" are "all ambitious, upward tending" (V, 876–80), and in a dynamic universe will go on forever, one stage leading to another which in turn is to be transcended. The insight permitted Paracelsus is that success is failure and failure is success enough: life is not having and resting, but being and becoming.

Although the revelation granted to Paracelsus is presented as a paradox, it nevertheless is meant to stand as final truth. And this works against the ironic arrangement of the parts and also Paracelsus' own discovery that all explanatory systems are inadequate because language can never be sufficiently refined to deal with ultimate truth. At this point Browning apparently was not yet ready to forgo formal closure, even though it was at variance with the ideas presented in the work.

The irony in both *Pauline* and *Paracelsus* is largely a matter of form—and elementary at that. The completion of *Paracelsus,* however, with its enunciation in Part V of the doctrine of becoming, provided Browning with a philosophical basis for his irony which allowed him to enlarge his conception of it to cosmic scope. For in a state of becoming, the principle of contradiction is not applicable: anything can be both itself and not itself at any specific moment, it being in the process of becoming something else. Once Browning accepted the idea of progress with its attendant idea that being is also becoming— that *a* is both *a* and not *a*—then the way was opened to the kind of irony which is to be seen not so much as a form of irony or as a device but as a way of presenting it, really the dramatization of irony. Many of the implications of such an irony were set down by Friederich Schlegel, some of whose works Browning may have known directly or, more likely, as mediated through Carlyle. It was, however, an Englishman who probably delineated for the young poet the dramatic possibilities of irony as a cosmic view. Writing on the irony of Sophocles in 1833, Connop Thirlwall observed that in the *Antigone,* Sophocles impartially presented two equal and opposite points of view and, expanding on this, remarked that irony may reside in the attitude of an ironic observer or, more precisely, in the situation observed:

> There is always a slight cast of irony in the grave, calm, respectful attention impartially bestowed by an intelligent judge on two contending parties, who are pleading their causes before him with all the earnestness of deep conviction, and of excited feeling. What makes the contrast interesting is, that the right and the truth lie on neither side exclusively: that there is no fraudulent purpose, no gross imbecility of intellect, on either: but both have plausible claims and specious reasons to alledge, though each is too much blinded by prejudice or passion to do justice to the views of his adversary. For here the irony lies not in the demeanor of the judge, but is deeply seated in the case itself, which seems to favour each of the litigants, but really eludes them both.

The most interesting debates or conflicts are not, Thirlwall writes, those in which evil is pitted against good. For this case . . . seems to carry its own final decision in itself. But the liveliest interest arises when by inevitable circumstances, characters, motives, and principles are brought into hostile collision, in which good and evil are so inextricably blended on each side, that we are compelled to give an equal share of our sympathy to each, while we perceive that no earthly power can reconcile them; that the strife must last until it is extinguished with at least one of the parties, and yet that this cannot happen without the sacrifice of something which we should wish to preserve. (*The Philological Museum*, 2 [1833], 489–90)

It was with such ironic possibilities in mind, whether gained from Thirlwall or not, that Browning sat down to write *Strafford*, probably the first play in English consciously designed as a dramatization of irony.

Once we understand the ironic intent of the play, even surface ironies become almost immediately apparent. The characters are far from being "the healthy natures of a grand epoch" of whom Browning spoke in the Preface. At best Strafford and Pym are monomaniacs, devoted, against all reason, to the furtherance of an idea—to the monarchial principle in the case of Strafford, to the parliamentary in the case of Pym. Yet if we investigate further, we find that what drives them, as well as Lady Carlisle, is not principle but love, in all three cases love frustrated.

Strafford is enchanted by the King. Despite every act of perfidy and disloyalty on Charles' part, Strafford remains utterly faithful to the King. Besottedly, like a romantic lover, he adores Charles, not the King but the man, has come "to love the man and not the king— / The man with the mild voice and mournful eyes" (II,ii,292–93). In the case of Pym there is a contrary movement. Where Strafford casts off notions of office in manifesting his love for the person, Pym puts aside the notion of love and friendship to serve the office. When he sees that Strafford devotes himself exclusively to Charles and denies his former friendship with the leader of the parliamentarians, Pym, like a scorned lover, becomes in his own mind "the chosen man that should destroy / The traitor" (IV,ii,159–60).

The dialectical movement of the antagonists shows that, in Thirlwall's words, "both have plausible claims and specious reasons to alledge, though each is too blinded by prejudice or passion to do justice to the views of the adversary." Both Strafford and Pym are led by belief in their causes to condone methods and actions of which they would otherwise disapprove. Strafford is loyal to a person whom he knows to be worthless and pursues a cause and courses of action which he knows to be futile. Pym places his faith in Strafford despite his former friend's known opposition to the parliamentary cause, and when it becomes plain that Strafford will support the King under all circumstances, Pym resorts to acts in total violation of parliamentary principles, including connivance with the King and collusion with the King's party. This means that the audience is faced with the paradox that the better man represents the worse cause.

Almost certainly the conflict between Pym and Strafford was the germ of the play: which is to say, the play was conceived as an ironic drama of character. It is of this, no doubt, that Browning speaks when in the Preface he refers to *Strafford* as a drama of "Action in Character, rather than Character in Action." Yet the young poet was unable to sustain or tolerate the openness and indeterminacy of ironic art. He was still at the stage where he felt compelled to offer some approximation of reconciliation and harmonious resolution. Throughout the play Pym and Strafford alike refer to a "meeting" between them which must take place. But both agree in the last scene that although this is the inevitable encounter, it is not to be the anticipated meeting: the tryst so long awaited will be better postponed till heaven (V,ii,291–310). Given the countermovement of their characters, no reconciliation can take place; yet Browning permits the possibility of a resolution by postponing the meeting till an afterlife: which is to say, he allows a certain sentimental pretense, something totally alien to the nature of irony.

In addition, Browning attempted to provide a stable center for this drama of dialectical movement: the "meaning" would focus on Lady Carlisle. Pym and Strafford were the historical *données:* the portraits of them are, Browning said, "faithful." "My Carlisle, however, is purely imaginary" (Preface). Why is this so? Because the dramatist initially conceived of his play as a struggle between, in Thirlwall's words, "two contending parties" in which "the right and the truth lie on neither side exclusively." Then came the afterthought that the play perhaps needed not only something of a conventional romantic interest but also a moral center. If everyone else in the play was to be fickle, self-serving, or blindly deceived, at least in Lady Carlisle there would be one "good" character who was faithful, selfless, and aware of the deceptions about her. What results, alas, is an incredible character.

31

Carlisle's love for Strafford is both selfless and hopeless. She loves a man who does not love her but instead loves another—the King. And she constantly hides from him all evidence of the King's duplicity so as to assure his love for Charles: "One must not lure him from a love like that! / Oh, let him love the King and die!" (II,ii,243–44). To the last scene she keeps up this deception, pretending that it is the King and not she who has made plans for Strafford's escape from the Tower. She speaks no more after Pym is discovered at the door by which Strafford is to leave his prison, so that the last ninety-three lines are devoted to dialogue between the two antagonists, a fact which alone suggests her lack of centrality to the action of the play.

It is only by linking her to the major ironic theme of the play—deception—that Browning escapes making her totally extraneous. More than the other characters she is aware of the discrepancy between things as they are and things as they seem. With her various pretenses Carlisle is conscious of playing a role. Indeed, she regards herself and others as actors in a play, a notion which the other characters share. As she says, "there's a masque on foot" (II,ii,260). This self-consciousness on the part of the *dramatis personae* means that the characters become ironic observers and, as well, victims of irony to the extent that they doubt the meaningfulness of their actions in the play. Strafford, for example, wonders at the end whether history will declare the chief part in this masque to have been played by an actor named "the Patriot Pym, or the Apostate Strafford" (V,ii,57).

The characters' sense of being observers and victims in a play is underscored by their reiterated belief that they are but puppets pulled by a master puppeteer. This is not limited to the Presbyterians, who, as good Calvinists, feel that their actions are predestined. Even the King feels, "I am in a net / And cannot move" (IV,iii,82–83). But there is really no question of the irony of fate at all: there is only the irony of falsely believing oneself trapped by a fateful irony: in actuality the characters are free to do as they choose.

The characters not only see themselves as actors in a play but also regard themselves and their circumstances as part of a text to be interpreted. Reports and communiqués are constantly read and studied and more often than not misunderstood. As Strafford says, only time, "the busy scribe" will provide the "curious glosses, subtle notices, / Ingenious clearings-up one fain would see" (V,ii,52–55).

In this play Browning is concerned with showing that because words are only signs and not the things themselves and because men use words to rationalize their actions, the text which is life and living can never be interpreted in a wholly satisfactory way. One speaks truly only when one has nothing to hide, from oneself as well as from others. In the phenomenal world this never happens, even though one can delude oneself like Pym, who believes that "the great word went from England to my soul" (IV,iii,99). The only time when word and thing become truly united is that which Strafford foresees:

> Earth fades, Heaven dawns on me: I shall stand next
> Before God's throne: the moment's close at hand
> When Man the first, the last time, has leave to lay
> His whole heart bare. . . . (V,ii,204–07)

Until that time language will remain a deceptive veil through which it is impossible fully to pierce.

The relationship of word and thing, veil and truth, body and soul touched upon in *Pauline, Paracelsus* and *Strafford* is given extended study in Browning's next poem. *Sordello* (1840) is well known, by title at least, as a difficult poem. It becomes more penetrable, however, when one recognizes it as one of the supreme examples of ironic art. For the poem has as its chief subject the impossibility of writing the kind of poem its author would like to write and yet is, at the same time, a brilliant example of the type of art to which he aspires. To borrow the paradox of *Paracelsus,* its failure is also its success.

Let us first consider what Schlegel called the ironist's recognition "of the impossibility and necessity of total communication" (*Lyceum Frag.* No. 108). Like his Sordello, Browning would say it "All at once" (II,626). Yet language is linear: a poem is a text to be inspected one word at a time, in a given sequence, while perception—and by perception Browning means abstract perception or idea or character as well as visual perception pure and simple—is simultaneous: that is, all the elements that contribute to a perception are grasped at once. Sordello finds that "perceptions whole, like that he sought / To clothe, reject so pure a work of thought / As language: Thought may take Perceptions's place / But hardly co-exist in any case, / Being its mere presentment—of the Whole / By Parts, the Simultaneous and the Sole / By the successive and the Many" (II, 589–95). This being the case, how may any verbal work of art achieve simultaneity? Sordello finds that it cannot, and so, unable to express his "whole dream" (II, 603), he gives up poetry entirely.

The poet, on the other hand, continues, both in his own voice and as the narrator of the poem, to write; and he learns, at the end of Book III, what Sordello learns in Book V—namely, that language is a social enterprise, poetry a dialogic art. Where Romantic bards sing to themselves—"All poetry is of the nature of soliloquy," said J. S. Mill in "What Is Poetry?" (1833), carrying Romantic theory to its logical conclusion—Browning's poet would engage his audience in the enterprise and demand, as Browning himself had in the Preface to *Paracelsus,* that the audience join in the construction of the poem. This may well be why Browning chose for his hero a poet-troubadour, one whose art depends on interaction with his audience. The form of such a work would depend on its language, "brother's speech," a language of sparseness and suggestiveness:

> a single touch more may enhance,
> A touch less turn to insignificance
> Those structures' symmetry the Past has strewed
> Your world with, once so bare: leave the mere rude
> Explicit details, 'tis but brother's speech
> We need, speech where an accent's change gives each
> The other's soul—no speech to understand
> By former audience—need was then to expand,
> Expatiate—hardly were they brothers! true—
> Nor I lament my less remove from you,
> Nor reconstruct what stands already: ends
> Accomplished turn to means: my art intends
> New structure from the ancient. (V,631–43)

But even this new kind of poetry, although it will allow more to be expressed than ever before, will prove inadequate to deal not only with all human experience but also with what the poet himself wants to say: the poet "must stoop contented to express / No tithe of what's to say —the vehicle / Never sufficient" (V,652–54).

Fully aware of the impossibility of total communication, Browning nevertheless has his go at "saying it all at once." As the narrator tells us in the beginning, a poet who would set forth "unexampled themes" and embody "quite new men" must be present in his work as well as absent from it, or, as he says in Book III, the poet works "as a god

[who] may glide / Out of the world he fills, and leave it mute / For myriad ages as we men compute, / Returning into it without a break / O' the consciousness" (610–15). The creations of such a poet are characterized both by fixity and looseness, enclosure and open-endedness. Thus the ironic poet is both like Eglamor, who sought to apprehend experience as "his own forever, to be fixed / In rhyme, the beautiful, forever" (II, 205–06), and also like Sordello, who penetrates to the perception that in all "true works" there is more energy than form can totally encompass (III, 619–30). This is why the narrator of the poem can dismiss and yet at the end embrace Eglamor and plead for and still condemn Sordello as artists; for the poet of *Sordello* is both a poet of closure and of openness, one whose "art intends / New structure from the ancient." Hence *Sordello* is organized on an epic pattern, the present action broken by a long flashback (in the first three books) to explain how the present moment of crisis (in the last three books) is reached. The first half of the poem covers thirty years in the life of the eponymous hero; the second half, three days. The details are realistic, historically accurate, and copious; in addition there is not one dangling motive. The verse form is rhymed couplets. In brief, the poem is carefully structured, the basic organization being temporal and sequential. Yet at the same time the poem *seems* disorganized, formless, the effect of the whole being one of unreality, of fantasy rather than history. The narrator even goes out of his way to contradict himself, such as his assurance in Book V that Eglamor has totally disappeared from history and in Book VI that Eglamor lives on. Sordello dies, a failure as a poet and as a man of action: "a sorry farce / Such life is, after all" (VI,849–50); yet the narrator invites our interest in and sympathy for him throughout the poem and even goes out of his way to speak on Sordello's behalf. The narrative is frankly unsatisfactory as plot. The language of the verse is highly colored, and the imagery runs the gamut from the delicately beautiful to the harsh and grotesque. There is a systematic derangement of tense, frequent ambiguity of referent, and highly elliptical syntax. The apparent organization of the poem, which seeks to concentrate its entire length into a single moment of simultaneous perception, is therefore largely spatial and nonsequential.

Being both linear *and* circular, sequential *and* nonsequential, *Sordello* is Browning's attempt at a poem which is both text and song, embodied in print and constrained by linearity but defying the rules of grammar and the expectations of logic. *Sordello* is, as I have said, a perfect example of the ironist's art, in that it shows how irony cannot accommodate itself to anything which seeks to limit it, how it wishes to be everywhere, to be all, or not to be, and how the ironist must be a comedian or buffoon who makes sport of himself, his reader, and his work. As Friederich Schlegel observed, in true ironic works "there lives a real transcendental buffoonery. Their interior is permeated by the mood which surveys everything and rises above everything limited, even above the poet's own art, virtue, and genius; and their exterior form by the histrionic style of an ordinary good Italian buffo" (*Lyceum Frag.* No. 42). In *Sordello,* Browning tries to "say it all at once" with the ironist's full recognition of the impossibility of such utterance. If, as Aprile discovered, only God is the perfect poet, then no mortal, even though he mimics in his art God's ability to be immanent and transcendent, can be a "whole and perfect Poet" (V,116). *Sordello* marks Browning's full disavowal of all Romantic notions of the bard.

Such a complex, playful work must almost inevitably strike the public as opaque and frivolous; and as all the world knows, this was exactly the fate of *Sordello.* To this very day *Sordello* remains undervalued, although Browning was surely right in considering it among his three or four most important works; and Ezra Pound, in the first of his *Cantos,* correctly discerned it as "an art-form" which is also "a rag-bag" such as "the modern world / Needs . . . to stuff all its thoughts in."

Following *Sordello,* Browning published a series of pamphlets under the overall title *Bells and Pomegranates.* These are shorter works than *Sordello* and are essentially dramatic rather than narrative in form. Formally less daring than the long poem, they are none the less ironic. *Pippa Passes,* the first (1841), is a series of four more or less discrete episodes united by Pippa's unknowing part in them. Structurally the poem proceeds by dialogically defined episodes between characters; thematically the poem pursues a dialectic of self and other. In such a way structure gives rise to theme and theme illuminates structure. Thus the adulterous, murderous pair in the first panel attempt to maintain the passion of illicit, romantic love but are brought by their misapprehension of Pippa's song to a sense of wrong destructive of their rapture. In each of the succeeding panels one of the characters is led by his misunderstanding of Pippa's lyrics to act in a way other than anticipated: each, in other words, interprets language in light of his own psychological needs. Where previously Browning had shown how as speakers we use words to fit our own requirements, he now goes further to suggest how as listeners we filter the language of others to fit our needs. As Paracelsus said, "We live and breathe deceiving and deceived" (IV,626); things are never as they seem. This is as true of Pippa as of the others: the characters in the four scenes are not "Asolo's happiest four," all is not right with the world, she has touched many lives on this day which she disappointedly believes to have passed without significance, she is not even a mere peasant working-girl, but the heiress to a fortune. Once again Browning calls on the reader's "co-operating fancy" not only to link the scenes but also to look beneath the surface and see that the apparent meaning of any word or thing is not be be relied on.

The other longer dramatic pieces of *Bells and Pomegranates* were, like *Strafford,* designed for stage presentation, although not all of them were produced. Dependent for their interest upon character development rather than action, they portray ironic themes and structures similar to those of *Pippa Passes.* The dialectic of self and other is the theme of *King Victor and King Charles* (1842). Power and will, represented by Victor, are set against love, in the person of Charles. In the end Charles discovers the value of power and Victor the meaning of love: each achieves a fuller self by reacting to the other. *The Return of the Druses* (1843), of less concentrated scope than *King Victor,* also pursues the dialectic of self and other for ironic effect. Djabal becomes through Anael the "divine" deliverer that he only pretended to be, and Anael discovers that divine love can be attained only through love of the human being. *A Blot in the 'Scutcheon* (1843), a melodrama which Browning called a tragedy, lacks the undiffused ironic effect of the two preceding plays. Though it contains all the ironies of melodrama—mistaken identity, misunderstanding of circumstances, etc.—it focuses on the moral blindness of Tresham, the intended tragic hero. *Colombe's Birthday* (1844) returns to the dialectic of love and power but this time with the result that, in the political arena at least, power cannot co-exist with love. *Luria* (1846) is concerned with the irony of loyalty: to question one's faith is a sign of faithlessness, yet to embrace it unquestioningly, as Luria does, may not show that one's trust is groundless. The protagonist kills himself so that Florence, the city in which he puts his faith and the city which

37

is the basis of his life, will not prove, in her execution of him, other than what he has believed her to be. In the case of *Luria* irony proves absurdity. *A Soul's Tragedy,* published in the same final pamphlet as *Luria,* presents the simpler ironic situation of the gentle-mannered man's being physically timid and the ill-conditioned braggart's being given to action, only to have the roles reversed in the end to the extent that the gentle man becomes the morally courageous one and the braggart is shown up as a "tragic soul" who does not rise above his own sophistries to act bravely when action is required. Though the plays are hardly worthy of stage presentation today, they are none the less among the finest ironic tragic comedies in English before Shaw.

Far better known among *Bells and Pomegranates* are the two pamphlets *Dramatic Lyrics* (1842) and *Dramatic Romances and Lyrics* (1845) containing some of Browning's finest monologues. We have already noted the increasingly dramatic quality of Browning's verse, his attempt to display ideas or motives in conflict with each other. Previously he had been able to reveal psychological conflict only in the form of the confessional soliloquy, as in *Pauline,* or in narrative, as in *Sordello.* Acting on his knowledge, most plainly set forth in *Sordello,* that point of view determines one's notions of truth and that one's sense of self necessitates special pleading, Browning hit on a form which would allow him to present the impetus to action from one angle of vision and at a special moment when a speaker would most likely reveal himself and this motivation. Hence it would be a "dramatic lyric," a song portraying conflict. With its opportunities for the representation of casuistries and sophistries, of tangled logic and torturous language as means of arriving at a position which justifies an intended or past action, the form would be a splendid vehicle for the ironist.

We see this to be almost obviously the case with "My Last Duchess." There is no compulsion upon the duke to reveal—to, of all people, the envoy from a prospective duchess—how he came to do away with his previous duchess. Yet at a moment when he is swept up into song he tells all and, furthermore, attempts to justify it. We the readers see, just as undoubtedly the envoy sees, that there can be no justification for the murder (if that is what it is) of a kind young lady whose only apparent error was that she was not sufficiently haughty to be (in the duke's mind) Duchess of Ferrara; yet at the same time we perceive—as presumably does the envoy, for he makes no demur—that the duke is a fascinating character, bigger than life and disdainful of the merely ordinary. With admirable irony Browning succeeds in giving us—and causing us to hold—two conflicting views of the same individual. And that is not all: making every attempt to locate the poem in time and place and thus force us to to accept it as the utterance of someone other than the poet, Browning in the end calls attention to the poem as a poem when he has the duke refer to Neptune, "Taming a sea-horse, thought a rarity / Which Claus of Innsbruch cast in bronze for me." In that passage we are invited to see the statue as a summarizing symbol of the speaker, this not by the duke himself but the poet, who remains in his work in spite of all disclaimers in the Advertisement to *Dramatic Lyrics* that the utterances in these poems are those "of so many imaginary persons, not mine." The ironic mode of the dramatic monologue thus allowed Browning the mutually enriching interaction of the objective and the subjective, the dramatic and the lyric modes.

Although there are superb pieces in *Dramatic Lyrics* and *Dramatic Romances and Lyrics,* only one other monologue has the ironic richness of "My Last Duchess." "The Bishop Orders His Tomb at St. Praxed's," from the latter collection, engenders the same tension between sympathy and judgment. The bishop has obviously broken almost every rule of conduct imposed by the Church upon her clergy; yet, so much caught up in the secular spirit of the Renaissance, he deludes himself that he has earned the right to a magnificent tomb in a choice spot in his own church. As readers we know full well how defective a cleric he has been and condemn him for his failure, but at the same time we are impressed by his exquisite taste and, further, pity him because he knows that his sons will bury him in a tomb of only "gritstone, a-crumble." The poem is not, however, merely the bishop's monologue. The poet intrudes into it by making the utterance a sermon on the text "Vanity, saith the preacher, vanity," which is the first line of the monologue. The poem thus becomes an exemplum preached by the bishop who, not incidentally, throughout the monologue constantly lapses into a homiletic style simply out of habit: the preacher proves his text, unknowingly, by the revelation of his character; his plea for sympathy becomes a literary form—a sermon—which stands in judgment of him. A poet can hardly go further in achieving so subtly in the work of art itself those reflections of the work of art which characterize the highest irony.

39

The final number of *Bells and Pomegranates* and Browning's marriage to Elizabeth Barrett, both in 1846, mark the end to the first period of Browning's career. Hereafter he was for a number of years to be a different kind of poet; indeed, during the years of his marriage he was, by comparison with the prodigious amount of work appearing in his earlier and later periods, to publish very little at all. As he wrote to his future wife (13 Feb. 1846), "I mean to take your advice and be quiet awhile and let my mind get used to its new medium of sight—seeing all things thro' you."

The work of his married years and that appearing soon after is generally regarded as his very best. And surely no one who loves literature can but love the monologues of *Men and Women* (1855) and *Dramatis Personae* (1864). Yet for the admirer of Browning's irony and radical formal innovations, seeing all things through the eyes of Elizabeth Barrett Browning had its limitations. In the first place, Mrs. Browning demanded of poetry that everything be spelled out—no loose ends, no parts unlinked by logical copula, no requirement that the reader employ his "co-operating fancy." For example, she said of *Sordello,* in a letter of 9 September 1845, "it wants drawing together & fortifying in the connections & associations . . . [sic] which hang as loosely every here & there, as those in a dream." This of course was precisely the effect that Browning intended, but at her urging he kept revising it to make it hang together more tightly and, for me at any rate, in the end diminished its liveliness. In the second place, Mrs. Browning wanted the "meaning" of the poem to be as clear as its form. As Browning wrote (13 Jan. 1845), she spoke out, while he only made men and women speak. Hereafter he would address himself more directly to the moral concerns of his fellow men, would bear in mind his "mission of humanity" (25 Feb. 1846).

I do not mean to imply that the great monologues of the fifties and sixties are reducible to their moral content, but I do say that they have more moral design upon the reader than do the earlier poems. "Cleon," "Karshish," "Childe Roland," "Abt Vogler," "A Death in the Desert," "Caliban," to name only some of the best—all are concerned with the communication of some moral or religious message. Admittedly there are ironies galore—Cleon and Karshish do not embrace the Christian answer to their problems which lies so readily at hand, Roland meets with both success and defeat in finding the tower, Abt Vogler accidentally discovers an image of heaven which he cannot recapture in soberer mood and which he doubts may have occurred—but they are ironies which point always to some moral. Even those monologues specifically concerned with art—"Fra Lippo Lippi" and "Andrea del Sarto," to me the most excellent of the monologues of this period—even they are designed to communicate something about the morality of art. There is never any question about their "meaning." Browning had reoriented his art to the point where he was ready and willing to assume the bardic mantle, something he had continually disavowed earlier, although this new idea of the bard involved not being *overheard* (as J. S. Mill said all true poetry should be) but heard directly. Speaking in "One Word More" in his own voice and out of his own experience of unappreciation, Browning tells of the poet who like Moses is both looked up to for guidance and deprecated for it. It is a wearying business, but "Never dares the man put off the prophet."

I have spoken only of the best poems of the fifties and sixties. If I were to speak of others—*Christmas Eve and Easter Day,* "Respectability," "Rabbi ben Ezra," "Gold Hair," the "Epilogue" to *Dramatis Personae*—I could make an even clearer case for the reorientation of Browning's art towards a religio-moral aesthetic. The demand that poets address themselves to the immediate religious and moral needs of their society was of course in the air throughout the forties and fifties—witness what happened to Tennyson—but in the case of Browning, who in Florence was living at quite a remove from his native country, the demand that he suppress the "frivolous" irony of his earlier verse was evidently formidably reinforced by his wife. I say this because the verse written after and not immediately influenced by Elizabeth's death is of a different nature. It is different in that the old sense of irony returns, never so wonderfully zanily as in the case of *Sordello,* but boldly and paradoxically nevertheless. It is different too in that Browning gives up working mainly with one form, the dramatic monologue, and begins again the formal experimentation of the ironist who, aware of the principle of becoming and the inadequacy of any form to serve for more than one occasion, must always be seeking for new vehicles to embody new ideas.

The first fruit of his new artistic freedom was *The Ring and the Book.* For years it has been customary to speak of this long poem as the culmination of Browning's art. If by "culmination" one means that it is the finest of his works, then I cannot quarrel with such an assessment, although I am inclined to put *Sordello* and the *Parleyings* on the same level. But if by "culmination" is meant the logical outcome of his earlier verse, as seems to be the case, then I must argue most vehemently against any such notion. For *The Ring and the Book* is very little like the poems of the 1850s and the sixties. To be sure, most of it is a series of dramatic monologues and some of them seem to have a moral design upon the reader, but it is also a great work of ironic art, a narrative which mixes genres and ultimately undercuts the moral statements made by the monologists. There are wonderful characters in it who exist, almost like the Duke of Ferrara, for the sake of the characters themselves—those of the second, third, and fourth books, for example, even Guido himself, a study first of covert then of open villainy; and there are characters who, splendid in themselves, are nevertheless designed to have a moral effect upon us. What could be more affecting than the monologues of Caponsacchi, Pompilia, and, as the authorative voice, the Pope? But then we read the twelfth and last book, which calls into question everything that has gone before. For in it the poet, apparently speaking in his own voice, tells us that all these "pleadings and counter-pleading" have been just so many words. Even the Pope, who has pronounced the innocence of Caponsacchi and Pompilia and who has claimed to evolve the final truth (a claim which most critics have accepted)—even the Pope's soliloquy is called into question in the last book. It is not that he lies; rather, it is simply that he may not have spoken the full truth, for the simple reason that, even in soliloquy, he has an axe to grind, must justify himself to himself. The narrator says, "our human speech is naught, / Our human testimony false, our fame / And human estimation words and wind." Only art, "wherein man nowise speaks to men," may tell a truth because it aims for ideal significance by pretending to be nothing other than itself. As I understand *The Ring and the Book,* it is not the culmination of Browning's work but a transitional poem re-introducing radically ironic notions of art.

Since, as I noted at the beginning of this essay, I have already written at some length on Browning's poetry after *The Ring and the Book,* I have chosen to use most of the space allotted me to discuss the poet's earlier work. In what follows hereafter I shall hastily try to indicate how in his later years Browning returns to something like the style and mode of the poetry prior to his marriage. Once again the poetry becomes daringly innovative. *Balaustion's Adventure* (1871) stretches the dramatic monologue to formal lengths unenvisioned even in the writing of *The Ring and the Book*: it contains a whole version of a play by Euripides, with the strong implication that Balaustion, the simple girl from Rhodes, has seen more in the material than has Euripides and that she in her innocence has discovered the evolving nature of deity in the phenomenal world. *Prince Hohenstiel-Schwangau* (1871), perhaps the most misunderstood of Browning's later poems, presents the case of a voluptuary talking to himself who seems to be a reasoning man speaking to a courtesan. *Fifine at the Fair* (1872), the poem which Browning called the most "metaphysical" he had written since *Sordello*, presents seventy-two ways (or there-abouts) of looking at and justifying adultery—all of them wrong. *Red Cotton Night-Cap Country* (1873), a first-person narrative, gives all the evidence why a manic-depressive has a religious impulse to do the impossible and why he is both right and wrong. *Aristophanes' Apology* (1875) carries the dramatic monologue to the breaking point: it contains, *inter alia,* a debate between Aristophanes and Balaustion about the relative merits of Euripides and Aristophanes, comedy, tragedy, and tragi-comedy, a transcription of the Euripidean *Herakles,* and finally a seeming vindication of Euripides *and* applause of Aristo-phanes—all within one monologue. In such poems Browning tried, as he had in *Sordello,* to concentrate a vast amount of time and space into a prolonged but single moment of simultaneous perception, at-tempting, as Aristophanes envisions a future poet doing, "to take in every side at once, / And not successively." The last of the long poems of the 1870s, *The Inn Album,* is a narrative composed of eight dra-matic scenes in which the melodramatic action becomes the text of the album at the inn ironically hailed as a "salubrious spot" of "calm acclivity." These six long poems in a highly ironic mode deserve more recognition as belonging among Browning's greatest achievements.

For a dozen years thereafter Browning turned to shorter works. Although they represent experiments with new forms—the idyl, for example—and examine from an ironic stance the function of evil as a contribution to ultimate good, by and large they are less interesting than the long poems of the period 1871 to 75. It may be that Browning was acting out in person his own sense of irony. Everyone knows how Browning loved to dine out and be taken not for a poet but for a successful financier, how Henry James thought that the man he met in society could not possibly be Robert Browning the poet. During the later seventies and early eighties Browning lived his irony as he had never before been able to do.

In his penultimate work, *Parleyings with Certain People of Importance in Their Day* (1887), Browning achieves a masterpiece of ironic art. He summons from the past a group of artists, satirists, moralists, politicians, philosophers, musicians, all of whom had a certain influence on the poet's early life, and then proceeds by means of a parleying with some contemporary figure to justify why these men of the past, insignificant though they may now be, have had a salutary effect on the poet's development even though their views may be outmoded or wrong. Thus with a kind of double vision the poet sets into motion a process of dialectic in which he is and is not present, one which he can sit back and enjoy. The main subject of each parleying is the nature of fact and fancy; and the answer, if indeed answer it is, is that fact either cannot exist "unfancifully" or is worthless unless imaginatively apprehended by fancy. For the ironist the parleying is an ideal form in that it allows the author to be both immanent and transcendent and, further, while advancing claims to philosophical seriousness, does not pretend to be anything other than a work of art.

In his last volume, *Asolando* (1890), there is a poem which may be taken as a summarizing statement of Browning's essentially ironic view of the world. In "Development" the poet speaks of how he had first learned of the *Iliad* from his father: from re-enactment in play of the siege of Troy, to reading of it in Pope's translation, finally to studying it in the Greek original: each phase of his acquaintance with Homer was suited to the proper stage of his development. By the time he reached young manhood he was so well acquainted with Homer that concerning the facts of the blind poet's life he was convinced "nothing remains to know." But then came the German "Higher Criticism" which proceeded to show that there had never been a Troy and, worse, "No actual Homer, no authenticated text, / No warrant for the fiction I, as fact, / Had treasured in my heart and soul so long." He should have not been surprised because he should have known that, in an evolving universe, nothing remains static. Yet today, in spite of this new knowledge, which he of course accepts, he will nevertheless guard in his soul's shrine the reality of Helen, Hector, Achilles, Ulysses, and the rest; in the life of the imagination he will retain "fact's essence freed and fixed / From accidental fancy's guardian sheath." It is irony which permits, in Friederich Schlegel's words, this "clear consciousness of an eternal agility, of the infinitely abundant chaos" (*Athenaeum Frag.* No. 69). It is irony which allows for the provisional negation of the "serious" or "objective" character of the external world and, correlatively, for the provisional affirmation of the creative omnipotence of the thinking subject; it is irony which, after the poet's declaration that "No dream's worth waking," returns us in the end to the world of quotidian reality where it is "boys' way" to soil a book "with bread and milk," "crumple, dogs-ear and deface." If there has been any "development," it is only that the gray-haired man doesn't disfigure a book.

From the time of *Paracelsus,* Browning had held firmly to what many regard as mindless optimism. As he relates in "Reverie," the last poem of *Asolando* excepting the "Epilogue,"

> Even as the world its life,
> So have I lived my own—
> Power seen with Love at strife,
> That sure, this dimly shown,
> —Good rare and evil rife.

Yet he has clung to the faith that eventually wrong will be righted. "Why faith?"

> but to lift the load,
> To leaven the lump, where lies
> Mind prostrate through knowledge owed
> To the loveless Power it tries
> To withstand, how vain!

We may speak of this as willed faith, but correctly we must name it irony, that philosophical and aesthetic mode (to borrow from Leo Capel's introduction to his translation of Kierkegaard's *The Concept of Irony*) aspiring to ideal significance whose meaning is contradictory, whose structure is dialectical, whose medium is the language of reflection, and whose style is antithetical.

No other Victorian poet is so thoroughly ironic in his view of the world or in the presentation of that view in his art. Among the early Victorians we have to go to Carlyle, mainly *Sartor Resartus* (written almost directly under the influence of the German romantic ironists), to find work similar to those "transcendental buffooneries" of Browning, yet Carlyle was unable or unwilling to sustain his irony for very long and so in the later 1830s lapsed into the prophet. Dickens was clearly working towards a thorough-going irony in *Bleak House,* yet he never developed it in his later works. What happened to both Carlyle and Dickens was what happened to Browning during his middle period, the twenty years from 1846 to 1866: they failed to maintain the double vision of the ironist. Browning however recaptured his old way of seeing and, with a remarkable outburst of energy, returned to the ironic mode in his later works.

Browning remained aware of the conflict between the old religious and the new positivist world-views and, more importantly, of the impossibility on his part to take either side or bring them into accord. In this respect he was not unlike, say, Matthew Arnold, who was well aware of wandering between two worlds. He was different from Arnold not in recognizing these conflicts but, in a large body of his work, presenting them ironically so as to transcend them. It was his irony that allowed Browning, unlike most of his contemporaries, to rise above mere argument or special pleading for this or that cause. It was his irony that permitted him to be among the least topical of English poets and yet simultaneously to be among the most fully grounded in the life of his time. In sum, it was his irony that makes him one of the most innovative and enduringly influential poets in English.

ARTHUR HUGH CLOUGH: PALPABLE THINGS AND CELESTIAL FACT

MICHAEL TIMKO

While no one up to now has been able to explain, the fact remains that Clough has always claimed attention. Certainly one could make a case for being just a bit puzzled as to why this should be, since nothing in his life and career seems to explain the interest he inspired in his own lifetime and continues to inspire among critics and readers today. Born in Liverpool in 1819, the son of a cotton merchant, Clough lived for a short time in Charleston, South Carolina (1822–28), where business had taken his father; but he returned to England to attend Rugby and Oxford, where he was both student and Fellow from 1837 to 1848. He resigned the Fellowship in 1848 because of his inability to subscribe fully to the various beliefs of the Church of England and spent the next few years teaching, traveling, and writing *The Bothie,* (1848), *Ambarvalia* (1849), *Amours de Voyage* (1850), *Dipsychus* (1850), finally taking on an Examinership in the Education Office, London, in 1853. The next year he married Blanche Smith, a cousin of Florence Nightingale's. The rest of his life was spent quietly enough working at the Education Office, writing (*Mari Magno*), and traveling for his health. He died in Florence on November 13, 1861, and is buried there in the Protestant Cemetery.

How does one, in the light of the apparent "failure" of this not so "eminent" Victorian, account for the attraction he has had in the past and still retains?[1] One might explain it by the people who were attracted to him, contemporaries and those who came after, who found in Clough himself and in his work something that inspired not only friendship but real affection and admiration. I have much to say about Matthew Arnold and Clough below, but Arnold was both a friend and an admirer of Clough. He wrote to his sister at one time that she and Clough were "the two people I in my heart care most to please by what I write"; and he wrote to Clough himself: "My dear old soul. I find that, au fond, when I compose anything, I care more, still, for your opinion than that of any one else about it." Henry Sidgwick also acknowledged the great influence of Clough: "The truth is," he stated, "if Clough had not lived and written, I should probably be now exactly where he was. . . . I can neither adequately rationalise faith, nor reconcile faith and reason, nor suppress reason. But this is just the benefit of an utterly veracious man like Clough, that it is impossible for any one, however sympathetic, to remain where he was."

Carlyle, Emerson, and Tennyson, personal friends, also had words of praise for Clough. There is, of course, the well-known story of Clough's telling Emerson that Carlyle had led them out of the desert and left them there, at which point Emerson, placing his hand on Clough's head, "consecrated" him "Bishop of all England" to lead the people out of the wilderness to the promised land. Emerson himself, after reading the *Bothie,* wrote to thank him: "I cannot tell you how great a joy to me is your poem. . . . [It] is a high gift from angels that are very rare in our mortal state. It delights and surprises me from beginning to end. I can hardly forgive you for keeping your secret from me so well. I knew you good and wise, . . . but how could I know or guess that you had all this wealth of expression, this wealth of imagery, this joyful heart of youth, this temperate continuity, that belongs only to high masters. It is a noble poem. Tennyson must look to his laurels." Carlyle, too, although Emerson in the same letter complained that Carlyle had never mentioned the poem to him, thought highly of Clough. J. A. Froude, Carlyle's close friend, wrote to tell Clough's widow that Carlyle had often told him that he thought more highly of Clough than of anyone else in his generation. Cecil Woodham-Smith, the biographer of Florence Nightingale, tells us that Florence Nightingale's grief over Clough's death was "second only to her grief for Sidney Herbert." Tennyson, with whom Clough spent some time in 1861, thought that Clough had "great poetic feeling." Perhaps the most appropriate comment, however, is that of Dean Stanley, writing in the *Daily News* shortly after Clough's death. "Those who knew him well," Stanley said, "know that in him a genius and character of no common order has passed away." Then he added these prophetic words: "They will scarcely be able to justify their knowledge to a doubting world."

One might, then, attempt to explain Clough's appeal to a doubting world in terms of pity or sympathy, but the real attraction, I would insist, resides in the work itself: its concerns and the sources of those concerns. It lies, too, in the poet himself, for there is, without question, a close connection between person and writer, believer and the articles of his belief. This close connection has in recent years caused some misunderstanding about Clough and his work. Different critics have tended to focus on certain aspects of the person or his writings, thus emphasizing far out of proportion one facet or another of his personality, his writing, or his interests. In recent years he has been called a quintessential Victorian or a pre-modern; a Carlylian or a democrat; an empiricist or an idealist. He is, of course, all of these and more, and it is the more that makes Clough the single Victorian writer who deserves our close attention at this time. Clough at the same time both defied and defined his age; he attempted to transform it and at times he succeeded in transcending it. To know more about him and his writing is to come to know more about the age in which he lived. Ultimately, of course, it is to come to know more about our own.

There are a number of characteristics of Clough and his work that account for his particular place in Victorian life and literature. He was always in touch with significant movements and important people. He was always aware of the importance of facts (of palpable things, as he called them), while never losing sight of the "spiritual" or celestial. Most important, perhaps, his chief concern was with human beings, their strengths and weaknesses, their foibles and fetishes. He never resorted to type or caricature. As a result, his writings reflect his own ideas as to exactly what human beings are like and how they act in a world that at times seems to be for them if not alien at least inhospitable. Clough does not write about systems or ideologies or movements or theories. He writes about human beings who have those qualities that we call human, and it is for this reason that we respond to him as artist and person.

Clough still remains elusive, however, particularly in his approach to human nature and to life itself. Part of this puzzlement is reflected, as I have already said, in our inability to "place" Clough, to label him, to categorize him. Part of this puzzlement is reflected in various attempts to classify his poems, especially the long ones, as satiric, lyric, narrative, or what you will. Ultimately, the understanding of Clough, I think, is closely bound with not only appreciating those characteristics I cite above, but also seeing the close connection between Clough's artistic and moral concerns. Here is the heart of the problem, for Clough the artist cannot be separated from Clough the human being.

In a recent essay Barbara Hardy has brought this problem into sharp focus. She mentions Richard Gollin's disagreement with Paul Veyriras about the moral and personal in Clough's work; then she writes: "Richard Gollin's remarks on Clough always command respect, and in a review . . . he takes Paul Veyriras to task for occasionally mistaking Clough's moral concern for his personal compulsion." She goes on to indicate her own disagreement with Gollin:

> I have to begin by admitting that I find myself unable to feel as confident as Mr. Gollin about distinguishing Clough's detached and controlled criticism from his "self-directed utterances." While acknowledging Clough's variousness and toughness, I see his analytic mode as inextricably bound up with his personal compulsions, and indeed welcome his attachment to the personal as a source of warmth and acceptance even in satire.[2]

We need, then, to be clear about this one important point concerning Clough and his writings, and I should think that to deny Clough his "detached and controlled criticism" is to deny him a great deal of his artistic skill. In this matter I find myself siding with Gollin, for to confuse "personal compulsions" with an artist's "analytic mode" is to create a false impression about that artist's art. Clough's moral concern is found throughout his writings, and it is a concern that is an important part of his critical and artistic stance. To dismiss it as an "attachment to the personal" is to fail to see one of Clough's strongest artistic and critical points. Clough's art is, in fact, one that has a very strong moral basis, a morality that is seen throughout his own critical statements and his poetry.

Professor Hardy's inability to grasp fully, as does Professor Gollin, Clough's "detached and controlled criticism" accounts for her failure, in an otherwise impressive essay on Clough's use of lyric and narrative structure, to perceive Clough's admirable use of "distancing"; she mistakes personal feeling for his keen insight into human nature. Thus she can write: "Clough's poems never give themselves up to feeling, but neither do they distance it. . . . A profound and sober respect for life holds him back from satire, as it held back George Eliot too." (p.

268) I am certain that many readers of George Eliot might want to dispute this point, and I know that many of Clough's readers would want to do the same thing. To fail to see Clough's skillful use of distancing in such poems as *Amours* and *Dipsychus* is a denial of one of the fundamental strengths of Clough's poetry, especially the long poems. I will say more of this later; let me begin with some of Clough's own statements about "fact" and feeling.

These are well enough known by this time, and I need not go into much detail here. I have, too, elsewhere written about the Clough-Arnold relationship and Clough's poetic theory.[3] However, a few points might be worth going over, if only to remind ourselves of several matters that seem consistently to be either ignored or forgotten. In the Clough-Arnold relationship it is worth keeping in mind that there is some evidence to suggest that Clough had a great deal of influence on Arnold's critical ideas, especially those concerning the moral aspects of poetry. This point is especially worth pondering since Arnold's influence on modern critical thought is so often stressed in our time. Clough's strong influence on Arnold's critical thought, and thus on our own, has up to now not been fully recognized; certainly, not so much as it should be.

From Arnold's early statements "condemning" Clough's lack of interest in aesthetics, Arnold gradually changes his position until he and Clough are in virtual agreement. In 1845 Arnold can write to Clough and tell him that, since they believe in "the Universality of Passion as Passion," they "will keep pure our Aesthetics by remembering its one-sidedness as doctrine."[4] He can condemn one of Clough's poems for being too "allegorical," and he can also lecture Clough on what is missing from his poetry; he writes to Clough in February of 1848:

> A growing sense of the deficiency of the *beautiful* in your poems, and of this alone being properly *poetical* as distinguished from rhetorical, devotional or metaphysical, made me speak as I did. But your line is a line: and you have most of the promising English verse-writers with you now: Festus for instance. Still, problem as the production of the beautiful remains still to me, I will die protesting against the world that the other is false and JARRING. (p. 66)

Arnold's emphasis on the beautiful is a plea for Clough to concern himself less with content and morality and more with form, and he continues this line in still another letter of 1848. He tells Clough in no uncertain terms:

You know you are a mere d_____d depth hunter in poetry and therefore exclusive furiously. You might write a speech in Phèdre—Phedra loquitur—but you could not write Phèdre. And when you adopt this or that form you must sacrifice much to the ensemble, and that form in return for admirable effects demands immense sacrifices and precisely in that quarter where your nature will not allow you to make them. (p. 81)

"The greatest wealth and depth of matter," Arnold tells his friend in a letter of early 1849, apparently attempting to drive home his point that form must take precedence over matter, "is merely a superfluity in the Poet *as such.*" He tells Clough in some detail:

If I were to say the real truth as to your poems in general, as they impress me—it would be this—that they are not *natural.*

Many persons with far lower gifts than yours yet seem to find their natural mode of expression in poetry, and tho: the contents may not be very valuable they appeal with justice from the judgement of the mere thinker to the world's general appreciation of naturalness—i.e.-an absolute propriety—of form. . . . I often think that even a slight gift of poetical expression which in a common person might have developed itself easily and naturally, is overlaid and crushed in a profound thinker so as to be of no use to him to help him to express himself.—The trying to go into and to the bottom of an object instead of grouping *objects* is as fatal to the sensuousness of poetry as the mere painting, (for, in *Poetry,* this is not grouping) is to its airy and rapidly moving life.

"Consider," Arnold concludes, "whether you attain the *beautiful,* and whether your product gives PLEASURE, . . . not excites curiosity and reflexion." (pp. 98–99)

In spite of this emphasis on formalism, Arnold was really not sure of his own position, and the various statements of Clough (statements we must surmise since Clough's letters were apparently destroyed) seemed to have their effect on the advocate of form and beauty. His shift from an "aesthetic" to a "moralistic" critic may be seen most clearly in his views towards style and in his very firm "moralistic" bias, and in both of these aspects his ideas and words are similar to Clough's. In the former, for instance, the views on style, one need only read some of Clough's comments to see their influence on Arnold's own critical theories. Clough defines style as "that permanent beauty of expression, that harmony between thought and word, which is the condition of '*immortal* verse.' "[5] He also emphasizes the necessity of the poet's keeping the style simple and severe, so that it contributes to the "total impression" of the poem. Since the thematic content (that which the earlier Arnold so much deplored and Professor Hardy has so much difficulty with) is, in Clough's poetic theory, the most important element of any poem, the poet must keep the style subordinate to it. He insists that other elements of the poem—form, metre, imagery, diction—not call attention to themselves, but, instead, contribute to the main drift of "what calls itself a single poem." (pp. 165–166) What Clough is objecting to, in this particular case, is the way Alexander Smith, one of the poets he is reviewing, keeps "perpetually presum[ing] upon" what should be the "real continuity of poetic purpose." In the light of Arnold's particular interest in the Romantics, it is of some significance that Clough concludes this aspect of his review with these words: "Keats and Shelley, and Coleridge, perhaps.... with their extravagant love for Elizabethan phraseology, have led to this mischief. Has not Tennyson followed a little too much in their train?" (p. 166)

Whether or not he would agree with Clough as to the causes, Arnold, the "later" Arnold, does emphasize the need for subordinating imagery, metre, and diction to the total impression of the poem. A letter to Clough in 1852 seems a complete turnabout from his earlier position; Arnold writes that

> modern poetry can only subsist by its *contents:* by becoming a complete magister vitae as the poetry of the ancients did: by including, as theirs did, religion with poetry, instead of existing as poetry only, and leaving religious wants to be supplied by the Christian religion, as a power existing independent of the poetical power. But the language, style, and general proceedings of a poetry which has such an immense task to perform, must be very plain direct and severe: and it must not lose itself in parts and episodes and ornamental work, but must press forwards to the whole." (p. 124)

Of course the insistence on the subordination of style to content reflects the firm belief in the moralistic basis of poetry, that which Gollin calls Clough's "moral concern." Arnold's later criticism reveals a moralistic bias as strong as Clough's, and one that is, as I have suggested, quite different from his earlier aesthetic bias. His rejection of *Empedocles* from the 1853 volume because of its failure to "inspirit and rejoice" the reader is surely a reflection of his later insistence that content be placed over form. Perhaps the clearest indication of the great influence that Clough's belief in the moralistic concern of poetry must have had on Arnold's own thinking is revealed in his essay on

Wordsworth. In this essay Arnold is now able to say boldly: "It is important, therefore, to hold fast to this: that poetry is at bottom a criticism of life; that the greatness of a poet lies in his powerful and beautiful application of ideas to life,—to the question: How to live. . . . A poetry of revolt against moral ideas is a poetry of revolt against *life;* a poetry of indifference towards moral ideas is a poetry of indifference towards *life*." And in *The Study of Poetry* Arnold can write: "More and more mankind will discover that we have to turn to poetry to interpret life for us, to console us, to sustain us."

It is of the greatest interest and significance that all of these ideas are found in Clough's statements about poetry and literature. What ultimately makes Clough a significant Victorian figure and one of the "major" writers of that period is his high regard and great respect for poetry. For Clough, as it came to be for Arnold, the greatness of poetry lay in its application to life, and it is the specific way that his own poetry demonstrates this belief that gives it its distinction, that enables it to have some meaning for us today. It explains, in fact, why he can be so many things to so many readers and critics; he can be, at one and the same time, as modern as any contemporary and yet, in the words of Barbara Hardy, remain a Victorian writer "visibly imprisoned in his Victorianism, breathing with difficulty under its glass dome." (p. 253)

Obviously, then, for Clough, poetry is more than the spilling out of emotions, the writing about "personal compulsions." In order to perform its role poetry must not simply reflect one's own feelings; the poet cannot be secluded from the real world. It was, in fact, his rejection of poetry as the revelation merely of feelings that caused Clough to have certain reservations about Wordsworth, whom he admired very much. For Clough, Wordsworth, who did at times seem to rely too heavily on feeling rather than fact, was occasionally guilty of sentimentality as well as of a certain seclusion from and evasion of the world. In his lecture on Wordsworth, after pointing out those positive aspects of the poet's writings that warrant our admiration and praise, Clough comments on what he considers to be the unfavorable ones, some of which are due to what he calls Wordsworth's "premature seclusion." He then explains as follows:

> And I cannot help thinking that there is in Wordsworth's poems something of a spirit of withdrawal and seclusion from, and even evasion of the actual world. In his own quiet rural sphere it is true he did fairly enough

look at things as they were, he did not belie his own senses, nor pretend to recognize in outward things what really was not in them. But his sphere was a small one, the objects he lived among unimportant and petty. Retiring early from all conflict and even contact with the busy world, he shut himself out from the elements which it was his business to encounter and to master. This gives to his writings compared with those of Scott and Byron a certain appearance of sterility and unreality. . . .

This also sadly lessens the value which we must put on that high moral tone which we have hitherto been extolling. To live in a quiet village, out of the road of all trouble and temptation, in a pure, elevated, high moral sort of matter is after all no such very great a feat. (p. 119)

This "arbitrary positiveness" in Wordsworth results in what Clough characterizes as "the triviality in many places of his imagery, and the mawkishness . . . of his sentiment." Clough's comments are indeed revealing, for they demonstrate his own awareness of the dangers of substituting one's personal feelings for one's own "moral concern," and they also show his own ability to distinguish "detached and controlled criticism" from "self-directed utterances." As poet and critic he is able to keep separate objective analysis from personal bias. Wordsworth's mawkishness, this excessive sentimentality, Clough explains, comes from his forgetting the importance of the real world; he elaborates:

instead of looking directly at an object and considering it as a thing in itself, and allowing it to operate upon him as a fact in itself,—he takes the sentiment produced by it in his own mind as the thing; as the important and really real fact.—The Real things cease to be real; the world no longer exists; all that exists is the feeling somehow generated in the poet's sensibility. This sentimentalizing over sentiment; this sensibility over sensibility has been carried I grant by the Wordsworthians to far more than Wordsworthian excess. But he has something of it surely. (p. 121)

It is instructive to view the Arnold-Clough relationship in terms of their attitudes towards Wordsworth's "sentimentalizing," his dependence on sentiment and feeling. While Clough deplores this vein in Wordsworth's poetry—"Instead of looking directly at the object . . . he takes the sentiment produced by it in his own mind as the thing; as the important and only real fact"—Arnold cites it as one of the positive aspects of Wordsworth's writing. He praises, as did John Stuart Mill, the "states of feeling" (the words are Mill's) generated by Wordsworth's poetry. Unlike Clough, who rejects the kind of writing that "sentimentalizes over sentiment" and insists that "feeling" is all,

55

Arnold accepts it wholeheartedly. The difference is crucial, I think, and one that has not yet been wholly accepted in discussions of the Clough-Arnold relationship. In this difference lies Clough's ability to see the object as it really is, to let the object operate upon him as a fact in itself, to be, sympathetically at times, detached and objective. Clough could never write, one can be sure, as Arnold did in "Memorial Voices":

> Wordsworth has gone from us—and ye,
> Ah, may ye feel his voice as we!
> * * * * * * * * * *
> He spoke, and loosed our heart in tears.
> * * * * * * * * * *
> Others will teach us how to dare,
> And against fear our breast to steel;
> Others will strengthen us to bear—
> But who, ah! who, will make us feel?

Who, indeed? Clough's own poetry, often misunderstood, had a much different goal, one that Arnold himself, as his words in "Thyrsis" make clear, failed to understand. Clough prized not a poetry of feeling, of "sentimentalizing," but one of consolation and interpretation, a poetry of truth, one that, indeed, in Barbara Hardy's words, has a "profound and sober respect for life."

A poet and critic who can speak and write as Clough is not very likely to substitute personal feelings and sentiment for moral concern. What Clough found as a major fault in Wordsworth was the absence of the real world: the fact that real things ceased to be real. For Clough, poetry had to teach the significance of and give purpose to life, and it had to indicate in some way one's relationship to what he called the "purer existence." Fittingly enough, or perhaps ironically enough, his fullest statement concerning the role of poetry is found in his review of poems by Smith and Arnold. After deploring the kind of "languid collectanea" being published so often in his time, the "pleasing stanzas on the beauties of Nature and fresh air," Clough asks rhetorically why is it that people prefer *Vanity Fair* and *Bleak House.* He then gives his own answer:

> Is it, that to be widely popular, to gain the ear of multitudes, to shake the hearts of men, poetry should deal more than at present it usually does, with general wants, ordinary feelings, the obvious rather than the rare facts of human nature? Could it not attempt to convert into beauty and

thankfulness, or at least into some form and shape, some feeling, at any rate, of content—the actual, palpable things with which our every-day life is concerned; introduce into business and weary task-work a character and a soul of purpose and reality; intimate to us relations which, in our un-chosen, peremptorily-appointed posts, in our grievously narrow and limited spheres of action, we still, in and through all, retain to some central, celestial fact? Could it not console us with a sense of significance, if not of dignity, in that often dirty, or at least dingy, work which it is the lot of so many of us to have to do, and which some one or other, after all, must do? Might it not divinely condescend to all infirmities; be in all points tempted as we are; exclude nothing, least of all guilt and distress, from its wide fraternization; not content itself merely with talking of what may be better elsewhere, but seek also to deal with what *is* here? . . . Cannot the Divine Song in some way indicate to us our unity, though from a great way off, with those happier things; inform us, and prove to us, that though we are what we are, we may yet, in some way, even in our abasement, even by and through our daily work, be related to the purer existence.

The modern novel is preferred to the modern poem, because we do here feel an attempt to include those indispensable latest addenda—these phe-nomena which, if we forget on Sunday, we must remember on Monday —these positive matters of fact, which people, who are not verse-writers, are obliged to have to do with. (pp. 144–145)

Clough makes a distinction, as do most perceptive critics, between mere verse-writers and poets, and for him poetry has to be both consolatory and interpretive. It must not only provide some under-standing of what we do here on earth, but it must also give us some insight as to how we "retain to some central, celestial fact." Poetry, for Clough, as critic and as poet, defines in universal terms those actions and ideas we see only as particulars.

From all of this emerge a number of significant matters concerning Clough's importance as critic and poet. One is his relationship to Arnold, one of the major critical influences in our own day. It is important, in this respect, to remind ourselves (or to learn) that Clough in fact was a crucial influence on Arnold's critical thinking. Arnold's heavy emphasis on poetry as a criticism of life owes much to Clough. It is also important to keep in mind the emphasis that Clough placed on what he saw as the ultimate end of poetry: its moral concern. To recognize this is to keep one from falling into the error of mistaking in Clough's own poetry "personal feeling" or compulsion for detached and controlled observation and criticism. Finally, it is especially important to recognize Clough's deep appreciation of "fact" and "reality" as both critic and poet, especially as it relates to his concept of what constitutes the truth. His great concern to avoid what he considered "false or arbitrary positiveness," a fault of which Wordsworth seemed guilty, is at times mistaken for timidity or indecisiveness. Indeed, Clough's reputation as one who failed comes from this very aspect of his thought, an aspect that, in fact, should be considered as one of his great strengths. It is this position that enables him to retain that supreme objectivity, that firm control of content and form, that withholding of judgment so often mistaken for indecisiveness of purpose. This is the Cloughian mark that deserves much more notice and respect than it has received up to now. It is that which constitutes most clearly his contribution to Victorian literature.

His own clearest statement regarding the need for it in poetry is found in his essay on Wordsworth. "There is," writes Clough, "such a thing in Morals as in all Science, as drawing your conclusion before you have properly got your premises. It is desirable to attain a fixed point: but it is essential that the fixed point be the right one. We ought to hold fast by what is true; but because we hold wilfully fast it does not follow what we hold fast to is true. If you have got the truth, be as positive as you please; but because you choose to be positive, do not therefore be sure you have the truth." (p. 120) It is this spirit that led Clough to praise the age of Dryden for its "austere love of truth," its "rigorous uncompromising rejection of the vague, . . . the merely probable." "Such a spirit," he concluded, "I may say, I think, claims more than our attention,—claims our reverence." (p. 137)

One of the best ways to illustrate these qualities is to compare one of Clough's poems with that of one of his contemporaries. A useful comparison, I think, might be made of *Amours de Voyage* with Tennyson's *Maud.* There is some justification for selecting these two poems. They both are poems that represented for their authors a special kind of poetic venture, reflecting some autobiographical concern and revealing their ideas about the period in which they lived. For Tennyson, the poem dealt with "the blighting influence of a recklessly speculative age," while for Clough the poem took place in a world that, "Whithersoever we turn, still is the same narrow crib." For both poets, too, the work dealt with a subject that suggested several important possibilities: a hero seeking redemption through a loved one in a world he finds difficult to understand, a world not of his own making. Tennyson described *Maud* in these terms:

This poem is a little *Hamlet,* the history of a morbid poetic soul, under the blighting influence of a recklessly speculative age. He is the heir of madness, an egotist with the makings of a cynic, raised to sanity by a pure and holy love which elevates his whole nature, passing from the height of triumph to the lowest depth of misery, driven into madness by the loss of her whom he has loved, and, when he has at length passed through the fiery furnace, and has recovered his reason, giving himself up to work for the good of mankind through the unselfishness born of his great passion.[6]

There is reason to think that Clough thought of his own poem in something of the same way. One of the mottos or epigraphs he rejected for the poem stated, "He who despairs of himself is mad," and he, like Tennyson, thought of the ending in a wholly positive way. Disagreeing with his friend, Shairp, who could find nothing to admire about the hero, Clough replied:

But do you not, in the conception, find any final Strength of Mind in the unfortunate fool of a hero? I have no intention whatever of sticking up for him, but certainly I didn't mean him to go off into mere prostration and defeat. Does the last part seem utterly skeptical to your sweet faithful soul?[7]

Shairp's response to the poem may be said to be the typical one to much of Clough's poetry. He saw the poem as a projection of Clough's own "state of soul"; he found it had too much introspection. It was too "Werterish," even though, as he confessed, he had never read Werter. Clough protested, of course, but he could never convince Shairp of what he considered to be the "rightness" of the ending and of his artistic control over the piece. One of the ways to approach the poem in order to appreciate fully this control is to see exactly how Clough presents the hero, Claude, a character who seems to many to be anything but heroic. One clue to Claude may be found in Clough's description of Walter, the hero of Smith's *Life-Drama,* a character who has, for Clough, some admirable qualities; in his review Clough writes:

Under the guise of a different story, a story unskilful enough in its construction, we have seemed to recognize the ingenuous, yet passionate, youthful spirit, struggling after something like right and purity amidst the unnumbered difficulties, contradictions, and corruptions of the heated and crowded, busy, vicious, and inhuman town. Eager for action, incapable of action without some support, yet knowing not on what arm to dare to lean; not untainted; hard-pressed; in some sort, at times, overcome,—still we seem to see the young combatant, half combatant, half martyr, resolute to fight it out, and not to quit this for some easier field of battle,—one way or another to make something of it. (pp. 146–147)

While Claude is not simply another Walter, he does have some of Walter's characteristics, especially in his struggle after something "like right and purity" in the midst of contradictions and corruptions. He is also determined to "fight it out, not to quit this for some easier field of battle," a point that Clough is eager to establish in his poem. It is useful, for instance, to compare the hero of *Maud* with Clough's Claude, for one instantly recognizes the truth of Clough's statement regarding the final "strength of mind" of his hero. The hero of *Maud,* in spite of Tennyson's own description, fails to convince anyone of his unselfishness. Throughout much of the poem he is given to a great deal of sentimentalizing and exaggeration, and there is much of the Spasmodic in him. It is difficult to take him seriously, and it makes little difference about or against what he happens to be railing: love, Maud herself, politics, burial fees, etc. The tone is always the same; the impression is that of one who is, in fact, acting a part rather than living a life. There is no real sense of change, no suggestion of either the resolution of Walter or the strength of mind of Claude; his speeches range from the slightly embarrassing:

> And sleep must lie down armed, for the villainous
> centre-bits,
>
> Grind on the wakeful ear in the hush of moonless nights,
> While another is cheating the sick of a few last gasps,
> as he sits
> To pestle a poisoned poison behind his crimson lights.[8]

to the sentimental:

Maud, with her venturous climbings and tumbles and childish escapes,
Maud, the delight of the village, the ringing joy of the Hall,
Maud, with her sweet purse-mouth when my father dangled the grapes,
Maud, the beloved of my mother, the moonfaced darling of all—

to the outright chauvinistic:

> Though many a light shall darken, and many shall weep
> For those that are crushed in the clash of jarring claims,
> Yet God's just wrath shall be wreaked on a giant liar,
> And many a darkness into the light shall leap,
> And shine in the sudden making of splendid names,
> And noble thought be freer under the sun,
> And the heart of a people beat with one desire;

It is not just that Tennyson's hero is able to tell exactly how God feels, or that he has no hesitation in identifying himself with "the heart of a people"; it is simply that he never stops posing and shouting.

This is not to deny the lyric quality of *Maud,* of course, the "masterpiece of rhythm" as it has been called. We know that Swinburne, a superb critic, praised it highly. However, in terms of the effectiveness of the piece, especially as a work the message of which depends on the meaning conveyed chiefly through the protagonist, the contrast with Clough's Claude is striking. Whether or not one agrees with the "message" of Clough's poem, the point remains that Claude as a character effectively conveys the meaning of *Amours.* In this respect Claude is a successful portrayal; his own speeches and the way he is described and seen by others combine to convey Clough's central meaning, convincingly and interestingly. Of that central meaning I shall say more below; let me simply note here that it has to do with Claude's "final strength of mind," his refusal to "go off into mere prostration and defeat," and the ultimate resolution of the poem in terms of Claude's particular experience and its meaning in the context of what Clough calls "some central, celestial fact."

Claude succeeds as a character, then, while the hero of *Maud* does not. In contrast to the strained rhetoric of the speeches in *Maud,* those by Claude seem both appropriate and convincing, especially as commentaries on the age, on places, on people, on the situation of the *Amours* itself. Claude's observations on religion, politics, love, and human nature itself are perceptive and, more important, contain no sense of straining after effect:

No, the Christian faith, as at any rate I understood it,
With its humiliations and exaltations combining,
Exaltations sublime and yet diviner abasements,
Aspirations from something most shameful here upon earth and
In our poor selves to something most perfect above in the heavens,—
No, the Christian faith, as I, at least, understood it,
Is not here, O Rome, in any of these thy churches,
Is not here, but in Freiburg, or Rheims, or Westminster Abbey. (I, iv)
* * * * * * * * * *
It is most curious to see what a power a few calm words (in
Merely a brief proclamation) appear to possess on the people.
Order is perfect, and peace; the City is utterly tranquil;
And one cannot conceive that this easy and *nonchalant* crowd, that
Flows like a quiet stream through street and market-place, entering
Shady recesses and bays of church, osteria, and cafe,

61

Could in a moment be changed to a flood as of molten lava,
Boil into deadly wrath and wild homicidal delusion. (II, ix)
* * * * * * * * * *
What with trusting myself and seeking support from within me
Almost I could believe I had gained a religious assurance,
Found in my own poor soul a great moral basis to rest on.
Ah, but indeed I see, I feel it factitious entirely:
I refuse, reject, and put it utterly from me;
I will look straight out, see things, not try to evade them;
Fact shall be fact for me; and the Truth the Truth as ever
Flexible, changeable, vague, and multiform, and doubtful—
Off, and depart to the void, thou subtle fanatical tempter! (V, v)
* * * * * * * * * *
Not as the Scripture says, is, I think, the fact. Ere our death-day,
Faith, I think, does pass, and love; but Knowledge abideth.
Let us seek Knowledge;—the rest must come and go as it happens.
Knowledge is hard to seek, and harder yet to adhere to.
Knowledge is painful often; and yet when we know, we are happy.
Seek it, and leave mere Faith and Love to come with the chances. (V, x)

Much of the success of the portrayal of Claude is due to the "execution" of the poem, an artistic matter of which Clough was very much aware. We know that Clough did much revision in order to achieve a better portrait of Claude, one that conveyed a rounded rather than a flat impression. The flatness is what ultimately undermines our faith in the hero of *Maud,* for the only voice we hear is his, shrill, strained, unreal. Clough made certain that that would not happen in *Amours;* indeed, Claude's is only one voice among many that help to convey his character. There is always the balance provided by what amounts to a chorus of voices telling us about Claude; one does not have only the narrator's word, as in *Maud.* Claude's own speculations, sometimes almost contradictory about certain subjects, are balanced by the comments of others, particularly Georgina and Mary Trevellyn. We hear Georgina saying at the very beginning: "Who can a Mr. Claude be whom George has taken to be with? Very stupid, I think, but George says so *very* clever." (I, iii) Of course, we soon form our own opinion of Georgina, so that her comments are taken in their own frame of reference, another indication of Clough's artistic handling of events and characters in the poem. Mary Trevellyn's first impression of Claude also adds to the portrait: "I do not like him much, though I do not dislike being with him./ He is what people call, I suppose, a superior man, and/ Certainly seems so to me, but I think he is frightfully selfish." (I, xiii) Claude himself, Mary, Georgina, and even implicitly George and Eustace—all these contribute to our final impression of Claude. In this way Clough avoids the trap Tennyson fell into, for we are not limited by the one voice. Arnold sensed this, too, for in writing to Clough at one point he felt it necessary to contrast Clough's and Tennyson's manner, although there were certain stylistic similarities; writing to him in 1855, after reading *Maud,* Arnold said:

> From the extracts I have seen from Maud, he seems in his old age to be coming to your manner in the Bothie and the Roman poem [i.e., *Amours*]. That manner, as you know, I do not like: but certainly, if it is to be used, you use it with far more freedom vigour and abundance than he does— Altogether I think this volume a lamentable production, and like so much of our literature thoroughly and intensely *provincial,* not European. (p. 147)

I have written elsewhere of Arnold's view of Tennyson's provincialism, and he is here writing with a certain amount of willingness to believe the worst of Tennyson's writing; however, in this particular case I think that one must acknowledge the correctness of his judgement. Clough's *Amours* is in many respects a poem that stands up well when contrasted with *Maud,* even if one does not agree with Arnold that the latter is "lamentable"; and a great deal of the attractiveness of the poem comes from Clough's manner, which indeed exhibits the "freedom vigour and abundance" praised by Arnold.

This manner also helps bring out in a positive way Clough's purpose, for he was most anxious, as his letters to Shairp and others indicate, that the "conception" as he called it be understood. There is no doubt that readers have had trouble understanding fully the meaning of both poems, and the largely unfavorable critical reaction to both, especially *Maud,* might be traced to this difficulty. Certainly the chauvinistic ending of *Maud* failed to satisfy many critics; there was one who insisted that the title might be better if one dropped either vowel. Tennyson, we remember, had said that the hero was giving himself up "to work for the good of mankind," but the ending, and the previous actions and words of the hero, failed to convince many of the readers and critics. Clough succeeded where Tennyson failed in this respect, for he was able to make his hero both believable and sympathetic. He was also able, as Tennyson was not, to make clear the reasons why one should find that "final strength of mind" in his hero, that strength which enabled him to avoid prostration and defeat. That some readers and critics did not understand these reasons, or chose to ignore them, is another matter, but they are clearly there, especially for the perceptive reader who understands the nature of Clough's manner and the full implications of his poetic theory.

What Clough stresses in *Amours* is the way that the hero responds to each situation and his final resolve to know, to face fact and not fall prey to illusion, of which war might very well be the greatest, and to false hope. The hero of *Maud,* it becomes clear, has in fact taken the easy way out, for it is not very difficult to identify one's cause as the right one and go on to use "God's wrath" to fight for it. It may indeed be better to "fight for the good" than "to rail at the ill," but, as Claude keeps reminding himself and others, what exactly is the good and what are the proper motivations for action? "Action will furnish belief,—but will that belief be the true one?/ This is the point, you know. However, it doesn't much matter./ What one wants, I suppose, is to predetermine the action,/ so as to make it entail, not a chance-belief, but the true one." (V, ii) At another point, Claude tells Eustace, "We are so prone to these things with our terrible notions of duty." (II, xi) For Claude it is indeed tempting to accept the illusion: "Ah, did we really accept with a perfect heart the illusion!/ Ah, did we really believe that the Present indeed is the Only!/ Or through all transmutation, all shock and convulsion of passion,/ Feel we could carry undimmed, unextinguished, the light of our knowledge!" (III,vi) Claude cannot, of course, for he knows that he finally must "look straight out, see things, not try to evade them:/ Fact shall be fact for me; and the Truth the Truth as ever." (V, v)

The hero of *Maud* has, one is tempted to say, evaded things, but that is not really the point of the comparison. Clough's idea of poetry, we recall, was one that was concerned with the application of poetry to life. It should, we remember, first, be able to teach us the significance of that life, give some purpose to it, and, second, indicate to us our relationship to the "purer existence," indicate to us our unity with that existence. In *Amours* it seems clear that he is attempting to do these things, and particularly so in terms of tracing the thoughts and actions of Claude, his "unfortunate fool of a hero." With what Arnold called "freedom vigour and abundance" of manner, Clough attempted to demonstrate what he saw as his hero's final strength of mind, a strength that refused to accept illusion and insisted on seeing things clearly. Claude's experiences and comments help bring into sharper focus the meaning of human existence. His own actions and words illustrate and give form and shape and feeling to what Clough calls the "actual, palpable things with which our every-day life is concerned." By having his hero resist the easy way, by having Claude insist on following the truth, Clough demonstrates how poetry can, indeed, confer both consolation and inspiration on human beings, how it can help define in universal terms those ideas and actions we tend to see only as particulars.

One recent writer has, in fact, come very close to stressing the qualities that I have cited as the essential ones in understanding *Amours de Voyage* and Clough himself, and she has done this, appropriately in terms of the Arnold-Clough relationship. "Although Arnold complained of Clough's fluctuation in the Time Stream," writes Dorothy Deering, "he realized that in his own sense of crisis he was constantly thinking of Clough as one of the 'children of the second birth,' acknowledging his 'still, considerate mind' and an individual power that 'the world could not tame.' . . . Furthermore, these qualities bore directly on the impact of his poetry, for they formed the basis of its sincerity, reality, and lack of self-conscious posturings, qualities Arnold admired in Clough's poetry and judged deficient in his own. . . . " So far, so good, but Professor Deering then goes on to mention the one element that I have implicitly emphasized as being also present in Clough's poetry, one not often noted. I refer to the optimistic note often found in his work. "In contrast to the 'beatific vision' of Arnold's romantic imagination," concludes Deering, "which produced joy from an intensely individualistic isolated moment of reception, Clough's epiphanies are public and communal, yet without despair."[10] Patrick Scott, interestingly enough, has called *Amours* Clough's "long-pondered, if tentative, testament of hope." (p. 14) Perhaps we do have, then, some notions about what makes Clough so fascinating a figure, and it should be of some interest to see how these are developed by future readers and critics.

NOTES

1. For the fluctuations in Clough's reputation see Michael Thorpe, ed., *Clough: The Critical Heritage* (New York: Barnes and Noble), 1972.

2. Barbara Hardy, "Clough's Self-Consciousness" in *The Major Victorian Poets: Reconsiderations,* ed. Isobel Armstrong (London: Routledge and Kegan Paul), p. 253.

3. "Corydon Had a Rival," *Victorian Newsletter,* No. 19 (Spring, 1961), 5–11; "The Poetic Theory of Arthur Hugh Clough," *English Studies,* 43 (August, 1962), 240–247.

4. *The Letters of Matthew Arnold to Arthur Hugh Clough,* ed. with an intro. by Howard Foster Lowry (Oxford, 1932), p. 59. All subsequent references to Arnold's letters are to this edition.

5. Buckner B. Trawick, ed., *Selected Prose Works of Arthur Hugh Clough* (University, Alabama: University of Alabama Pr., 1964), pp. 113–114. All future page references to Clough's criticism will be to this volume; I have ignored the editor's silent corrections of Clough's text.

6. Hallam Lord Tennyson, *Alfred Tennyson: A Memoir* (London, 1897), I, 396.

7. *The Correspondence of Arthur Hugh Clough,* ed. F. L. Mulhauser (Oxford: Oxford University Press, 1957), I, 278.

8. All quotations from *Maud* are from *The Poems of Tennyson,* ed. Christopher Ricks (London: Longmans, Green and Company Ltd., 1969); all quotations from *Armours de Voyage* are from the volume edited by Patrick Scott (Queensland: University of Queensland Press, 1974).

9. "Arnold, Tennyson, and English Idyl: Ancient Criticism and Modern Poetry," *Texas Studies in Literature and Language,* 16 (Spring, 1974), 135–146.

10. Dorothy Deering, "The Antithetical Poetics of Arnold and Clough," *Victorian Poetry,* 16 (Spring/Summer, 1978), 30.

MATTHEW ARNOLD:
"ALL ONE AND CONTINUOUS"

MIRIAM ALLOTT

My familiarity with Matthew Arnold began late in life, in fact not much more than six or seven years ago when I took over some of the work on nineteenth-century poetry in general and Arnold in particular left unfinished at his death by Kenneth Allott. The "experience" has been curious and significant in a number of ways. My own early interests as a university teacher were formed by a sedate academic progress from a master's thesis on E. M. Forster and a doctoral thesis on Henry James to a teaching post on the staff, which led in due time to directing specialist courses on the traditional nineteenth-century novel, with George Eliot figuring prominently and predictably as a high-Victorian sage struggling to forge an honorable answer to the question "how to live" in an age "Of change, alarm, surprise." Arnoldian quotations of this nature came readily even then, the affinity between these eminent agnostic angels being something of which necessarily one had long been aware. But the self-confessed representative of the "main movement of mind" of the age was still seen more or less out of the corner of my eye—"somewhat sideways," as Keats said of certain artistic achievements whose power he sensed but did not properly understand.[1]

Now it is Arnold who has moved to the foreground, though George Eliot, once known, cannot be confined to the peripheral areas of anyone's vision. Her work is a central *massif* linking two vast ranges of English fiction and marked by configurations which belong to both. It obeys the missionary impulse of the early Victorian novelists while

67

yielding, even if unwittingly, to the demand to be heard urged by a pressingly personal and largely sombre vision of things, a demand which her late-Victorian successors, repudiating didacticism and the utilitarian view of literature, responded to as the imaginative writer's real, right and only thing. Similar conflicting impulses shape Arnold's writing career and help to explain why these two figures so readily come together in one's thinking about the peculiarities of their age. It is generally accepted that their shared missionary sense is associated with the early-Victorian and high-Victorian conviction that a writer's duty in that "iron time" was to exhort and encourage others, to "animate," as Arnold has it in a celebrated letter,[2] which meant doing as much as possible on these lines for oneself as well. It is recognized, too, that many writers whose creative gifts were stimulated by feelings of melancholy and loss feared that putting these principles into practice might mean artistic suicide. But it is perhaps less often said that for certain other writers the exercise was not at all out of keeping with their native gifts. George Eliot's finest achievements stem from her novelistic gifts finding at their service a natural bent for lofty, humane, profoundly earnest, "evangelical" proselytizing. This is apparent in the phrasing, the movement, the cadences of even her earliest letters. When as a novelist she permits ingredients from her spiritual autobiography to dominate her exemplary fictional style, her readers can experience more uneasiness than they do even when she is at her most governessy. The anomaly was recognized some time ago by F. R. Leavis when he complained about the damagingly "sentimental" and "immature" elements in the drawing of her heroines (notably the idealistic ardours of Maggie Tulliver and Dorothea Brooke, whom she presents as finely-tuned spirits homeless in an uncomprehending world). The effect is still more pronounced in the religiose passages of *Daniel Deronda,* where she gives head at last to the suppressed religious yearnings of the Dinah Morris in herself, transmogrifying them, so to speak, into Mordecai, with no holds barred.

Fiction is one thing and poetry another, and what works in the former may not work in the other, especially so far as the management of personal feeling is concerned; but a revealing peculiarity in George Eliot, for this reader at any rate, is that alone among Wordsworth's Victorian readers her lifelong admiration for him never faltered, whether his hand was in his breeches pocket or not.[3] She was twenty when she first read his poetry in her recently acquired copy of the six-volume Moxon edition and declared, "I never before met with so many of my own feelings just as I could like them." She must have been thinking chiefly of the poet of the *Lyrical Ballads* (and perhaps Margaret in *The Excursion*) when in 1861 she wrote of *Silas Marner* that no one would be "interested in it but myself (since Wordsworth is dead),"[4] but it is to the "philosophical" Wordsworth whom Arnold deplored that she most consistently turns, especially as he appears in *The Excursion*. It is the case that certain dominating movements in the intellectual and imaginative history of the Victorians can be followed through the complications of their feelings about Wordsworth; and it is important to this history that her fellow devout skeptics from Mill to "Mark Rutherford," whom Arnold liked so much,[5] experienced very mixed feelings about him indeed. Arnold's ambivalences make themselves felt early, as we know from "Resignation," begun about 1843, which looks towards "Tintern Abbey" at the same time that it dissents from it, replacing a Nature which is a constant source of joy and consolation with one that "seems to bear rather than rejoice." The "Obermann" poem of 1849 and the two poems written at the time of Wordsworth's death in 1850, "Memorial Verses" and "The Youth of Nature," are similarly ambiguous in saluting a poet who brought hope by celebrating the freshness and delight of the natural world in his own

> iron time
> Of doubts, disputes, distractions, fears . . .,

but was unequal to the needs of the age into which he lived, when

> the complaining millions of men
> Darken in labour and pain . . .,

so making it hard not to claim, as we read in the Obermann poem, that

> . . . Wordsworth's eyes avert their ken
> From half of human fate . . .

At the other end of his life, in the 1880 introduction to his one-volume edition of selections designed to rescue Wordsworth from the Wordsworthians, Arnold delivered his broadside:

> The Excursion abounds with philosophy, and therefore the Excursion is to the Wordsworthian what it never can be for the disinterested lover of poetry,—a satisfactory work. 'Duty exists', says Wordsworth in the

Excursion; and then he proceeds thus—

> ... Immutably survive
> For our support, the measures and the forms,
> Which an abstract intelligence supplies,
> Whose kingdom is, where time and space are not.

And the Wordsworthian is delighted, and thinks that here is a sweet union of philosophy and poetry. But the disinterested lover of poetry will feel that the lines carry us really not a step further than the proposition which they would interpret; that they are a tissue of elevated but abstract verbiage, alien to the very nature of poetry ...[6]

The passage moves us in a special way when we recollect that the man writing had for some twenty years abandoned poetry for prose and was now celebrated as his country's foremost critic of its current cultural short-comings, a critic moreover with his own governessy ways who was displaying some of them now. The reproof found its way to the heart of Wordsworth's other famous admirer, sitting at home in the Priory shortly before moving into Cheyne Walk with her new husband John Cross, and there encountered resistance. A selection of Wordsworth is unsatisfactory "except for travelling and popular distribution," she notes dismissively in her April 1880 letter to Frederic Harrison, because it cannot give "the perfect gems to be found in a single line, or in a dozen lines, which are to be found in the 'dull' poems." She quotes a good passage from Book VIII of *The Prelude* (11. 60-8–15) but, an unrepentant "Wordsworthian" still, she offers as "much to your purpose" the pronouncement,

> There is
> One great society alone on earth:
> The noble living and the noble dead ...,

and regrets Arnold's omission of the sonnet "I grieved for Buonaparte ...," She quotes from the poem "these precious lines," which display the "sweet union of philosophy and poetry" prompting Arnold's amused scorn (the italics are hers):

> 'Tis not in battle that from youth we train
>   The governor who must be wise and good,
> And temper with the otherness of the brain
>   Thoughts motherly, and meek as womanhood.
> *Wisdom doth live with children round her knees.*[7]

One's affection for Arnold owes a good deal to differences of the kind signalled by these reactions to Wordsworth, and it is clear to me now that the effect produced by his poetry on my own sensibility is governed by a feeling for the whole movement of his creative intelligence. When we speak of "George Eliot" we mean the author of an entire body of writing, and the same goes for Arnold. H. F. Lowry agrees that Arnold's efforts in the two fields of poetry and prose "are *inseparable*":

> . . . the reader who knows only one body if his work can hardly know even that. Voices reverberate back and forth between the verse and the essays; the questions raised in the one are answered in the other . . .[8]

Furthermore, as I was once led to add in another context, "the tone of the one is answered by the tone of the other."[9] The experience of reading Arnold is as much as anything else a matter of responding to a particular temper. Some years ago Douglas Jefferson, in distinguishing Fielding's and Richardson's contrasted styles, singled out the play of humor and the strategic ironic withdrawals of the former and the equally impressive but totally divergent "awful directness" of the latter.[10] It is not far out of the way to see a parallel in Arnold and George Eliot, since she belongs securely in the English Puritan tradition which Professor Jefferson has in mind when discussing Richardson, while Arnold of course engaged in a running battle with the narrowing effects of the tradition in contemporary England. He gathered his forces in the late 1860s for culminating attacks on them in *Culture and Anarchy* and its more polished companion, *Friendship's Garland,* where he bounces them up and down with a fresh access of gaiety and wit. His initial forays in the first series of *Essays in Criticism* show him attempting to draw out some response to European culture from "that powerful but at present somewhat narrow organ the modern Englishman" by introducing him to a number of unfamiliar minor foreign figures—Joubert, Maurice de Guérin, Maurice's still less known sister Eugénie—whose shared "excellence" lay above all in their ownership of, and power to express, a spirit subtly self-scrutinizing, honest, imaginative, melancholy and gallant. He felt at home with those writers because he had a good measure of their qualities himself, although in his early Oxford days he might not have wished to acknowledge the affinity. There were reasons in any case why he should have felt the need to dissemble. It is notable that in assuming during his Oxford days his youthful dandyish disguise he drew on other qualities, gaiety and high spirits above all, which he never refers to in any of the people—from Marcus Aurelius to Heine and from Falkland to Senancour—of whom he writes so admiringly and plangently. He was to employ precisely these qualities when seeking "to instruct, elevate, and to amuse" the British public once he had left behind the ten years or so of his poetic career and become "a master of prose and reason" (or at any rate imaginative reason).[11] That phrase referring to the '*utile* and *dulce*' of art is used dismissively by Joyce's cocky Stephen Dedalus, who reminds us of Arnold's supercilious self-protective pose when he announces in *Stephen Hero,* "Everyone . . . who has a character to preserve must have a manner to preserve it with." Art would "never yield its secret to one who is enmeshed with profanities," he declares loftily, and the chief of these is

> the antique principle that the end of art is to instruct, to elevate, and to amuse. I am unable to find even a trace of this Puritanic conception of the aesthetic purpose in the definitions which Aquinas has given of beauty. . . .[12]

Charlotte Brontë, whose peculiar fusion of passionate earnestness and earnest passion gave a new dimension to nineteenth-century English Puritanism, was close to recognizing a reason both for the disguise and the need to make unfrivolous use of the qualities on which it drew when she met Arnold in 1850 and felt that "the shade of Dr. Arnold seemed to frown on his young representative."[13] This sort of attitude is neatly captured by Max Beerbohm in the sharp inquiry, "Why oh why Uncle Matt will you never be wholly serious?" which he fancifully ascribes in his Matthew Arnold cartoon to the disapproving little girl later to be Mrs. Humphry Ward. It still survives here and there today, especially in quarters where the combination of airy polemics in Arnold's serious essays and the melancholy temper of his poems produces unsettlement and misgiving. There is something in the English—if not also the American—Puritan spirit which can still suspect that to amuse and be amused is a frivolous way of carrying on and certainly incompatible with a proper seriousness of purpose.

And yet the co-existence of wit and serious feeling is increasingly noticeable in English post-modernist literature and it arises for the most part from a brand of stoicism which Arnold would have recognized and understood. At Oxford, as we know from his friend Clough, he was "full of Parisianism" entering a room "with a song of Béranger on his lips," walking with an "air of parading the Rue de Rivoli," letting his hair grow long and regularly cutting chapel."[14] But from the

> hidden ground
> of thought and austerity within . . .,

he was at this time composing the poems which surprised everyone when they appeared in his first volume, *The Strayed Reveller* (1849), because of their reflective melancholy and their "knowledge of life and conflict . . . *strangely like experience,*" as his favourite sister Jane put it, underlining the phrase for emphasis.[15] His own crisis of faith, unlike that of many of his contemporaries among the "lost generation" of the 1840s, seems to have taken place off stage but, as with Joyce's artist as a young man, "the episode . . . had resulted in a certain outward self-control which was now found to be very useful."[16] There was additionally an inner "self-control" to which as poet and moralist he also schooled himself. His austere self-commands hint at the hidden turbulence to be brought under discipline. The itinerant preacher, the "restless fool" of the early "In Harmony with Nature," is scorned for exhorting us "To be like Nature strong, like Nature cool," since Nature is "cruel," "stubborn," "fickle," "forgives no debt and fears no grave." But it is the longing to be indeed "strong" and "cool" which lends force to the lines. Echoes of this are felt as far on as 1873 when Arnold's thinking about "Nature" is still governed by misgiving, for the term is "full of pitfalls," as he says in *Literature and Dogma,* and if "we are to give full swing to our inclinations" which self is it in us that wer are to follow—"our *apparent* self or a higher real self"?[17] Whether "apparent" or "higher" and real" the self most urgently present in the early poems is restless, emotional, passionate, lonely and uncertain. Images suggesting longed-for calm arrive together with those suggesting the threatening opposite as in "In Utrumque Paratus," written about 1846, where the Plotinian debate rises in poetic temperature at the end of the third and the start of the fourth stanza:

The solemn peaks but to the stars are known,
But to the stars, and the cold lunar beams;
Alone the sun arises, and alone
     Spring the great streams.
But if the wild unfather'd mass no birth
     In divine seats hath known;

> In the blank, echoing solitude if Earth,
> Rocking her obscure body to and fro,
> Ceases not from all time to heave and groan ... (11.18–26)

Calm may perhaps be found on mountain slopes or "some high station," but down in the world are fever, sickness, distress, the distraction from distraction by distraction:

> Not milder is the general lot
> Because our spirits have forgot
> In action's dizzying eddy whirl'd,
> The something that infects the world. ("Resignation," 11.275–8)

His need for self-schooling is still more urgently present in the 'Switzerland,' poems. His temperament is,

> Too strange, too restless, too untamed ...,

he owns "a starting feverish heart," forsees "a life alas! / Distracted as a homeless wind ...," and fears that there is no help for it but to face,

> This truth—to prove and make thine own:
> Thou hast been, shalt be, art, alone. ...

The forces ruling his world are as arbitrary as they are implacable, urging wrathfully, "Be counsell'd and retire" and placing eternally between himself and the other—in these poems the figure we know as "Marguerite"—"The unplumb'd salt estranging sea," a line which concentrates, with a peculiarly individual Arnoldian "natural magic," the essence of the sorrowful, hard-fought-for stoicism of the 1849 volume.[18]

Nearly a quarter of a century later, facing as so often before the recognition that though people cannot do without religion neither can they any longer do with it as it is, he offers in place of the arbitrary powers ("A god, a god, their severance ruled") and of "the preternatural, which is now [religion's] popular sanction" but will have to be given up in the "scientism" of the times, "the mighty forces of love, reverence, gratitude, hope, pity, and awe—all that host of allies which Wordsworth includes under the one name of *imagination.*"[19] The gaiety, which in the 1840s was a protective armor for the disturbed self struggling to bring its emotions into creative order, now reappears in fine fettle, this time to safeguard in Wordsworth the poet of *"imagination"* from the poet of "the 'scientific system of thought' " who offers us "at last such poetry as this which the devout Wordsworthians accept" (the passage is from *The Excursion,* Book IX, 11.219–302):

> O for the coming of that glorious time
> When, prizing knowledge as her noblest wealth
> And best protection, this Imperial Realm,
> While she exacts allegiance, shall admit
> An obligation, on her part, to *teach*
> Them who are born to serve her and obey;
> Binding herself by statute to secure,
> For all the children whom her soil maintains,
> The rudiments of letters, and inform
> The mind with moral and religious truth.

He goes on,

> Wordsworth calls Voltaire dull, and surely the production of these un-Voltarian lines must have been imposed on him as a judgment! One can hear them being quoted at a Social Science Congress; one can call up the whole scene. A great room in one of our dismal provincial towns; dusty air and jaded afternoon daylight; benches full of men with bald heads and women in spectacles; an orator lifting up his face from a manuscript written within and without to declaim these lines of Wordsworth; and in the soul of any poor child of nature who may have wandered in thither, an unutterable sense of lamentation, and mourning, and woe![20]

As it happens, the National Association for the Promotion of Social Science (first established in 1856 and featured in 1861 as the Pantopragmatic Society of Peacock's *Gryll Grange*) was dissolved for want of funds six years after this, but these days we have our Further Education courses and our extra-mural seminars in English Literature and some of us may without difficulty "call up the whole scene." We must remember too that George Eliot's spirit was invoked as often as Wordsworth's at meetings of Moral Improvement Societies up and down the country. Her work was similarly culled for "gems," and anthologies of wise sayings were put together from her novels. It is hard now to realise the almost total eclipse of this hugely popular reputation after her death in the 1880s, but from the first beginnings of its revival (a landmark was David Cecil's *Early Victorian Novelists* of 1934), it became a habit to salute her as our first "modern" novelist. But how "modern" is "modern"? The work of our internationally known novelists since the 1950s—Graham Greene, Iris Murdoch, Angus Wilson, Muriel Spark, let us say, along with our university wits, David Lodge and Malcolm Bradbury, who are well known in America—has as its highest common factor a combination of satirical wit with serious, even tragic, feeling, a form of tragi-comedy which, as I have said elsewhere, may well come to be seen as the twentieth-century's dominant literary "kind." It is also present with variations in English contemporary poetry, notably in Philip Larkin's wry verse and the more exuberant but denser, because more deeply sculptured, poems of Seamus Heaney. If this temper is "modern," then George Eliot is certainly not "modern." The claim for her modernity rested on the reach of her psychological insight and her capacity to drama-tize inner movements of mind and feeling and at the same time to enliven with her lion's share of the traditional novelist's gift for realis-tic detail the life of ordinary human beings in an often disappointing everyday world. But with the calling into question of nineteenth-century narrative procedures ("realistic" characterization, plot as a causal sequence consonant with a recognized outward order, the re-luctance to bring out into the open bleak feelings of disturbance and conflict), not even her insight into the erosions of a spirit confronting with dismay an increasingly complicated world can make her seem other than resolutely committed to steadying course in that time and place, with as little as possible of disheartening allusion to the "dead world" behind and the alarming world about "to be born."

Arnold's claims to "modernity" are less vulnerable. This is largely because as poet he unflinchingly confronts, while contending with, his own "imagination of disaster," so that his poetry certainly becomes as candid a "dialogue of the mind with itself" as any other in the age. And when the moralist in himself can no longer countenance what he feels to be "morbid" introspection, he directs his critical intelligence to the practical business of safe-guarding values threatened by the order of things which brought the poetry into being in the first place. I must make it clear that I am not using the term "modern" to mean "adequate" in Arnold's evaluative manner, but the fact remains that for new readers—I am thinking especially of my own students—what Arnold writes commands sympathetic response for its authenticity and for its engagement with problems whose far-reaching effects are recognised at every turn of their own road. The response is quickened by their recognition of the interplay between the poet, the critic and the personality of the man who, in his latest years, brought a flavour of his everyday personal self into his engaging and touching dirges for lost household pets (a canary, a cat, a beloved dog). Such readers light up at his remarks about coal in the Elizabethan Age, his mickey-taking in "The Dissidence of Dissent and the Protestantism of the Protestant Religion," his amusement at the lapses in his own "disin-terestedness" ("Ruskin was dogmatic and *wrong*"), his failed efforts to emulate the Barbarians in field sports and his insouciant jokiness —for example at the expense of the unfortunate Mr. Wright, who protested about Arnold's remarks on him as a translator of Homer,

> One cannot always be studying one's own works, and I was really under the impression, till I saw Mr. Wright's complaint, that I had spoken of him with all respect . . .,

and, as a son and brother, in an affectionate letter home at the time of the Chartist riots in 1848 and the fear of the French invasion,

> Tell Edward I shall be ready to take flight with him the moment the French land, and have engaged a hansom to carry us both from the scene of carnage . . .[21]

(There is no such kicking up of heels, alas, anywhere in George Eliot or Charlotte Brontë). With a more immediate personal concern, since many will become, or are already, members of the teaching profession, these readers are held by his still all too pertinent views about the English educational system, and, with some wryness, his hard slog as a school inspector. Perhaps the most surprising discoveries are his "democratic" ideas about state government[22] and his struggle to for-mulate a system of belief capable of meeting spiritual needs without resting on "miracle, mystery and authority," in both of which the effort towards clarity is saluted as well as the limitations in the think-ing, most of them stemming from the same traditions of English liberal humanism governing George Eliot's favorite themes and the "outmoded" narrative procedures which accommodate them. But Arnold confronts more explicitly and practically than George Eliot the problem of how to live in an increasingly secular age. His view that poetry must take the place of religion to light up morality is responded to as an anticipation of modern existentialist movements towards the retention of warmth behind our moral perceptions in an age of de-mythologized religion and increased secularity. (Camus puts this in his own terms in *La Peste* through Tarrou's celebrated inquiry, "Can one be a saint without God?")

This liking for a temper which can be serious without pomposity and amusing without being frivolous has made it easier for new read-ers to respond sympathetically to Arnold as a poet. In any case, of course, one no longer has the sense of addressing the unconverted when talking about the Victorian poets, though it has taken time for the vast proliferation of nineteenth-century studies during the past twenty years or so to produce its effect. This is partly because scholar-ship has done everything to uncover information about the social, political and religious background of the age and has devoted itself to minute exegesis of the poetry and the prose, but has done relatively little to illuminate the nature and quality of the literature itself. Things have not been helped, either, by the recent fashion, largely promoted in Britain by television drama and the antiques trade, for what in feeling, stance and style is really "Edwardian" but nevertheless is commonly described as "Victorian." This means that it is all the more imperative to distinguish among the three phases of the period—Early, Middle (or High) and Late—which are as strikingly differen-tiated in temper and climate as comparable phases in any other period of history. Even so, I think 'Victorian' is beginning to be recognized as a term we can reserve for those aspects of the age which have become part of our post-Strachey folklore about it but have little to do with the writers and thinkers who "represent the age's main move-ment of mind." (The stock ingredients of this lore include among other things sexual prudery, sweated labour, frilled piano legs, an-timacassars, poker-work mottoes, Sunday observance, hypocritical relativism, religiose poetry, and a literature consistent with wayside pulpit exhortation).

With much of this débris cleared away, critical response is freer and more flexible (there is a parallel in the case of D. H. Lawrence, who used to be condemned or passionately admired for extra-aesthetic reasons). At the same time, the relative novelty of this "discovery" of the Victorian poets has the effect of heightening appreciation of their curiously wide tonal range. It comes to be accepted, with some critical alertness to the reasons for the inequalities, that for instance, Tenny-son is sometimes sentimental and silly, but can be magical; that Browning substitutes bluster for the hard graft of thinking out difficult ideas, but is boldly colloquial, delighted by the drunkenness of things being various and a subtle love poet; and that Clough—well Clough can still be an enormous surprise. Few readers in this largely non-churchgoing generation have been familiar since childhood with "Say not the struggle nought availeth ..." (though it is sung in church services yet) but even without these animating Rugbeian lines to afford a comparison it is still an arresting experience to come upon a Victorian "poet of doubt" whose uncertainties stimulate witty inventiveness, as they do in *Amours de Voyage*—whose diffident hero Claude is Clough's version of the nineteenth-century Hamlet figure (found at his most disenchanted in Flaubert and his most alarming in Dostoevsky)—and again in "Dipsychus," probably the most brilliant and original of the manifold "dialogues of the mind with itself" of the age. Then there are the light-hearted *vers-de-société* ("How pleasant it is to have money, heigh ho! ..."),[22] the animated salute to the lifeforce in "Natura Naturans," and the erotic contributions to the youthful *Ambarvalia* (which upset Mrs. Clough so much). To be able to recognize something of the quality of these varied talents, the unevennesses of which are often traced to a worried engagement between the writer's individual temper and his preoccupation with his public role, is invaluable equipment in the matter of understanding Arnold's poetic gifts. The absence from these of Tennyson's "natural magic," Browning's dynamism and Clough's wit comes to be seen as the necessary concomitant of a poetry essentially elegiac and melancholy, but not passively so, since it is precisely against nostalgia and inactive melancholy that Arnold's formal and stylistic constraints are posed. When for Clough religious certainties disappeared, the initial sense of desolation and loss was urgent, explicit and plangent, and found expression in what is probably the most powerful of the poems of the "lost generation":

> Christ is not risen!
>
> Christ is not risen, no;
> He lies and moulders low;
> Christ is not risen.
>
> As circulates in some great city crowd
> A rumour changeful, vague, importunate, and loud,
>   Or authorship exact,
>   Which no man can deny
>   Nor verify;

> So spread the wondrous fame;
>   He all the same
> Lay senseless, mouldering, low,
>   He was not risen, no,
>   Christ was not risen!

Ashes to ashes, dust to dust;
As of the unjust, also of the just—
    Yea, of that Just One too.
This is the one sad Gospel that is true,
    Christ is not risen.

("Easter Day," 11.5–8, 48–63)

The reply in the second part of "Easter Day" is still sombre:

> Joy with grief mixes, with despondence hope.
> Hope conquers cowardice, joy grief;
> Or at least, faith unbelief

("Easter Day" II, 11.32–4)

Arnold's lines in "Stanzas from the Grande Chartreuse" on a similar subject are characteristically more reflective, the low-keyed style signalling the taut self-discipline to which the lines themselves refer:

> Wandering between two worlds, one dead,
> The other powerless to be born,
> With nowhere yet to rest my head,
>   Like these, on earth I wait forlorn.
> Their faith, my tears, the world deride—
>   I come to shed them at their side.
>
> O, hide me in your gloom profound,
> Ye solemn seats of holy pain:
>   Take me, cowled forms, and fence me round,
> Till I possess my soul again;
>   Till free my thoughts before me roll,
>   Not chafed by hourly false control!

(11.85–96)

The tone of voice is unmistakable and is sustained throughout the ten or so years of Arnold's poetic career. We become accustomed, as not in Clough, to a particular register. This is not to take away from Clough's brilliances in his still smaller handful of poems, but one sees why Arnold grumbled about his friend's fits and starts and told him to settle to his own *assiette.*[23] It has been said that in arranging and classifying Arnold's poetry there are two possible methods.[24] One is to group together the *Weltanschauung* poetry, direct or dramatized, the "pure subject" narrative poems and the love poems, together with the personal elegies. The other is to classify them by style, say the "Keatsian" poems and the "Wordsworthian" poems, the former having more particularity and colour ("The Scholar Gypsy," "Thyrsis," some of "Tristram and Iseult") and the latter more severity and drive in the movement of the argument ("Mycerinus," "Stanzas from the Grande Chartreuse," the Obermann poems). But the truth is that the work is consistent with itself in a way that resists these ready taxonomic procedures. Even when it is recognized that the stylistic influences are mixed, that they include something of Goethe in the reflective poems and the unrhymed recitations of "Sohrab and Rustum," "Rugby Chapel," "Howarth Churchyard" and "Heine's Grave," and something of Tennyson too here and there in passages from "Mycerinus," "The Forsaken Merman" and "The Scholar Gypsy," it is still the case that whatever the play of various influences, Arnold forges a personal style, less flowing and hypnotic than Tennyson's, less abrupt and diffuse than Browning's, rarely given to *èlan* and incandescence, but always emotionally honest, in command of tone and temper and sometimes, through the operation of strong feeling under constraint, transcending self-consciousness to produce a fine unimpeded poetic expressiveness. The consistency of this poetic tone and temper sees to it that the melancholy severity of Empedocles's hexameters,

> Riches we wish to get,
> Yet remain spendthrifts still;
> We would have health, and yet
> Still use our bodies ill;
> Rafflers of our own prayers, from youth to life's last scenes ...
>
> We do not what we ought,
> What we ought not, we do,
> And lean upon the thought
> That chance will bring us through;
> But our own acts, for good or ill, are mighty powers. ...
>
> (I ii 222–6, 237–41)

is still felt in the "Keatsian" poetry of "The Scholar Gypsy":

> No, no, thou hast not felt the lapse of hours!
> For what wears out the life of mortal men?
>   'Tis that from change to change their being rolls;
>   'Tis that repeated shocks, again, again,
>   Exhaust the energy of strongest souls
>   And numb the elastic powers.
> Till having used our nerves with bliss and teen,
>   And tired upon a thousand schemes our wit
>   To the just-pausing Genius we remit
> Our worn-out life, and are—what we have been.
>   (11.141–50)

But then again both the "austere" and the "Keatsian" poems express
with particularity and poignancy Arnold's characteristic feeling for
the beauty of a natural world which saddens as it delights, for, though
separate from man and indifferent, it is subject to the same laws of
change and transience. The feeling is not unlike Hardy's and moves
the reader as the description of Egdon Heath moves him at the opening of *The Return of the Native,* though Arnold, when all is said, has
a more captivating "natural magic." So in "Resignation,"

> The self-same shadows now, as then,
> Play through this grassy upland glen;
> The loose dark stones on the green way
> Lie strewn, it seems, where then they lay;
> On this mild bank above the stream,
> (You crush them!) the blue gentians gleam,
> Still this wild brook, the rushes cool,
> The sailing foam, the shining pool!
>   (11.98–107)

In spite of the resigned sadness of the poem the "eye is on the object"
with the same pleasure that it rests on the natural landscape in Calli-
cless's songs, which set against Empedocles's overtaxed mind the
youthful poet's balance of thought and feeling:

> The track winds down to the clear stream,
> To cross the sparkling shallows; there
> The cattle love to gather, on their way
> To the high mountain-pastures, and to stay,
> Till the rough cow-herds drive them past,
> Knee-deep in the cool ford, for 'tis the last
> Of all the woody, high, well-water'd dells
> On Etna; and the beam

Of noon is broken there by chestnut-boughs
Down its steep verdant sides; the air
Is freshen'd by the leaping stream, which throws
Eternal showers of spray on the moss'd roots
Of trees, and veins of turf, and long dark shoots
Of ivy-plants, and fragrant hanging bells
Of hyacinths, and on late anemonies,
That muffle its wet banks; but glade,
And stream, and sward, and chestnut-trees,
End here; Etna beyond, in the broad glare
Of the hot noon, without a shade,
Slope behind slope, up to the peak, lies bare;
The peak, round which the white clouds play.

(I ii 36–56)

The keenness of the feeling is invariably heightened by the contrast
with another order of being, imaged here in "the broad glare/Of the
hot noon," as it is with the green, shaded "Keatsian" retreats in "The
Scholar Gypsy," where the lines are penetrated with elegiac nostalgia
and the "hot noon" is held at a distance while the eye rests on the
well-memoried scene.

Screen'd is this nook o'er the high, half-reap'd field,
    And here till sundown, shepherd! will I be.
        Through the thick corn the scarlet poppies peep,
And round green roots and yellowing stalks I see
        Pale pink convolvulus in tendrils creep;
            And air-swept lindens yield
Their scent, and rustle down their perfumed showers
        Of bloom on the bent grass where I am laid,
            And bower me from the August sun with shade;
And the eye travels down to Oxford's towers.

(11.21–30)

Feeling and the landscape are brought together and associated as in
Tennyson, and also as in Tennyson the sense of loss can be made
poignantly explicit, though constrained still, and often by formal
narrative procedures. Arnold sings of his personal sense of loss
through his deserted merman's "lyrical cry"—

Call her once before you go—
Call once yet!
In a voice that she will know:

83

> Margaret! Margaret!
>
> Children's voices wild with pain—
> Surely she will come again!
> Call her once and come away;
> This way, this way!
> Mother dear, we cannot stay!
> The wild white horses foam and fret!
> Margaret! Margaret!
>
> (11.10–13, 16–22)

—or through the Breton narrator in the third part of "Tristram and Iseult" reflecting upon what it is that "wears out the life of mortal men":

> ... we may suffer deeply, yet retain
> Power to be moved and soothed, for all our pain,
> By what of old pleased us, and will again.
> No, 'tis the gradual furnace of the world,
> In whose hot air our spirits are upcurl'd
> Until they crumble, or else grow like steel—
> Which kills in us the bloom, the youth, the spring—
> Which leaves the fierce necessity to feel,
> But takes away the power—this can avail,
> By drying up our joy in everything,
> To make our former pleasures all seem stale.
> This, or some tyrannous single thought, some fit
> Of passion, which subdues our souls to it,
> Till for its sake alone we live and move—
> Call it ambition, or remorse, or love—
> This too can change us wholly, and make seem
> All which we did before, shadow and dream.
>
> (III 116–32)

The setting for the sorrowing Iseult, "dying in a mask of youth," is still beautiful and in its particularized detail even cheerful:

> ... This cirque of open ground
> Is light and green; the heather, which all round
> Creeps thickly, grows not here; but the pale grass
> Is strewn with rocks, and many a shiver'd mass
> Of vein'd white-gleaming quartz, and here and there
> Dotted with holly-trees and juniper.

In the smooth centre of the opening stood
Three hollies side by side, and made a screen,
Warm with the winter-sun, of burnish'd green
With scarlet berries gemm'd, the fell-fare's food.
Under the glittering hollies Iseult stands,
Watching her children play; their little hands
Are busy gathering spars of quartz, and streams
Of staghorn for their hats; anon, with screams
Of mad delight they drop their spoils, and bound
Among the holly-clumps and broken ground,
Racing full speed, and startling in their rush
The fell-fares and the speckled missel-thrush
Out of their glossy coverts . . .

(III 13–31)

The salute to the everyday hum of things here and in "Lines Written in Kensington Gardens" is regrettably rare in Arnold's poetry. It belongs to the daylight side of his temperament which kept anhedonia at bay in his earlier years and is clearly visible in what we know of his life as an affectionate husband and father. It is the "unburied self" of the family man, the educationist who earned his living as an inspector of schools, the public figure who lectured at Oxford, and the polemicist who took on the hosts of Midian in a zestful campaign against the Philistines. The "buried self" operated on its hidden ground with equal consistency, so that an attempt to group the poems by subject matter and approach is no more successful than the attempt to do so by their prevailing style. There are the poems which might be said on the face of it to support explicitly Arnold's statement that his work represented the main movement of mind in the last quarter of a century—the poems, that is, which reflect not only the issues of the time, but the feelings, mixed and uncertain, which the issues generated. These, I suppose, would always be thought of as including "Empedocles on Etna," the two Obermann poems, many of the lyrics, including the "Memorial Verses" which speak of

> this iron time
> Of doubts, disputes, distractions, fears . . .,
> (11.43–4)

and "The Scholar Gypsy" which censures

> This strange disease of modern life
> With its sick hurry, its divided aims
> Its heads o'ertaxed, its palsied hearts . . .,

(11.203-205)

and the "Stanzas from the Grande Chartreuse," referring to himself as

> Wandering between two worlds, one dead,
> The other powerless to be born . . .,

(11.85-6)

the dead world being the old world of settled social relations and religious certainties (before 1832, even before 1789), and the "unborn world" being the age of settlement into new social problems and a religion purged of myths and dogmas. There are also two other kinds of poetry: the love poetry and the long poetic pieces, "Sohrab and Rustum," "Balder Dead" and *Merope,* where Arnold, against his own poetic grain, tried to get back to an earlier role of the poet as one who tells stories and teaches implicitly, who "makes something" rather than "thinks aloud." But we have already noted the presence of "public" themes in the "Marguerite" love poems—is communication possible? what part can love have in producing the happiness difficult to find with a skeptical consciousness in the modern world?—and the themes link them with the *Weltanschauung* poems. The finest of the love poems, Arnold's most famous lyric "Dover Beach", similarly unites the issues of the time and the theme of love and displays at its best Arnold's gift for expressing the feelings of the transitional times —the indecision, the confusion, the regret. The scene is beautiful, the moonlight and the sea are calm, but the mood once again is one of quiet resigned sadness because the natural world is indifferent to man, beauty is evanescent, and to "see life steadily and see it whole" can only be saddening since the "sea of faith" is ebbing, life is like a night-battle in which confusion reigns and the only consolation is in personal relationships. The poetic temperature rises with the pain and regret of the "melancholy, long, withdrawing roar" and "The vast edges drear/And naked shingles of the world," and the description of the landscape expresses above all loneliness and loss.

In the long narrative poems "Sohrab and Rustum" and "Balder Dead," or in the would-be "Sophoclean" *Merope,* Arnold is resolute to stop "tearing himself to pieces" in the effort to speak honestly in "confessional" poems and to devote himself to "the fascination of what's difficult" in solving the exclusively formal problems posed by dealing with given, objective themes. And yet the familiar voice is still heard, especially in the recurrent natural imagery, which is among the most intimately revealing of all poetic resources. The moonlit landscape of "Dover Beach" expresses the characteristic Arnoldian combination of delight in and longing for calm and lucidity: it is present in the final lines of "The Forsaken Merman," where desolating pain gives way to resigned acceptance of the way it must be:

> When soft winds blow,
> When clear falls the moonlight,
> When spring-tides are low . . .
>
> We will gaze, from the sand-hills,
> At the white, sleeping town;
> At the church on the hill-side—
> And then come back down.
>
> (11.125–7, 136–9)

The flat finality of the monosyllabic closing line places it a distance from the active unrest of that other closing line, "The unplumbed, salt, estranging sea" (the bitterness constantly on the tongue, no deepest there is none, isolation constantly pressing on the sensibility), which is the state most resolutely fought against because most frequently experienced. A little later in the same period, in "A Summer Night," the "moon-blanched land" is recalled by the "moon-blanched street" where the thought arrives "Of a past night, and a far different scene":

> And the calm moonlight seems to say:
> *Hast thou then still the old unquiet breast,*
> *Which neither deadens into rest,*
> *Nor ever feels the fiery glow*
> *That whirls the spirit from itself away,*
> *But fluctuates to and fro,*
> *Never by passion quite possessed*
> *And never quite benumbed by the world's sway.*
>
> (11.26–33)

87

Unrest, palpable and urgent, consolidates itself in this poem into a physical being, a beleaguered *doppelgänger,* a Flying Dutchman:

> . . . the pale master on his spar-strewn deck
> With anguished face and flying hair
> Grasping the rudder hard,
> Still bent to make some port he knows not where,
> Still standing for some false, impossible shore.
> And sterner comes the roar
> Of sea and wind, and through the deepest gloom
> Fainter and fainter wreck and helmsman loom
> And he too disappears and cares no more.
>
> (11.65–73)

Against this wild and dark fated figure is set the conjuration,

> Plainness and clearness, without shadow of stain!
> Clearness divine!
>
> (11.76–7)

The moonlight, then, is lucid, plain, clear, and associated with the stars, which carry a similar charge of feeling, unquestionably heightened by sympathetic response to their presence in Keats's poetry. The "same, bright, calm moon" of "A Summer Night" is near in more than one sense to "the same bright, patient stars" upon which Hyperion gazes in his trouble. Arnold's stars are always patient and steadfast, like the star in the "Bright star" sonnet, which he frequently and lovingly echoes in poems of the 1840s and early 1850s and wrote out in his copy of Moxon's 1851 selection of Keats's poetry (from which it had been excluded).[25] In "Quiet Work" the sonnet beginning "One lesson, Nature, let me learn of thee . . .," he echoes Keats's "nature's patient, sleepless eremite":

> Still do thy sleepless ministers move on,
>
> Their glorious tasks in silence perfecting;
> Still working, blaming still our vain turmoil,
> Labourers that shall not fail when man is gone.

The last words in "Empedocles on Etna" belong to Callicles's celebration of the harmony and order of the self-dependent universe which ends in quietude:

> The night in her silence,
> The stars in their calm.

Moon, stars and mountains are the constants in this moral universe, the mountains standing for the steep climb to truth, though from the heights, once reached, the traveller gazes downwards, looking out over the earth to see it steadily and whole (and if not "deep" at least "wide"),[26] rather than upwards to find after all no marked lessening of the distance to the remote serenity of moon and stars. The mountain scenery is insistent and seized upon as early as the Lucretius-inspired Rugby Vulgus exercise, "Juvat ire jugis,"[27] to suggest the arduous climb towards the "lofty station" and its perspectives. It recurs in poems from the earliest to the latest phases of this poetic career, from "In Utrumque Paratus,"

> The solemn peaks but to the stars are known,
> But to the stars and the cold lunar beams . . .,
>
> (11. 18–19)

and the setting in "Empedocles on Etna" (1852), where the journey from youth to the disenchantment of middle age is symbolized in the climb from "the wooded region" of Etna to the "melancholy waste" at its summit, to the "mountain-tops" in "Thyrsis" (1861),

> . . . high the mountain-tops, in cloudy air,
> The mountain-tops where the throne of Truth,
> Tops in life's morning-sun so bright and bare!
>
> (11.143–6)

Mediating between these self-dependent objects, "too great for haste, too high for rivalry," and the restless, uncertain, diminutive human figure, always wandering, climbing, gazing, longing, there is water. Arnold saw himself as "one who looks on water as the mediator between the incarnate and man," and water when clear is especially loved: "Now I have a perfect passion for clear water: it is what in a mountain country gives one, I think, most pleasure."[28] But clearness is not its only attribute in the poems. It flows and moves, it may run in hidden channels or on the surface, or again, ceasing to be a river, may widen out into a vast sea, where again it may be stormy or calm. The contrarieties are consistent with themselves for they image the uncertainties producing that desire for calm focussed in the imagery of moon, stars, mountain heights; uncertainties, that is, about our origins and destiny, about how to live and act in a world where the thinking self is, if I may put it so, increasingly "at sea," since now there is "no coherent social faith and order" (the phrase is used by George Eliot in her Prelude to *Middlemarch*). In Arnold the river of life at its calmest flows out to the wide sea of eternity, as Oxus flows into the Aral Sea; or it flows away from its source in the pure origin of things and it is for us to remount the stream of time, as Henry James has it in another context; or else again rivers are hidden currents of the buried self and, divided and unselfknowing as we are, we must attempt to distinguish the kinds and relative authenticities of these different levels of being:

> If what we *say* we feel—below the stream,
> As light, of what we *think* we feel—there flows
> With noiseless current strong, obscure and deep
> The current stream of what we feel indeed.[29]

The complex of feelings generating these images penetrates the "Keats." poems, the *Weltanschauung* poems, the lyrical and personal poems, and finally, breaking through their constraint, the public and "objective" poems, where the aim is to make something instead of thinking aloud. The voice of the youthful Callicles singing of traditional wisdoms and the brightness and harmony of the natural world is heard again in Aepytus whose recollections of youth enliven the painstaking *Merope,*

> We bounded down the swarded slope, we plunged
> Through the dense ilex-thickets to the dogs.
> Far in the wood ahead their music rang;
> And many times that morn we coursed in ring
> The forest round that belt Cyllene's side ... (11.790–94)

and, in his mother's lines,

> ... he, in the glens
> Of Lycaeus afar,
> A gladsome hunter of deer,
> Basks in his morning of youth,
> Spares not a thought to his home. (11.518–22)

The sense of oppression and longing for calm reappears in "Balder Dead" where the willed "animating" lines prophesying the arrival of "The second Asgard," and "an earth / more fresh, more verdant than the last" (III 521, 528–9), are countered by the authentic voice grieving at its own sickness and unrest,

Mine eyes are dizzy with the arrowy hail;
Mine ears are stunned with blows, and sick for calm ... (III 507–8).

The interplay of these motifs, each heightening the other—youthful vitality and its brevity, longed-for calm and the anxieties which heighten the longing and make it hard to find—gather together in the final part of the first long "public" poem "Sohrab and Rustum" (which "in its own way animates" according to its author). The course of an individual life—the course of this particular poetic life we should perhaps rather say—is imaged in the lines reaching to the coda from Sohrab's death-blow at the hands of his father (in Keats's terms a "man of power" rather than a "man of achievement"),

> ... from his limbs
> Unwillingly the spirit fled away,
> Regretting the warm mansion which it left,
> And youth, and bloom, and this delightful world ..., (11.855–8)

The celebrated coda becomes a paradigm for the impending obstacles of age and time as vitality ebbs ("The Scholar Gipsy," we remember, grieves at "The foot less prompt to meet the morning dew, / The heart less bounding at emotion new ..."), and for the looked-for but perhaps never achievable end:

> The shorn and parcell'd Oxus strains along
> Through beds of sand and matted rushy isles—
> Oxus, forgetting the bright speed he had
> In his high mountain-cradle in Pamere,
> A foil'd circuitous wanderer—till at last
> The long'd-for dash of waves is heard, and wide
> His luminous home of waters opens, bright
> And tranquil, from whose floor the new-bathed stars
> Emerge, and shine upon the Aral Sea. (11.10–18)[30]

It is the consistent, authentic, enactment in the whole work of an entire process of being which is so remarkable in Arnold, from the anxious son who wrote "Mycerinus," thinking that his legacy might include the weakness of heart which killed his father, to the man of morality and character who dedicated himself with his father's purposiveness to the moral and imaginative education of his fellow-countryman. But among the weapons he used for his polemics were those individual "vivacities" which he displayed in his Oxford days and which disquieted his father as they certainly disquieted earnest contemporaries, most keenly, naturally enough, when they came under attack. This son of Thomas Arnold would probably not have approved of "the literature of experience," especially as we have come to know it since Joyce and *A Portrait of the Artist as a Young Man,* a book which lingers under a cloud of disfavour for present-day inheritors of a tradition which requires the firm provision of moral signposts to this and that, but "the literature of experience" is what Matthew Arnold's work as a whole really is. What he did not care to contemplate or act upon—how could he? The *Zeitgeist* was working for and in him but with its lineaments not completely revealed—was the possibility that exploration of the sombre, the dark, the uncertain, might be as fruitful and enriching as the effort towards sweetness and light, that the one indeed hardly has significance without confronting the possibilities of the other. His views about "adequacy" in art illustrate only too well that his public self firmly censored this pressing theme. But his creative self, "flowing/With noiseless current, strong, obscure and deep," knew better and saw to it that the poet would survive long enough for as much as possible of the whole "experience" to find forms of expression which would afford the succeeding age the peculiar delight that accompanies "the shock of recognition."

NOTES

1. See Keats's letter to Benjamin Haydon, 8 April 1818 (*Letters,* ed. H. Rollins 1958, i 245) and for "the main movement of mind" Arnold's letter of 5 June 1869, "My poems represent, on the whole, the main movement of mind of the last quarter of a century and thus they will probably have their day as people become conscious to themselves —of what that movement of the mind is . . ." (*Letters of Matthew Arnold,* ed. G. W. E. Russell (1895) ii 9). Arnold goes on to compare himself with Tennyson and Browning.

2. "I am glad you like the Gypsy-Scholar—but what does it *do* for you? Homer *animates*—Shakespeare *animates*—the Gypsy-Scholar at its best awakens a pleasing melancholy. But this is not what we want." (Arnold to Clough, 30 November 1853, *Matthew Arnold's Letters to Arthur Hugh Clough,* ed. H. F. Lowry (1932) 146).

3. Keats to J. H. Reynolds, 3 February 1818, "We hate poetry that has a palpable design upon us—and if we do not agree, seems to put its hand in its breeches pocket . . . I will cut all this—I will have no more of Wordsworth" (*Letters* i 244).

4. Letter to Blackwood of 24 February 1861, *The George Eliot Letters* ed. Gordon Haight, and for the earlier reference *Letters* i 34.

5. Recorded in J. W. Gullard's unpublished letter of 24 June 1913, cited Irvin Stock, *William Hale White (Mark Rutherford)* (1956) 3n.

6. "Wordsworth," *The Complete Prose Works of Mathew Arnold,* ed. R. H. Super (1960–77), ix 48–9. The lines quoted are from *The Excursion* iv 73–6.

7. Letter of 19 April 1880, *Letters* vii 261–2.

8. *Letters to Clough,* 36.

9. *Matthew Arnold: Selected Poems and Prose,* ed. Miriam Allot 1978, xvi.

10. Douglas Jefferson, *Eighteenth-Century Prose 1700–1780, The Pelican Book of English Prose,* ed. Kenneth Allott (1956) III xxii.

11. See "Pagan and Medieval Religious Sentiment," ". . . the imaginative reason . . . the element by which the modern spirit, if it would live right, has chiefly to live" (*Complete Prose Works* iii 230).

12. James Joyce, *Stephen Hero,* ed. Theodore Spencer (1944) 67, 135.

13. Letter to James Taylor, 15 January 1851, *The Brontes: Their Lives, Friendships and Correspondence* (ed. Wise and Symons, 1932) iii 199.

14. *Letters to Clough,* 25.

15. Quoted in Mr. Humphry Ward's *A Writer's Recollections* (1918) 44. The lines of verse are from Arnold's "Austerity of Poetry" (1867).

16. *Stephen Hero, ed. cit.* 22.

17. *Literature and Dogma* (1873) repr. *Complete Prose Works* ix, vi, 389, 391–2.

18. Quotations from "A Farewell" (11.20, 32, 49–50), "Meeting" (11. 29–30, 12), "Isolation. To Marguerite" (1.24).

19. Preface to *God and the Bible* (1875), *Complete Prose Works* vii 377.

20. "Wordsworth," *Complete Prose Works* ix 50.

21. Letter of 24 February 1848, *Letters to Clough* 66. On Mr. Wright, see Preface to *Essays in Criticism, Complete Prose Works* iii 286.

22. *Dipsychus,* Sc. iv, 130–203.

23. Letter of 12 February 1853, *Letters to Clough* 128.

24. Kenneth Allott, unpublished lectures. I owe more then I can say to these for many points made in this part of the paper.

25. I am deeply indebted to Mrs. Mary Moorman who generously made a gift to me of Arnold's copy of this edition, which contains his transcription of "The Bright Star!" sonnet.

26. "Resignation," 1.214.

27. See *Matthew Arnold. The Complete Poems* (ed. Kenneth Allott, 1965), second edition, 1979, Appendix I, pp. 714–16.

28. *Letters to Clough* 34, 92.

29. *Letters of Matthew Arnold,* ed. George Russell (1895) ii, 28; Poems, 1979 edition, 588.

30. For a commentary on these lines, including their expression of "a deep organic need for release from conflict and tension," see *Poems,* 1979 edition, 354.

THE FEMINIZATION OF D. G. ROSSETTI

BARBARA CHARLESWORTH GELPI

Dante Gabriel Rossetti's mother, like her mother before her, was a governess. To be a governess in nineteenth-century England was to act as the socializing medium through which children of the middle and upper classes were schooled in those elaborate rituals of speech, dress, and social behavior which served as outward symbols of their class. Her reward was not so much her meagre salary as the tenuous and grudging admission that she too was of the class whose mores it was her function to instill. According to a certain logic, it was imperative that she be granted such a position, however anomalous for one performing a salaried service, because unless she were to the manner born, she could not properly teach the manner.

Although when she was twenty-six Frances Polidori gave up her position to marry Gabriele Rossetti, a very much older Italian with a "romantic" revolutionary past, it was a match described by her usually hyperbolic fiancé in surprisingly rational terms: "It was necessary for me to engage in a more regular system of life in order to give proper attention to my studies, and that helped me to come to such a decision."[1] One takes it as likely that the future bride also had certain practical motivation and that it stemmed not so much from dislike for her profession with all the values which it represented as from disquietude at the prospect of spinsterhood. A sign at least of her belief in the suitability of governessing is that she planned to have Maria, her oldest daughter, follow that career in what by then was a family tradition.

The Rossetti family with its four children, living on Gabriele's small and fluctuating salary as a language teacher, could not afford a governess, but Frances Rossetti took on that function, and given the competence of her management in other matters, she was in all likelihood a highly effective teacher. Descriptions, then, of the Rossetti living room where excitedly gesticulating Italian exiles might be found in revolutionary conversation with Gabriele, or of Gabriele's study filled with the hermetic texts of his obscure Dantean researches must be balanced with R. D. Waller's observation on the house: "the family (i.e. the children) that lived there must surely have been among the most efficiently regulated and disciplined."[2] His mother's influence on D. G. Rossetti—as on all the children—was much stronger than his father's,[3] and that influence, despite her own Italian father, was genteel and English. Rossetti's attitude toward foreigners throughout his life was as insularly British as that of his somewhat older contemporary, Charlotte Brontë. In 1878, for instance, he wrote to Ford Madox Brown, "Could you tell me of any male model you use? I prefer English to Italian."[4] The editors of his letters, commenting on this statement, note that Rossetti cared little for the French and even less for Italians, adding, "Amusingly, he prided himself upon his Englishness!" The amusement can only come from a predisposition to see him as un-English, a man living out of his proper setting; perhaps we should take him seriously on what he says were his true cultural terms.

A central tenet of the culture and the household in which Rossetti was raised was that of the separation between masculine and feminine "spheres": the father's was the outer world of competitive wage-earning, political concern, and public affairs; the mother's was the domestic area of household management, child rearing, and social intercourse.[5] Because so many of Gabriele Rossetti's letters recount the doings of his children and because his scholarly research was done largely at home, we might get the mistaken impression that this typical Victorian pattern did not characterize the Rossetti household. But as Waller points out, Gabriele Rossetti was away from home teaching for most of the day,[6] and his voluminous manuscripts and extensive correspondence show that his spare time too was taken up with the masculine life of active scholarship and not with the womanly concerns of child-care. Occasionally Frances Rossetti was ill, at which times she might take a vacation from some or all of her family

95

duties at her parents' home in the country, but Gabriele did not then take over feminine tasks in her stead. Frances' sister, Margaret— "Your substitute," Gabriele calls her[7]—undertook those.

Within this domestic and feminine sphere the Rossetti children on their London city street were virtually as isolated as were the Brontës beside their Yorkshire moor, and for much the same reason. There were other children to play with in Haworth, but they were not of the proper class,[8] and children undoubtedly on Charlotte Street, but that neighborhood lacked gentility.[9] Frances Rossetti might not be able to change her children's circumstances by moving to a more refined (and expensive) area, but she could arrange matters so that her children played together under her eye. Rossetti's school experience did not begin until he was eight, and there, after such years of family seclusion, his only brother, who was also his school companion, remained his single friend. More than many boys of his class, then, Rossetti lived in youth within a feminine circle whose circumference was his mother, his aunts, his elder sister Maria, and his younger sister Christina.

It is within the setting of this Victorian, feminine, middle-class culture that I propose to place D. G. Rossetti. Critics in the past, myself included, have often taken him and his work out of that culture and seen him as a Bohemian or counter-culture figure defying all the norms of Victorian respectability, or seen him out of any cultural context whatever—an explorer of the collective unconscious, brooding among the archetypes. Although these approaches have their usefulness, they keep us, each in its way, in the dark, either of London night-life or of the unconscious. At least as important is, so to speak, a daylight view of Rossetti; the sources of his art are clearer there as are the sources of his conflict.

Although Rossetti's life-long devotion to his mother has often been noted, surprisingly little has been written in analysis of its effect upon the themes and forms of his art, whether painting or poetry. His first major painting, *The Girlhood of Mary Virgin* (1848), used both his mother and Christina as models, the one for St. Anne and the other for Mary. The painter's stance in the work is outside the serene, enclosed woman's world he is depicting, watching it while St. Anne, hands calmly folded, watches Mary, supervising her work, and Mary, also calm but a little self-conscious, scrutinizes the lily whose form her needlework reproduces. There is a masculine figure in the picture: outside the women's curtained enclosure St. Joachim prunes a vine. Rossetti's difficulties with perspective cause the form of St. Joachim to jump to the eye, but the figure's rough clothing and somewhat homely features make him thematically as well as pictorially a somewhat jarring contrast to the women's quiet elegance.

In a painting, the medium necessarily leaves the observer outside the scene (unless, as Velasquez did in *Las Meninas,* he contrives participation through mirrors). In a poem, on the other hand, Rossetti can—and does—move at times into virtual identification with the women he watches. In "The Bride's Prelude," for instance, a fragment which also dates from 1848, Amelotte, the bridesmaid who will hear her sister's tragic story, is first watched by the unseen, voyeuristic observer as she makes a gesture which is innocent enough yet also highly erotic in its unselfconsciousness and privacy:

> Against the haloed lattice-panes
>   The bridesmaid sunned her breast;
> Then to the glass turned tall and free,
> And braced and shifted daintily
>   Her loin-belt through her côte-hardie.[10]

As the poem progresses, Aloyse, her sister, speaks in the first person, and of course as we listen we move into a kind of identification with her, but actually it is Amelotte, the listener, with whom we become most closely identified. The poem gives details of her physical experience which no outside observer could know:

> Her fingers felt her temples beat;
>   Then came the brain-sickness
> Which thinks to scream, and murmureth,
> And pent between her hands, the breath
>   Was damp against her face like death. (p. 25)

A woman's feelings in two senses come into those lines. Her physical sensations are there as well as her emotional tension and linking them the cause of both: a life in which the desire to scream must be disciplined to a murmur.

Precisely the same feminine discipline is a central theme in another early poem, "My Sister's Sleep" (1847–49). Written when Rossetti was much under the influence of Elizabeth Barrett Browning,[11] the poem both in its situation and in its message of calm acceptance in

97

the face of death has parallels with Barrett Browning's "Isobel's Child," much praised in its time—as with many other similarly lugubrious poems which were the particular hallmark or specialty of women writers of the period. As one among such poems it is remarkably restrained and effective, chiefly because the minutely noted naturalistic details—the click of knitting needles, the hiss of the fire—made almost preternaturally vivid by the speaker's extreme fatigue, give edge and clarity to what might otherwise be a sentimental blur. Fine analysis of the work in these terms already exists[12] and does not need further discussion, but the character of the speaker of the poem deserves a moment's thought.

Because we know the poet to be a man, we take the speaker to be one—i.e., to be a brother who with his mother has been keeping watch over the sickbed of his sister. It adds a dimension to the poem and makes it a much more incisive study of the feelings and attitudes of Victorian women if we consider the possibility that throughout the poem (rather than in parts of it only as in "The Bride's Prelude") Rossetti is placing himself *within* a feminine consciousness.[13] It was, after all, more customary in Victorian society for women than men, particularly young men, to keep watch beside sick beds. Then, too, the restraint and self-discipline of the speaker's response in the face of death is that which characterizes the "angelic" Victorian woman: "I but hid my face, / And held my breath, and spoke no word" (p. 166) —as is the quick resignation to the sister's death, almost equalling that of the even more angelic mother.

If we imagine that quiet room as peopled only by three hushed women, something very interesting happens to the "pushing back of chairs" which Harold Weatherby complains of as "quasi-supernatural" in that highly naturalistic setting. The sound is at least equally naturalistic and impels the question, "Would a group of *women* be sitting up in talk past midnight in a well-run Victorian household?" Not likely. "And if there were women in a household where one lay seriously ill, would they be so thoughtless as to push their chairs back noisily at such an hour?" Indeed not. Thus the noise overhead becomes the only appearance in the poem of a rough, thoughtless, intrusive masculine presence, and the only flicker of anger or irritation on the mother's part lies in her hasty response to it as she checks to see whether the sleeper has been disturbed. The point is admittedly speculative: if true, it serves as one more piece of evidence for the way in which Rossetti's feeling for his mother creates in him at least imaginative membership in the feminine "sphere"; even if untrue, the poem nonetheless shows Rossetti's intense interest in women's responses to life.[14]

"The Blessed Damozel" (1847) is another early poem whose meaning takes on new significance in the light of Rossetti's feeling for his mother. In it for the first time is sounded the theme most central to Rossetti's work: a love once possessed but now lost, leaving behind only the "one hope," tenuous and unfulfilled, that it may eventually be recovered. Other major expressions of this theme—"Love's Nocturne," "The Stream's Secret," and many of the sonnets in *The House of Life*—were written during or after Rossetti's involvement in frustrating love affairs and might seem, therefore, to have "real" passions as their emotional source. When he wrote "The Blessed Damozel," on the other hand, he had never loved any woman, much less lost her —except, of course, his mother.

A sibling's acerbity creeps into William Rossetti's tone when describing Rossetti's relationship to his family, "warm and equable, and (except in relation to our mother, for whom he had a fondling love) not demonstrative" (p. xi). The fondling, clinging child is the one not loved enough, and evidence seems to point to the fact that William himself was actually his mother's favorite.[15] Rossetti as the second of four children appearing in as many years would in any case early have had to receive less of his busy mother's attention than was his at birth and in the first months of life.

In the past I have argued, as I still do, that C. G. Jung's identification of " 'beyond the grave' or on 'the other side of death' " with a state "beyond consciousness"—i.e., with the unconscious—should be used to interpret the "Heaven" in which the Blessed Damozel waits. The coupling of sense and spirit in the poem becomes with such a rubric more open to explication.[16] But my former description of the Damozel herself as, rather generally, an "anima" figure gains in precision if we see her, not specifically as a mother figure, and certainly not as the figure of Frances Rossetti translated skyward, but rather as an image of the relationship between mother and infant, once enjoyed but now broken and only persisting in the unconscious, creating thus in consciousness an obscure sense of loss.

The motherliness of the Blessed Damozel is present in her very stance, the subject of so much critical comment. She leans a very real bosom against a really warm barrier, and infant-like, "the lilies lay as if asleep / Along her bended arm" (p. 3). Rossetti's choice of details invites us to feel the bar—and the bosom—as well as to lie with the lilies, but our imaginative position when we do so becomes an infant's. Mother-like too is her attitude toward the earthbound beloved: deeply concerned for his welfare, she is nonetheless in a sphere transcending his, possessed of knowledge he does not yet have. On his eventual re-union with her, his role will be that of child-pupil, hers of mother-teacher in the ultimate process of education. Even the learning is an eroticized lullaby:

> "And I myself will teach him,
>   I myself, lying so,
> The songs I sing here; which his voice
>   Shall pause in, hushed and slow." (p. 5)

Other elements may also inform the erotic feeling of "The Blessed Damozel," but the permitted and even idealized eroticism of the mother/infant relationship in the Victorian period has to be considered as an important subliminal source for the poem and a cause, equally subliminal, of its success at the time.

The poems considered so far were written, at least in first versions, when Rossetti was still very young, but many of the sonnets of *The House of Life,* written in his maturity and emotionally based in his love for young women, bear the suggestion that the *real* muse, the "onlie begetter," is again the mother/child bond. Erich Neumann has a description of this "primal relationship" which, though its Jungian vocabulary may be different, closely parallels the ideas of many neo-Freudian psychologists about the first year of life:

> In the post-uterine phase of existence in unitary reality, the child lives in a total *participation mystique,* a psychic motherfluid in which everything is still in suspension, and from which the opposites, ego and Self, subject and object, individual and world have yet to be crystallized.[17]

Elsewhere in his book on the child, Neumann points out that the infant's identification with the mother, since she as source of all his well-being seems a suprahuman figure, a goddess, gives him *through her* a sense of supernatural powers. Having her the infant has—and is—a whole world, or in Margaret Mahler's words:

> The essential feature of symbiosis is hallucinatory or delusional, somato-psychic, omnipotent fusion with the representation of the mother and, in

particular, delusion of common boundary of the two actually and physically separate individuals.[18]

Such theories seem designed as rubric or gloss for reading a poem such as "Heart's Haven." In the octave the beloved and the lover interchange roles, he the mother at first and she the child, then the reverse. Their personalities interchange as it were but all, as the sestet describes, within a relationship in which both are a single mother/child being and "Love" their "participation mystique." The warbling tune and the watching face which symbolize this experience are not those of a particularized mother but are the mother aura, her enfolding presence. Rossetti, following the tradition of Dante in the *Vita Nuova,* calls this presence "Love" and makes it masculine, but "his" attributes are feminine, and the connotations of the phrases call up a nursery scene:

> And Love, our light at night and shade at noon,
>   Lulls us to rest with songs, and turns away
>   All shafts of shelterless, tumultuous day.
> Like the moon's growth, his face gleams through his tune;
> And soft as waters warble to the moon,
>   Our answering spirits chime one roundelay. (p. 82)

The same relationship informs the sestet of "Mid-Rapture":

> What word can answer to thy word,—what gaze
>   To thine, which now absorbs within its sphere
>   My worshipping face, till I am mirrored there
> Light-circled in a heaven of deep-drawn rays? (p. 83)

and it appears in "Heart's Hope," "Heart's Compass," "Her Gifts," and "Soul's Beauty."

Although psychological theory acts as an appropriate gloss to these poems, the tautological nature of the interaction between theory and text needs constantly to be kept in mind. Nor is the connection accidental or synchronistic; both the modern psychological theory, whether Freudian, neo-Freudian or Jungian, and the nineteenth-century poetic myth have a common source in nineteenth-century beliefs about the relationship between mother and child and about the god-like power, euphemised as "influence," of motherhood. Lydia Sigourney, writing of motherhood in 1838, puts a mother "in point of precedence ... *next to the Creator*" (emphasis mine) in order to

101

remain religiously orthodox but continues with phrases which virtually deify her nonetheless:

> ... in power over her pupil, limitless and without competitor; in faculty of teaching, endowed with the prerogative of a transforming love; while the glorious department allotted is a newly quickened soul, and its immortal destiny.

Other examples of the sort might be multiplied from the prescriptive literature of the period.[19]

So far we have considered the mother/child bond only in its positive aspects. Central to it, however, is the dependence of the infant/lover on the goddess/beloved, and if from dependence in its happy aspect spring trust, well-being, and the ability to love, from it also arise negative feelings of fear, anger, hatred, self-pity, and a host of those other "bogeys" which caused Rossetti so much pain. Omnipotence in mothering creates ambivalence in children, particularly that ambivalence toward feminine power which so characterizes Rossetti's poetry and painting. The goddess of one painting turns siren or betrayer in another—or, depicted as Pandora or Venus Astarte, she seems a combination of the two. She is the "Lady Beauty," holding whom one has all the heart's desire; yet she withdraws, she withholds herself to the bitterness of her child/lover's heart.

In 1869 when he was falling deeply in love with Jane Morris, Rossetti wanted to paint her as Fortune, "seated full-faced dealing cards on which will be visible the symbols of life, death, etc."[20]—an image much resembling the "fatal woman" whom he had described many years before in an early poem called "The Card Dealer" who rules the game we call life, but "When she shall speak, thou'lt learn her tongue / And know she calls it Death" (p. 175). During the summer of 1869 he wrote a prose summary and a few stanzas of a projected poem "The Orchard Pit," his strongest expression of mixed attraction and fear for a hypnotically beautiful, powerful, and dangerous woman: "Life's eyes are gleaming from her forehead fair, / And from her breasts the ravishing eyes of Death" (p. 240).[21]

Philip Slater in *The Glory of Hera* has juxtaposed a study of Greek myth and literature with analysis of the family structure of classical Athens. Young Greek women, kept virtually illiterate, were after marriage segregated completely from all the concerns of the larger political community and, with their young children, lived in the women's quarters of the house. A male child, Slater theorizes, thus closely bound to his mother in infancy, imbibed all his mother's conscious or unconscious frustrations and while dependent on her was filled with the need to fight free of her influence—thus continuing when he came to manhood the society's oppression of women.

Although Slater limits his study to Greek society, he allows it to be clearly understood that he sees the applicability of his theory to "many historical and contemporary social systems"[22]—i.e., to an American middle-class culture in which women, not illiterate but on the contrary highly educated, are balked in the effort to use that education and isolated with their children in suburban homes while their husbands work in the relatively distant city. Victorian society offers another version of the same situation: an oppressed mother who is, nonetheless, made the all-powerful figure in the "sphere" assigned her—a not unsurprising parallel since the Victorian ideology continues to operate into modern times.

With Slater's theory as analytic instrument it would be possible to examine Rossetti's work in detail, showing that his Victorian upbringing within his strong mother's sphere produced an ambivalence reflected in the pictures he painted and the poems he wrote. His themes, moreover, however morbid or melancholy or strange, spoke to a Victorian consciousness which was ambivalent about women for the same reason as he.[23] Such a thesis is, I believe, perfectly sound, but I would like to strike off in a somewhat different direction to explore not how early confinement to the domestic sphere influenced Rossetti's attitude toward women and thus his portrayal of women but how it influenced his concept of himself as an artist.

The art critic John Berger begins an essay on the nude with an analysis of the difference between men's "presence" and women's: a man's presence is "dependent upon the promise of power," that is upon the sense he gives of being able to act in some capacity toward others; a woman's, on the other hand, is created by her own attitude toward herself. He continues:

> To be born a woman has been to be born, within an allotted and confined space, into the keeping of men. The social presence of woman has developed as a result of their ingenuity in living under such tutelage within such a limited space. But this has been at the cost of a woman's self being split into two. A woman must continually watch herself. She is almost continually accompanied by her own image of herself.

103

His admittedly simplified conclusion is that "*men act* and *women appear.* Men look at women. Women watch themselves being looked at."[24] One sees instantly the applicability of this statement to Rossetti's art. Most of the women depicted in the oil paintings which he began in the late 1850s and continued to paint to virtually the end of his life, know that they are being looked at and have a "presence" born of the commodity they have for sale: dreams, whether voluptuous or sweetly melancholy or tender or a complicated mixture of all three. They gaze out at or pensively look past the men who come to buy— businessmen for the most part whose "presence" is a creation of their power as buyers. But what of Rossetti, the man who stands beside the easel? What is his presence, and of what is it born?

He creates the pictures, as he writes the poems, by watching women either in reality or in his mind's eye, just as the customer with him is watching the painted woman. Yet in the artistic process he also imaginatively becomes the woman. True, this identification, obvious enough in poetry, is hard to verify in a painting, but an anecdote suggests its presence in Rossetti during the creation of both art forms. At the height of his passion for Elizabeth Siddal he sketched her constantly and could be heard repeating his pet name for her while at his easel, "Guggum, Guggum, Guggum"[25]—an incantation, as it seems to me, which hints at the fusion of personalities. And certainly the completed painting, as a product of his imagination, is *his* dream for sale. The expression of his ability to act upon others in that he "catches" such-and-such a pose, it is also the exposure of his own fantasy, a part of himself being watched.

Or to put the matter in another way: in Victorian society the arts were becoming feminized. As amenities conducive to the comfort, refinement, and recreation of men during those times in which they were freed from labor in the commercio-political sphere, they were classified as activities proper to the domestic sphere. If, since Rossetti was a man, we put aside the complicated and interesting situation of a woman artist, the question remains, What position does the man who is an artist have in such a society? What, particularly, is the position of a man whose art, like Rossetti's, is sourced imaginatively in the woman's sphere?

Henry James felt the strains involved in such questions, although he allowed as little strain as possible to creep into his urbane discussion of them. Musing, amused, he describes himself as a young writer living in "up-town" New York. The business world "down-town" seemed the world of true action and endeavor and thus the proper setting for a grand work in "the major key," but to James it was also "a monstrous labyrinth" from which, not to put too fine a point on it, he fled. (Rossetti's single venture into the "down-town" world was his application for a position as a telegraph operator; faced with the machine, he too fled—or, as he recounted it, walked away.)[26] This left for James the "minor key" of the uptown world "with the music-masters and French pastry-cooks, the ladies and children—immensely present and immensely numerous these, but testifying with a collective voice to the extraordinary absence (save as pieced together through a thousand gaps and indirectednesses) of a serious male interest."[27]

For James the position is a difficult but not, it would seem, a false one. While describing with ironic detachment the acrobatic agility needed to make the most of his material, he does not admit to being demeaned or unmanned. Rossetti's image is much stronger, but then his artistic conscience was not so clear. As an artist he compares himself not once but many times to a prostitute and his "down-town" business patrons to her clients. To his fellow artist and old friend Ford Madox Brown he wrote as follows in 1873:

> I have often said that to be an artist is just the same thing as to be a whore, as far as dependence on the whims and fancies of individuals is concerned. . . . The natural impulse is to say simply—Leyland* be d--d! —and so no doubt the whore feels but too often inclined to say and cannot.[28]

The comparison is not special to Rossetti, of course; it is virtually a cliché. Yet Rossetti uses it with particular vehemence and personal feeling.

Even in this rather casual moment of irritation Rossetti pauses, seeing things or attempting to see them with the "whore's" sensibility, just as in "Jenny" the speaker tries to imagine what Jenny is thinking. Thoughts melodramatic or pathetic are what the poem conjures up;[29] the letter's brief flash of "negative capability" has the ring of greater truth. With the prostitute imaginatively conjured up by his compari-son he feels the frustrated, silent anger of one economically dependent and thereby manipulated.

*F. R. Leyland, a wealthy Liverpool shipowner.

105

Rossetti's grumble is rational and sociologically astute. A society which separates woman into a sphere in which she is as wife and mother given homage as superior to men yet is also, again as wife and mother, used by men and totally dependent on that use for her subsistence, will treat its artists, sharers with women of the domestic sphere, in the same way. It will give them adulation, but in turning their works into commercial objects upon whose sale their existence is dependent, it will prostitute them.[30] Rossetti admits his own complicity in this system and its attendant guilt, allowing that poetry is less subject to corruption than painting, but only because it pays so badly that the artist cannot depend on it for a livelihood:

> My own belief is that I'm a poet (within the limit of my powers) primarily, and that it is my poetic tendencies that chiefly give value to my pictures: only painting being—what poetry is not—a livelihood—I have put my poetry chiefly in that form. On the other hand, the bread-and-cheese question has led to a good deal of my painting being pot-boiling and no more-whereas my verse, being unprofitable, has remained (as much as I have found time for) *unprostituted*.[31] (emphasis mine)

In working out the implications of Rossetti's metaphor I do not mean to suggest that he himself followed his thought out to any feminist conclusion. If he felt himself used by his merchant clients, he in turn was making use of the women who, whether as models or as lovers or as "inspiratrices," fleshed out his dreams.

These uses, however, cannot all be lumped together. The most obvious one is Rossetti's use of women as models for the oils of what he himself calls "that sensuous realistic type."[32] The first of these, *Bocca Baciata* (The Kissed Mouth), was painted in 1859 with Fanny Cornforth, a mistress, as his model. After the first two oil paintings of his specifically Pre-Raphaelite years, both with religious subjects (*The Girlhood of Mary Virgin* and *The Annunciation*) and both with family members as their models, Rossetti had worked for nine years in the media of watercolor, chalk, or pen-and-ink only. The work of that period is now generally considered to be his most truly imaginative and innovative, but it brought him little money and that little only through the kind but maddeningly overbearing patronage of Ruskin. Oswald Doughty follows a Victorian tradition in juxtaposing Rossetti's new subject matter of "women and flowers" and his renewed use of oil with his fascinated admiration for the voluptuous Fanny, whom Doughty takes, on circumstantial evidence, to have been a prostitute.

He also implies that Rossetti's relationship with Fanny has a connection with the much-repeated theme of prostitution in both Rossetti's poetry and his painting, although since several works related to the subject date before his meeting with Fanny, the connection is unclear.[33]

However shaky in its facts, Doughty's sense of a connection between oil painting (at least as Rossetti practiced it) and prostitution may have a certain validity. John Berger associates the medium of oil with the "avid and ambitious desire to take possession of the object" which Lévi-Strauss considers a dominant characteristic of art appreciation in Western civilization, oil paintings themselves being "sights: sights of what he [the painting's owner] may possess."[34] A similar tradition described in Robert Rosenblum's *The International Style of 1800* associates purity of style (the phrase having a moral as well as an aesthetic connotation) with emphasis on the clear line and with the use of watercolor, while the "virtuoso illusionism potential to the oil medium" makes it potentially more sensual as well as sensuous.[35] Besides the pleasure given by oil's realistic rendering of physical objects, one should perhaps take into account its greater durability over other possible media, making it thus a better investment;[36] certainly oil was what the newly wealthy Victorian manufacturers wanted, and Rossetti, once he took up the medium again, fairly quickly began to earn—and spend—large sums of money. And it is at least worth considering that Rossetti in his use of the more voluptuous medium to paint *The Kissed Mouth* turns Fanny, its model, into an object offered, for a price, to her buyer. Yet if he makes her an object (and thus, in a sense, a prostitute no matter what her actual occupation) he makes himself a pimp.

Two important disclaimers must be brought in to balance this line of argument. First, Rossetti himself makes a distinction between the paintings he did with "Titianesque" subjects, which, as noted earlier, he characterizes dismissively as "that sensuous realistic type" and those painted with "high aim." His example of the first is *La Bella Mano* as contrasted with *Pandora* "the model for which is Mrs. Morris . . . it will be immeasurably my best work yet. I intend that both form and drapery shall be thorough studies and the work monumental as far as in me lies."[37]

Here as at other times, Rossetti's respect for or dismissal of the painting becomes mingled with his feeling for the model, his guilt projected upon or deflected by a feminine "screen." For instance, of *La Donna della Finestra* he writes, "I had written it down a *thing,* but won't, because of the sitter [Jane Morris] to whom I owe the best of my art such as it is."[38] Although the grounds upon which Rossetti makes his judgment may be confused, the distinction itself is just: there are paintings in which the women with their typical Rossettian features of heavy hair, full lips, and long throat are empty of all expression, vessels for kinetic fantasy—e.g., *Veronica Veronese, La Ghirlandata, A Sea-Spell, Roman Widow*—and the list might be much extended. Then there are other paintings, Jane Morris indeed usually the model—*Astarte Syrica* perhaps the most striking example and *La Pia de'Tolomei* another—in which voluptuous features express *her* sexuality and are thus challenge and mystery, not passive invitation.

Another positive aspect of Rossetti's relationships with women, one which tends to get lost in all the speculation about his passionate attachments, is the number of good and equable friendships he had with women, particularly with women artists. Anna Howitt, the daughter of William and Mary Howitt, was one of these. In 1854 Rossetti writes indignantly to Thomas Woolner that one of her pictures has been rejected by the British Institution, "The wretches have not hung it. It was an open air picture, in sunlight, a most difficult task, and a very good picture."[39]

Barbara Leigh Smith and Bessie Parkes were also his friends at this time, and the former, strong feminist that she was, remained a helpful friend for many years, lending Rossetti her country house in 1869 so that he could have a quiet place to write. There are instances in which Rossetti betrays that unconscious patronage of women which underlies our culture. After his marriage to Elizabeth Siddal he writes of her work, "She will I am sure paint such pictures as *no woman* has painted yet."[40] Yet even here he is not using the locution, "very good —for a woman" but making a statement whose intention is historical. It offers no judgment on women as painters in the future, were they to be given real opportunity to paint. And on the whole, his respect for women as writers, artists and, in one instance, as architects is greater than that shown by most Victorian men.[41]

From this digression in the interests of justice we must return to consideration of the ways in which Rosetti struggled against his sense of himself as an effeminized victim dependent upon masculine capital. The first, as noted, was to use women as objects in his turn, much as from his viewpoint[42] his buyers used his paintings. The second was to become, like his clients, a collector of objects himself. Advances that he received on commissions were spent long before the paintings were completed, and often before they were begun, on his collections of exotic animals and of blue china. He took no proper care of the animals and though knowledgeable about the china and, one imagines, appreciative of its beauty, he showed more pleasure in outwitting a rival buyer than in the strictly aesthetic joy given him by a rare find.[43]

Far from being effective, these strategies exacerbated the problem. His relationship to women filled him with guilt, and his attempt to play the capitalist involved him in even greater dependence upon his business patrons because it put him more deeply in debt. These having failed, Rossetti's ultimate recourse was that of many Victorian middle-class women whose sphere he imaginatively shared. It was the recourse taken by two of the women he loved, Elizabeth Siddal and Jane Morris, and it was, I believe, Rossetti's as well: "hysterical" illness.

Hysteria or "womb sickness" has been classified as an illness since ancient times, the numbers of those afflicted with it rising and falling in interesting and surely significant patterns. In the Victorian period it was epidemic through the industrial West, including America, and was considered to be an affliction peculiar to upper- and middle-class girls and women. (Actually, it appeared among the poor as well, as Jean-Martin Charcot's research at the Salpêtrière Hospital shows clearly enough, but whereas symptoms of the disease among the wealthy were softened by the term neurasthenia, among the poor they were labelled insanity and treated as such.)[44]

The nature of the disease made its symptoms almost as variable as the individuals suffering from it, but certain ones appeared often: digestive upsets, often leading to weight loss but sometimes causing sudden gains or changes in weight, insomnia, headaches, extreme fatigue and depression leading to dependence on stimulants: "Then comes the mischievous role of bromides, opium, chloral, and brandy," writes S. Weir Mitchell, the most renowned medical specialist on the disease in America.[45] Often associated with it too were motor and organic disturbances, varying from violent paroxysms to the sense that individual limbs or organs could not function. By the end of the century Pierre Janet had isolated certain mental stigmata characteristic of hysterics as well, among which he included a diminished number of emotions because "these patients are in general very indifferent, at least to all that is not directly connected with a small number of fixed ideas."[46]

Elizabeth Siddal and Jane Morris had symptoms in common as well as different symptoms related to hysteria, their affliction a circumstance which suggests that Rossetti was a malign influence on the woman he loved. But if he communicated these symptoms, it must be noted that he also shared them—a fuller range of them, indeed, than that suffered by either of the two women.

Through much of the century, doctors, despite evidence to the contrary, believed the disease peculiar to women and, while recognizing its roots to lie in repressed emotion (the very word "hysteria" has been changed in modern medical terms to "conversion syndrome") thought that emotion to be virtually inevitably sexual.[47] These theories were modified as the century progressed, yet not nearly so fully as one might expect, when one considers the fact that the disease reached epidemic proportions not only among Victorian women but also among soldiers fighting in the American Civil War. (S. Weir Mitchell, who had a large and lucrative practice among American society women, first became interested in the disease when working as an army doctor.) In the First World War again, authorities became concerned when hysteria cut into fighting capacity by disabling soldiers in all armies.[48]

Even given these observations, Freud's analysis of hysteria in terms of sexual repression and his emphasis on women as typical hysterics continued to give widespread credence to what were in fact the Victorian assumptions about the disease, Freud's contribution being in the realm of treatment. Only recently has a renewed feminist analysis reconsidered the diagnosis already offered by Victorian feminists: the emotion being repressed was not sexuality but rage.[49] Helpless and inexpressible anger at finding themselves pawns whose lives were on the line (reproductively or militarily) within a giant system which denied them any personal control: might this feeling not be the link between women and soldiers?

In 1869 as he experienced the symptoms which foreshadowed his breakdown of 1872—insomnia, the belief that he was going blind, delusions of various kinds—Rossetti imagined himself to be in communication with, indeed possessed by, Lizzie Siddal's spirit. Lingering guilt over her suicide compounded by guilt over his new passion for

Jane Morris and his determination to retrieve his poems from Lizzie's grave may well, as is commonly believed, lie behind these manifestations.[50] But perhaps Lizzie's bitter spirit possessed Rossetti in another way as well. As an artist he lived "uptown," sharing woman's sphere, patronized like a woman by men upon whom his livelihood depended. From the sidelines only could he watch the conduct of worldly affairs which, nonetheless, were crucial to his own life. He wrote his mother:

> I hear there is a decided improvement in trade. Even cotton at Manchester, which seemed the most hopeless, is looking up decidedly and rather rapidly. Iron, copper, and coal mines, also on the mend. You may perhaps think this report not much in my line, but I view it as vitally wound up with the picture market.[51]

An artist in the picture market like a woman in the marriage market *must* be aware of these things.

To sum up: Rossetti's dependence on the feminine, stemming from his strong attachment to his mother, moved him imaginatively into the feminine sphere and made it possible for him to identify with women's feelings. That same dependence, however, in its creation of ambivalence caused him to fear and resent women's power. Out of this complex of identification mingled with fear arose his art.

Yet again, his imaginative centering in the feminine sphere made it impossible for him to join in the masculine world of commerce, academic philosophical discussion, scientific thought or its technological adaptation. For these matters he felt the ironic contempt which women, denied achievement in such areas, might also use as solace. Such contempt did not save him, though, from the sense of being used by those with masculine power, a feeling made all the more bitter by his envy of that power and its possessors.

We can see now that the separation of spheres killed, drove mad, and, whether physically or emotionally, crippled many thousands of Victorian women. Rossetti's history shows that its effect could be equally deadly upon a Victorian man.

NOTES

1. Quoted in R. D. Waller, *The Rossetti Family, 1824–1854* (Manchester: Manchester University Press, 1932), p. 37.
2. Waller, *Rossetti Family*, p. 75. Waller, who has the most detailed study of D. G. Rossetti's childhood, repeatedly stresses the importance of his relationship with his mother; cf. also pp. 121, 132, 137.

3. It was an influence, too, of which Rossetti was conscious throughout his life. In 1876 he wrote to his mother, "I assure you that your first inculcations on many points are still the standard of criticism with me, and that I am often conscious of being influenced correctly by these early-imbibed and still valuable impressions."—*The Letters of Dante Gabriel Rossetti,* ed. Oswald Doughty and John Robert Wahl (Oxford: Clarendon Press, 1967), III, 1402.

4. *Letters,* IV, 1602.

5. Walter E. Houghton, *The Victorian Frame of Mind, 1830–1870* (New Haven: Yale University Press, 1957), pp. 341–353.

6. *Rossetti Family,* p. 134.

7. *Rossetti Family,* p. 128.

8. Cf. Elizabeth Gaskell's comments on the social make-up of Haworth and the Brontës' reaction to it in *The Life of Charlotte Brontë,* ed. Alan Shelston (Penguin Books, 1975), pp. 85–86.

9. *Rossetti Family,* p. 42.

10. *The Works of Dante Gabriel Rossetti,* ed. William M. Rossetti (London: Ellis, 1911), p. 17. Future reference to this edition will be incorporated in the text.

11. Writing to Elizabeth Barrett Browning about *The Blessed Damozel* which dates, like "My Sister's Sleep," from 1847, Rossetti says: "Bearing in mind my favorite readings when I wrote it, I feel some slight misgiving lest there should be any property of his [Robert Browning's] or yours in it."—*Letters,* I, 273.

12. Harold L. Weatherby, "Problems of Form and Content in the Poetry of Dante Gabriel Rossetti," *Victorian Poetry,* II (Winter, 1964), 12–14; Ronnalie Roper Howard, *The Dark Glass: Vision and Technique in the Poetry of Dante Gabriel Rossetti* ([Athens]: Ohio University Press, 1972), pp. 2–5.

13. Howard opens up this possibility briefly by noting that the speaker is "presumably" a son (*The Dark Glass,* p. 2) but then drops it.

14. Several other Rossetti poems achieve interesting and sometimes very powerful effects through the way in which they use identification with feminine characters: "Jenny," "Sister Helen," "Stratton Water," "Troy Town," "Rose Mary" and "The King's Tragedy."

15. Brian and Judy Dobbs, *Dante Gabriel Rossetti: an Alien Victorian* (London: Macdonald and Jane's, 1977), p. 12.

16. Barbara Charlesworth Gelpi, "The Image of the Anima in the Work of Dante Gabriel Rossetti," *The Victorian Newsletter,* no. 45 (Spring, 1974), p. 3.

17. Erich Neumann, *The Child: Structure and Dynamics of the Nascent Personality,* tr. Ralph Manheim (New York: G. P. Putnam's Sons, 1973), p. 15. Neo-Freudians call this the period of "symbiosis" and define it as "that state of undifferentiation, of fusion with the mother, in which the 'I' is not yet differentiated from the 'non-I' and in which inside and outside are only gradually coming to be sensed as different."—John McDevitt and Calvin Settladge, "Editors' Forward" to *Separation/Individuation: Essays in Honor of Margaret S. Mahler* (New York: International Universities Press, 1971), p. 4. An excellent bibliography of sources on this theory can be found in Nancy Chodorow, *The Reproduction of Mothering* (Berkeley: University of California Press, 1978), pp. 241–256.

18. *The Child,* p. 14; Margaret Mahler, "On Human Symbiosis and the Vicissitudes of Individuation," *Journal of the American Psychoanalytic Association,* 15 [1967], 742.

19. L. H. Sigourney, *Letters to Mothers* (New York: Harper & Bros., 1845 [6th edition]), p. 16. Sarah Stickney Ellis in her chapter "Authority, Influence, and Example" also makes implicit comparisons between the mother's relationship to the child and God's to humankind. —*The Mothers of England: their Influence and Responsibility* (London: Fisher, Son & Co., 1843), pp. 27–60.

20. *Dante Gabriel Rossetti and Jane Morris, their Correspondence,* ed. John Bryson and Janet Camp Troxell (Oxford: Clarendon Press, 1976), p. 25.

21. Interestingly, Rossetti may have been given the image of eyed breasts from an incident involving Percy Bysshe Shelley and recounted by John Polidori, Rossetti's uncle, in a diary owned by the Polidori family. One night in the summer of 1816 when he heard Byron recite the lines from Coleridge's "Christabel," "Behold! her bosom and half her side, / Hideous, deformed, and pale of hue," Shelley went into hysterics. He told Polidori, who went to his aid, that, "He was looking at Mrs. S[helley], and suddenly thought of a woman he had heard of who had eyes instead of nipples."—*The Diary of Dr. John William Polidori,* ed. William Michael Rossetti (London: Elkin Mathews, 1911), p. 128.

22. Philip E. Slater, *The Glory of Hera: Greek Mythology and the Greek Family* (Boston: Beacon Press Paperbacks, 1971), p. xv. Several books show the applicability of Slater's theory to modern America: Adrienne Rich, *Of Woman Born* (New York: W. W. Norton & Co., 1976); Dorothy Dinnerstein, *The Mermaid and the Minotaur: Sexual Arrangements and Human Malaise* (New York: Harper & Row, 1976); Chodorow, *The Reproduction of Mothering.*

23. The early furor over Pre-Raphaelite art and Rossetti's decline in his last ten years through addiction to chloral make us forget the receptivity of his fellow Victorians to his themes. During the 1860s and into the 1870s his paintings commanded high prices, and when his *Poems* was published in 1870, the book went into six editions—small editions, to be sure, in order to create the need for more, yet with enough copies sold to make Rossetti jubilant.—*Letters,* II, 884.

24. John Berger, *Ways of Seeing* (Harmondsworth: Penguin, 1972), pp. 46–47.

25. Oswald Doughty, *A Victorian Romantic: Dante Gabriel Rossetti* (London: Oxford University Press, 1960 [second edition]), p. 130. Cf. also Dobbs, *Rossetti,* p. 101.

26. My interpretation of the incident follows Dobbs, *Rossetti,* p. 76. Stanley Weintraub believes Rossetti's application for the job to have been simply a gesture "to lower the implicit pressure on him to become a wage earner."—*Four Rossettis: A Victorian Biography* (New York: Weybright and Talley, 1977), p. 59.

27. Henry James, "Preface to 'Daisy Miller,' " *The Art of the Novel* (New York: Charles Scribner's Sons, 1934), p. 273.

28. *Letters,* III, 1175.

29. In "Jenny" the narrator speculates:

> What is the thought?—conjectural
> On sorry matters best unsolved?—
> Or only is each grace resolved
> To fit me with a lure?—or (sad
> To think!) perhaps you're merely glad
> That I'm not drunk or ruffianly
> And let you rest upon my knee. (*Works,* p. 37)

113

30. Recognition that the institution of marriage as codified in Victorian society was a form of legalized prostitution was not uncommon among feminists of the period and present in other thinkers as well.—cf. Charles Fourier, *Oeuvres Complètes* (Paris: Éditions Anthropos, 1966), I, 148–150.

31. *Letters,* II, 849–850. There is a similar sexual metaphor in Rossetti's note to Ford Madox Brown in 1864: "Are you not making water colours or pot-boilers of some kind and could you not let me have one here (if at disposal) to show to blokes or even buggers?"—*Letters,* II, 498.

32. *Letters,* III, 1324.

33. *A Victorian Romantic,* pp. 251–252, 254 and 682. Brian and Judy Dobbs have a different assessment of Fanny.—*Dante Gabriel Rossetti,* pp. 126–127.

34. Berger, *Ways of Seeing,* pp. 84–87.

35. Robert Rosenblum, *The International Style of 1800: a Study in Linear Abstraction* (Ann Arbor, Michigan: University Microfilms, 1956), p. 111.

36. I am grateful to my colleague Anne Mellor for this good suggestion.

37. *Letters,* III, 1324–1325.

38. *Letters,* IV, 1847.

39. *Letters,* I, 174.

40. *Letters,* I, 384 (emphasis mine).

41. Rossetti describes to his mother with excitement and no trace of condescension the work of an architect, Miss Losh, which he had seen during a visit to William Bell Scott in Newcastle.—*Letters,* II, 716.

42. I can recall scarcely an instance in which Rossetti writes of a manufacturing patron with anything but contempt, either open or hidden. His assessment, while understandable given his sense of powerlessness, is not charitable and may not be just, for often the patrons seem, on their side of the financial bargain, fairly long-suffering, and one of them, William Graham, gave Rossetti significant help at the time of his most severe breakdown.—*Letters,* III, 1048.

43. *Letters,* II, 508. The incident in which Rossetti most obviously betrays a commercial and objectifying lust turns upon his purchase (for £1) of a topiary box-tree that an old woman had worked on for thirty-three years. Transplanted to his Chelsea garden, it quickly died.—*Letters,* II, 609.

44. Ilza Veith, *Hysteria: the History of a Disease* (Chicago: The University of Chicago Press, 1965), p. 232; Lorna Duffin, "The Conspicuous Consumptive," *The Nineteenth Century Woman,* ed. Sara Delamont and Lorna Duffin (London: Croom Helm, 1978), pp. 39–40.

45. S. Weir Mitchell, *Fat and Blood; And How to Make Them* (Philadelphia: J. B. Lippincott & Co., 1877), pp. 27–28.

46. Pierre Janet, *The Mental State of Hystericals: A Study of Mental Stigmata and Mental Accidents,* trans. C. R. Carson (New York: Putnam & Sons, 1901), pp. xiv–xv.

47. Robert Brudenell Carter, *On the Pathology and Treatment of Hysteria* (London: John Churchill, 1853), p. 21.

48. Veith, *Hysteria,* pp. 213–214, 255.

49. Barbara Ehrenreich and Deirdre English, *For Her Own Good: 150 Years of the Experts' Advice to Women* (Garden City: Anchor Books, 1979), pp. 102–107.

50. Weintraub, *The Four Rossettis,* p. 157 and pp. 161–163; Dobbs, *Rossetti,* p. 171.

51. *Letters,* IV, 1688.

SIFTING AND SORTING MEREDITH'S POETRY

WENDELL HARRIS

Meredith is one of the curiosities of literature: few would seriously challenge his place as a major nineteenth-century writer, yet almost no one champions him enthusiastically as novelist, as essayist, or as poet. Only *The Egoist* and *The Ordeal of Richard Feverel* among the novels are much read; the "Essay on Comedy" offers little pleasure or enlightenment (the comic spirit is there defined primarily by negatives—a something other than wit, punning satire, humor, or irony); and the poetry is rarely examined in depth. Oscar Wilde's comment on Meredith has become so well known because though ironical it is also apparently unexceptionable (a situation which would likely have alarmed Oscar): "As a writer he has mastered everything except language: as a novelist he can do everything except tell a story: as an artist he is everything, except articulate." The quotation sums up much critical wisdom about Meredith's poetry and prose.

Barring *Modern Love,* the critical consensus about his poetry solidified early, has remained remarkably durable, and is considerably weighted toward the negative.[1] The Meredith of the *Poems* of 1851 was seen as setting out somewhat awkwardly down the Keatsian road: Meredith is "a limited kind of Keats" wrote William Michael Rossetti, a view echoed by Charles Kingsley. Meredith's delight in nature prompted the comparison; the roughness of his versification and lack of melody prompted the qualification. "The versification of these poems is frequently careless and unmusical to a degree that nothing can excuse; and in general we complain of a want of that care and

115

thought which a true poet would bestow upon his trifles," complained the reviewer for the *Leader.* Kingsley also suggested that the poet avoid "too-muchness" by curbing his loquaciousness.

Modern Love and Other Poems (1862) having found little enough favor, it was Meredith's novels which began to make him known. In reviewing *Poems and Lyrics of the Joy of Earth,* Mark Pattison wrote in 1883, "The circle (a select one) of the readers of these novels, knows that Mr. Meredith is a poet—in prose. Perhaps some of them may not know that he is a poet in the more usual acceptation of the term." *Ballads and Poems of Tragic Life* (1887) received somewhat the same reception. *The Pall Mall Gazette* reviewer remarked that "Mr. Meredith excels in these odd little gargoyles upon the fabric of his fantasy. If only he would keep contortion and grotesqueness in their right places, and not have them cropping out irrelevantly, here, there, and everywhere." W. E. Henley's review of the volume, which greatly annoyed Meredith, was summed up epigrammatically in the first paragraph: "There *is* genius, but there is *not* felicity." Slight as the eminence to which Meredith the poet was granted title as the result of these middle volumes, the collections that followed—*The Empty Purse* (1892), *Odes in Contribution to the Song of French History* (1898), and *A Reading of Life* (1901) were seen as declining from it.

Meredith's obscurity has been widely censured, often in metaphors contrasting light and dark. The 1883 *Pall Mall Gazette* reviewer wrote, "We are dazzled by a succession of shifting lights, coming from points a little off the usual range of sight." The *Saturday Review* in 1901 remarked that "in prose he would have every sentence shine, in verse he would have every line sparkle," but found instead "a somewhat exasperating semblance of lucidity, which still lurks mockingly about his work." G. M. Trevelyan spoke of both poetry and prose "illuminated by flashes of the same exquisite beauty . . . troubled by the same faults of uncouth and obscure expression" and of "a great body of work where the dark and lucid are mixed in various degrees."[2] Thus Oscar Wilde's "His style is chaos illumined by flashes of lightning" is only the most epigrammatic version of a common judgment. Wilde's "Meredith is a prose Browning, and so is Browning" not only transmogrifies Pattison's "Mr. Meredith is a poet—in prose" so that it is now impossible to read it without a double meaning probably not originally intended, but succinctly sums up the place assigned Meredith's poetry by 1890. There has been remarkably little change in

Meredith's standing as poet or the accepted roster of his poetic faults since Wilde's well-known formulation. Later critics have been more concerned than the original reviewers about understanding and explaining the causes of his obscurities, but even they have given little effort to defending the poetry as poetry.[3] In the case of Meredith's poetry, the history of critical response is thus more admonitory than encouraging—warning of thorns more often than delights. On the other hand, there is a continuing, if vague, general regard for Meredith as a poet. An anthology of Victorian poetry that did not include him would be heretical indeed.

Evidencing Meredith's status as a classic, little read and discussed as he may be, is the excellent new edition of his poetry, edited by Phyllis Bartlett, that appeared in 1978.[4] A reading of this edition suggests two general observations. First, reading right through the 707 pages of the first volume, which contains all the poems Meredith himself thought worth collecting, is much more a pleasure than an ordeal.[5] Meredith's poetry as a whole remains quite readable, which is not such faint praise as it sounds. (Try the experiment on the great majority of poets being reviewed by reputable periodicals in the years Meredith's poems were appearing.) Minor pleasures are plentiful. For instance, the reader smiles even while regretting the waste of wit on the subject of "Jump-to-Glory Jane." While one is wishing there were more substance to "The Shipwreck of Idomeneus" (and other of Meredith's classical subjects), one is admiring the ring of the Homeric similes.

Nevertheless, the best of Meredith, which stands out clearly from the merely acceptable, deserves the good office of being separately and clearly commended to the members of that endangered species, the lay readers of poetry. The handsome new edition is one for which scholars will be grateful, and one which Meredith, long accustomed to publishing his collected volumes at his own expense, would have been delighted to see. But at the same time, what such a careful, comprehensive edition offers the ordinary intelligent reader for whom poets presumably write is a higher proportion of chaff to grain. Meredith more than other nineteenth-century poets still requires winnowing. The best of Meredith's poetry has never come to stand out clearly from the bulk.

Second, reading through even the select best of the Meredith corpus suggests why so much of the critical commentary on his poetry seems either vague or reductionist. A major difficulty in setting out the case for that poetry is that it does not coalesce into a coherent cluster of impressions. Something relatively more definite is suggested, for instance, by the phrases "Tennyson's poetry," "Arnold's poetry," or "Hardy's poetry"—or "Meredith's novels"—than by "Meredith's poetry." No single, central virtue or mood can be urged. The fact is, I believe, that Meredith is not one poet but three. The best of his poems will be found to fall into three quite different groups, each of which repays the reader in its own coin. The result has been to disorganize critical evaluation and diffuse commendation.

One of the three groups is made up of scattered ballads, narratives, and sonnets which, though hardly of sufficient significance to make a poet's reputation, nor of sufficient likeness to suggest a single poetic personality, are obviously good in their kind. Many have received acceptance from the time of their publication: "Juggling Jerry" and the revised version of "Love in the Valley" are central examples. One can neither dismiss these poems nor derive any unity of impression from them.

The second group consists of the most poetically successful of the many poems in which Meredith stated his view of the lessons to be learned from "reading the earth." These give immediate pleasure in their handling of language as well as the more reflective pleasure which comes from recognizing their importance in the 100-year exploration of the relationship between man and nature which began at the end of the eighteenth-century. It is unfortunately not demonstrable that the poems we read with the most pleasure reflect the highest reach of the author's intellect. But to the extent Walter Pater was correct that all writing is translation of thought, to praise fineness of style is to praise accuracy of translation. The reader of poetry may thus have warrant for disregarding the unsuccessful and unappealing as too clumsy in its representation of whatever was in the poet's mind to be of any greater intellectual than aesthetic value. However, if a poem is of sufficient intrinsic merit to be worth reading, its relation to other poems and poetic traditions becomes a source of enriching interest. There are fortunately a double handful of Meredith's nature, or "earth," poems which are successful as poems as well as intriguing as heroic efforts to confront a major nineteenth-century intellectual dilemma.

The third set of poems to be commended to any reader of poetry consists of the single fifty-sonnet sequence, *Modern Love.* The censures of the original reviewers were for the most part based on criteria of good taste rather than poetic impact, and have accordingly suffered a sharp reversal. "There is a deep vein of muddy sentiment in most men, but they should let the mud settle, and not boast of it to the world. Mr. Meredith evidently thinks mud picturesque," wrote R. H. Hutton of *Modern Love*. J. M. Marston struck in: "We are not sure that, after great labour, we have arrived at Mr. Meredith's drift; but we are quite sure that, if we have, we do not care for it." Perhaps remembering Carlyle's famous description of Coleridge, Marston went on to say that the poem "contains passages of true beauty and feeling; but they are like the casual glimpses of a fair landscape in some noxious clime, where the mists only break to gather more densely." But Swinburne's public defense of *Modern Love* in the 1862 *Spectator* has been amply vindicated, and indeed by 1887, when the sonnet sequence was included in the collection *Ballads and Poems of Tragic Life*, the *Westminster Review* singled it out as "a most remarkable poem [which] has never received anthing like due recognition at the hands of critics or public." Further, "The poem stands alone, not merely in Mr. Meredith's work, but in all antecedent literature."

The poems which make up my winnowings extend in time from "South-West Wind in the Woodland" (1851), Meredith's earliest undeniably successful poem, to two pieces from the volume of 1892 (*Poems: The Empty Purse,* etc.), thus excluding the poetry of his last seventeen years. Also excluded are almost all the ballads, all the poems based on Greek myths, all the early sonnets, and the poems on French history. Of the two dozen or so poems on which I feel Meredith's poetic reputation most squarely rests, half appeared in *Poems and Lyrics of the Joy of Earth* (1883) or *A Reading of Earth* (1888) (the intervening *Ballads and Poems of Tragic Life* [1887] stands a somewhat desolate monument to misdirected effort). This slim harvest turns out to be only about one-tenth of the titles collected by Meredith, but not a few poets might be happy with the percentage.

I

In no century is there so much good poetry that we can afford to neglect any which commends itself to thoughtful pleasure by the fireside; anthologists looking for Victorian poetry that deserves to be better known may draw on Meredith for a rather interesting variety. The earliest would be "The Rape of Aurora," one of the most successful poems expressive of physical sexuality in English. It is a young man's outburst of amorous imagery. The least known is likely "The Song of Courtesy," a retelling of the curious legend of Sir Gawain and the loathly lady transformed into a beautiful maiden by his courteous kisses. In this poem, not republished for thirty years after its appearance in 1859, the inherent didacticism which would otherwise be absurd is made charming by the touches of humor controlling the versification. Much better known, a success from its first publication (1859), is "Juggling Jerry," the brief sketch of a travelling juggler's last hour. The danger in such a poem is an excess of sentimentality; here the antidotes to the sentimental are lightly understated folk imagery and unusually tight control at key points. An example of the first is this:

> Hand up the chirper! ripe ale winks in it;
>   Let's have comfort and be at peace.
> Once a stout draught made me light as a linnet.
>   Cheer up! the Lord must have his lease.
> May be—for none see in that black hollow—
>   It's just a place where we're held in pawn,
> And, when the Great Juggler makes as to swallow,
>   It's the sword-trick—I ain't quite gone! (148)

The control of tone is well illustrated by the multiple implications of the final image of a bird circling briefly above her fallen mate:

> the second
> Wheeled round him twice, and was off for new luck:
> There in the dark her white wing beckon'd:—
> Drop me a kiss—I'm the bird dead-struck! (149)

Then there are poems as various as "Martin's Puzzle" (1865), "The Nuptials of Attila" (1879), and "A Stave of Roving Tim" (1888). "Martin's Puzzle" is the most sentimental of Meredith's poems and the most Browningesque. The older poet's use of the dramatic monologue and fascination with theological speculation are here joined with the tone of "Pippa Passes." "The Nuptials of Attila" is the gem among Meredith's treatments of old legend. His other attempts in this genre somehow lack the vividness necessary for successful legendary narrative; here a succession of images creates scenes which remain in the memory. The procession of chiefs: "Chosen warriors, keen and hard; / Grain of threshing battle-dints." The fierce campaigns: "Men were flocks we lashed and spurned: / Fast as windy flame devours, / Flame along the wind, we burned." And the crazed bride hunched in a corner: "She, the wild contention's cause, / Combed her hair with quiet paws."

The jolly tramp of "A Stave of Roving Tim," speaks in quite a different accent:

> Lord, no, man's lot is not for bliss;
>   To call it woe is blindness:
> It's here a kick, and it's there a kiss,
>   And here and there a kindness.   (636)

Different yet are "Night of Frost in May" and "Empedocles" (both 1892). The first is Romantic response to nature—emotion recollected in tranquillity—at Meredith's best. Pure description unvexed by the verbal economies of which the poet is frequently so fond, it partakes generously of Wordsworth.

> Then was the lyre of earth beheld,
> Then heard by me: it holds me linked;
> Across the years to dead-ebb shores
> I stand on, my blood-thrill restores.   (541)

"Empedocles," quintessentially Meredith in its puzzling syntax, imagery, and phrasing, responds ironically to Arnold's "Empedocles on Etna." "The last of him was heels in air" observes the poet of Empedocles' leap into the volcano, the result of which desperation is nothing but "a more peculiar cinder." Meredith's brief treatment sums up Arnold's objection to his own poem as set forth in the 1853 Preface with considerably greater cogency and succinctness.

There are two very good and very different sonnets: "To J. M." (1867) and "Lucifer in Starlight" (1883). The first, to John Morley, is an excellent handling of the dedicatory sonnet, memorably dismissing men without aspiration "who what they are would be," while the well-known "Lucifer in Starlight" achieves a sonority and power of imagery hardly found elsewhere in the century's sonnets. And finally there is the inescapable "Love in the Valley," which compares the beloved by turns to winsome, to striking, and to soothing images from the natural world while tincturing natural scenes with eroticism until Mother Nature becomes Mistress Nature. The second version is better, but in both the beauty of nature and woman, human sexuality and natural fertility, blend into one another until the reader is carried, as

121

sometimes in Swinburne, on a stream of images which makes one heedless of precise meanings.

In addition to the variety of tone and subject, echoes from many a nineteenth-century poet are heard in these miscellaneous poems. They tend to be undervalued: poems which do not directly set forth what is understood as a central portion of a poet's view of life are generally regarded as of second-order importance. (This might be called the fallacy of the invariable theme.) But scattered in mood and genre, diverse in inspiration, frequently derivative as they are, I think they can confidently be commended to all true readers of poetry. If poetry is as important as critics say it is, it has many mansions.

II

Meredith does of course have a primary poetic theme, the relationship between nature and man, or more precisely, between love of nature and human contentment. His repeated excursions into this relationship are intriguing partly because they come so late in the afternoon of a century-long preoccupation. Wordsworth and Coleridge had begun to wonder whether beneficent and edifying powers actually dwelt in nature almost as soon as they had proclaimed their existence; the cruelty Tennyson saw in nature by the light of evolutionary doctrines finally became acceptable only through faith; Arnold the poet found strange and alien qualities in the same nature through which Arnold the pedestrian loved to tramp.

Meredith shifts the question; it is not whether nature holds some benign intercourse with the human spirit, but whether the beauty of nature is not of itself a compensation for much of the inevitable sorrow of life and, more important, whether the belief that human life deserves more pleasure and less pain than nature's processes afford the rest of earth is not man's greatest folly. Meredith's choice of the word "earth" over "nature" suggests the attempt to escape those transcendental overtones with which the Romantic Poets had imbued the latter word.

There are a generous dozen of these "poems of earth" deserving special consideration and commendation. Meredith's "South-West Wind in the Woodland," his first poetically substantive contribution to the on-going debate, accepts the violent and menacing as well as the grand, beautiful, and picturesque. In the beginning the Romantics had assumed the calm and beautiful as the norm of nature. But to choose a summer day as a paradigm leaves one open to the kind of question Aldous Huxley would ask some hundred years later in "Wordsworth in the Tropics." (Meredith himself did not escape Huxley's disapproval in that essay, but if Meredith's view of nature won't quite do in Huxley's tropics, it nevertheless does acknowledge the unpleasant and destructive.) Bad weather was hard on the Romantic poets: one recalls that it is when the wind rises outside that Coleridge writes the Dejection ode, and it is the storm swirling around Peele Castle which reminds Wordsworth that he has lost the power to summon "The light that never was, on sea or land." But Meredith delights in the storm as well as the calm; though the sound is of flapping, screaming, and wailing, celebration of the violence of the natural world is possible because "The voice of nature is abroad this night." Nature neither surrounds us with beneficence nor offers us any model for moral action. The model she in fact offers is how things will be, not how they should be—sun and storm, pleasure and pain are to be expected; the lesson we are to learn is that the egoism which expects special dispensation will be sadly disappointed. The contrast with Coleridge's "Dejection" may not have been consciously intended, but it is instructive. In his seventh section Coleridge imagines "a scream / Of agony by torture lengthened out," and a child who "now moans low in bitter grief and fear, / And now screams loud, and hopes to make her mother hear." Meredith describes the wind as "Now screaming like an anguished thing / Chased close by some down-breathing beak" and "wailing like a breaking heart, / That will not wholly break." Coleridge formulates a wish for the woman to whom his poem is addressed: "To her may all things live, from pole to pole, / Their life the eddying of her living soul!" Meredith writes "every elemental power / Is kindred to our hearts, and once / Acknowledged, wedded, once embraced, / Once taken to the unfettered sense, / Once claspt into the naked life, / The union is eternal." For all these similarities the radical difference is that from the beginning Meredith accepts the storm with joy: the approach of the storm is felt with as much expectation as foreboding. Meredith is well in control of his craft:

> The storm-cock warns the dusking hills
> And villages and valleys round:
> For lo, beneath those ragged clouds

123

> That skirt the opening west, a stream
> Of yellow light and windy flame
> Spreads lengthening southward, and the sky
> Begins to gloom, and o'er the ground
> A moan of coming blasts creeps low
> And rustles in the crisping grass;   (25–26)

That "lo" is one of the unnecessary archaisms Meredith was never able to shed, and "windy flame" and "crisping grass" sound better in passing than they appear on closer examination, but the poem is nevertheless effective in its description, while the joyful welcome of the storm in the last section knits all together.

Trevelyan's edition of Meredith's poems points out that "Ode to the Spirit of Earth in Autumn" is a second attempt to use a storm as a vehicle for arguing that man's oneness with nature includes turbulent nights as well as idyllic days. Meredith's characteristic strength and weaknesses are equally apparent in this second attempt. No poem with forced images like the following is today likely to find full favor:

> A lustrous heavenly orchid hung the West,
> Wherein the blood of Eden bloomed again:
> Red were the myriad cherub-mouths that pressed,
> Among the clusters, rich with song, full fain,
> But dumb, because that overmastering spell
> Of rapture held them dumb . . .   (194)

But no poem that ends as triumphantly as this can fail to seem worth the reading.

> Behold, in yon stripped Autumn, shivering grey,
>   Earth knows no desolation.
>   She smells regeneration
>   In the moist breath of decay.
>
> Prophetic of the coming joy and strife,
>   Like the wild western war-chief sinking
>   Calm to the end he eyes unblinking,
> Her voice is jubilant in ebbing life.
>
>   He for his happy hunting-fields
>   Forgets the droning chant, and yields
>   His numbered breaths to exultation
>   In the proud anticipation:
>   Shouting the glories of his nation,

> Shouting the grandeur of his race,
> Shouting his own great deeds of daring:
> And when at last death grasps his face,
> And stiffened on the ground in peace
> He lies with all his painted terrors glaring;
> Hushed are the tribe to hear a threading cry:
> Not from the dead man;
> Not from the standers-by:
> The spirit of the red man
> Is welcomed by his fathers up on high.   (199–200)

Though the last stanza was taken from an earlier, and quite different, unpublished poem, its position here is only less masterly than the effect achieved by Arnold some years earlier with the shift at the end of "The Scholar Gypsy" to the richly extended image of the "grave Tyrian trader."

Victorious assaults on the theme occur in three poems of *Poems and Lyrics of the Joy of Earth:* "The Woods of Westermain," "The Lark Ascending," and "Earth and Man." "The Woods of Westermain" is perhaps the critical test dividing those who happily immerse themselves in Meredith's poetry from those who find its eccentricities more chilling than bracing. That one's own mind determines whether nature—for which read *life*—is menacing or pleasurable is the argument of what seems to many an artificially difficult poem and to others a cleverly cast chant whose condensed seven-syllable (trochaic catalectic) irregularly rhymed lines drive its wisdom home. "Enter these enchanted woods, / You who dare" may seem as much a challenge to the potential reader as to the metaphoric woodsman. Alternatively, however, the brief opening section serves as reassuring epigraph, advertisement, summary, and sample. Wisdom for Meredith is not discursive and syllogistic but epigrammatic; his comic spirit has a gnomic rather than anecdotal wit. These qualities are faithfully reproduced in "The Woods of Westermain." The best-known passages are those describing egoism, the "scaly Dragon-fowl," the necessary but dangerous force on which Meredith keeps so strict a watch. However, such passages as the sketches of opposed alternatives at the close of the third section and opening of the fourth are marvels of condensation.

> Discords out of discord spin
> Round and round derisive din:

Sudden will a pallor pant
Chill at screeches miscreant;
Owls or spectres, thick they flee;
Nightmare upon horror broods;
Hooded laughter, monkish glee,
    Gaps the vital air.
Enter these enchanted woods
    You who dare.

IV

You must love the light so well
That no darkness will seem fell.
Love it so you could accost
Fellowly a livid ghost.
Whish! the phantom wisps away,
Owns him smoke to cocks of day.   (212)

This translates of course into an acceptance of the menaces and uglinesses not only in nature but surrounding human life. The dual aspect cannot be denied, but for Meredith the balance falls on the possibilities of beauty and delight. There is a well-known passage on this theme in *Diana of the Cross-ways* which reads in part, "As she grows in the flesh when discreetly tended, nature is unimpeachably flowerlike, yet not too decoratively a flower; you must have her with the stem, the thorns, the roots, and the fat bedding of roses." The same view of the world is more fully argued in two famous essays by a writer who has left his admiration for Meredith on record: Robert Louis Stevenson's "Æs Triplex" and "Pulvis et Umbra."

"The Lark Ascending" employs the standard tetrameter couplet to present much of the thought of "The Woods of Westermain" in more musical forms. The success of the poem is such as to require little comment. Forced rhymes are few while apt alliteration and assonance and a grammatical structure congruent with the tetrameter line carry one on. Each section (the first of which is sixty-four lines in length) is a single breathless sentence. (Though Ralph Vaughn Williams' musical romance echoing Meredith's title seconds the beauty of the poem, it misses, I think, the sense of upward force given by the structure of the poem.) The skylark having become an almost obligatory subject for nineteenth-century poets, Meredith's meeting of the challenge in a non-stanzaic form seldom used for lyric and his rejection of the customary personal note in which the poet attempts either to identify himself with the bird or finds in its song a personal message are substantial novelties. (The edifying application in the last section, however, is perhaps more traditional than welcome.) While "The Woods of Westermain" warns against egoism and asserts that nature will be found a source of joy or fear as we choose, it also celebrates change, a change seen on a long view as uni-directional. Blood rises to brain which rises to spirit, "Each of each in sequent birth." That impulse to change is what we are to hear in "The Lark Ascending": The man or woman able to remain at ease in Westermain extends human possibility, "More spacious making more our home, / Till lost on his aërial rings / In light."

"Earth and Man," like "The Woods of Westermain" denies mystic visions, beneficent intervention, or moral lessons. The earth is a source of nourishment, pleasure, beauty, and comfort; but it is the source of no secret wisdom, active spiritual force, or sentient power. Human success as a race or individual, the long slow evolutionary process which moves from blood to brain to spirit, is man's responsibility, "She who urged the start / Abides the race." "Westermain" alludes to the wisdom of "the deepest gnomes of Earth"; in "Earth and Man" man is imaged as "peering in Earth's entrails, where the gnome / Strange themes propounds." It seems important not to misread that image—the tone may seem satirical where actually it is ironical, and the irony is that true wisdom is indeed gnomic. It comes in units, not concatenated systems. And so it is packaged in the strange stanza Meredith chose for "Earth and Man": the rhyme is *abba* but the lines in each group are made up of a tetrameter, two pentameters and a concluding trimeter. Bringing the reader up short in the ultimate line of each stanza, the poem becomes a series of aphorisms quite different in effect from the onward flow of "The Woods of Westermain" and "The Lark Ascending" though the viewpoint is the same. Earth defines the conditions of life; there are no visible powers beyond her; what man may aspire to is human spirit grounded in earth's conditions.

G. M. Trevelyan has compared "Earth and Man" with Swinburne's "Hertha"; in fact a long series of poems reaching back to the early eighteenth century springs to mind. Meredith's argument as summed

127

up in stanza xix lies near the end of a tradition of poetic meditation reaching back to the earliest extant literature but of special significance for the nineteenth century.

> Behold his wormy home!
> And he the wind-whipped, anywhither wave
> Crazily tumbled on a shingle-grave
> To waste in foam.   (268)

Pope's "Essay on Man," or apologia for Deity, both recognizes the painful tension of man's "middle state," his place on the great chain of Being, and accepts it on the authority of hoary theological argument,

> Created half to rise, and half to fall;
> Great lord of all things, yet a prey to all;
> Sole judge of Truth, in endless Error hurled:
> The glory, jest, and riddle of the world!

The great effort initiated in 1798 was to justify a faith in the beneficence of nature either without such theological scaffolding (Wordsworth) or with a renewed sense of mystery and creativity (Coleridge). Tennyson can struggle through to faith in deity; Arnold can redefine it into a form his mind can accept; Hardy turns the concept of diety over and over, trying to escape the old sophist's dilemma that deity must be either without existence, without power, or without benevolence. But Meredith follows Swinburne in replacing a faith in deity with a faith in the possibility of living so as to maximize the pleasures earth offers.

By the time of *A Reading of Earth* (1888), Meredith is ready to rely simply on the cycle of seasons, sinking man's egoism in Earth's own rhythms. "Seed-Time" (first published in this volume) lacks both the ecstasy and the personal identification of Shelley's "West Wind"; it is closer to the classical acceptance of the mysterious cycle summed up but not explained by the Persephone myth. Meredith's descriptive powers are at their height:

> . . . a coat of frieze
> Travels from North till day has waned,
> Tattered, soaked in the ditch's dyes;
> Tumbles the rook under grey or slate;

> Else, enfolding us, damps to the bone;
> Narrows the world to my neighbour's gate;
> Paints me Life as a wheezy crone. (399)

The argument which led up to the affirmation "Earth knows no desolation. / She smells regeneration / In the moist breath of decay" ("The Spirit of Earth in Autumn") is now more briefly imaged: "The fuel, decay, / Brightens the fire of renewal." "Hard Weather" in the same volume moves from the description of a storm—which Meredith has always done well and now can do more succinctly and more powerfully—to a new facet of his argument.

> Bursts from a rending East in flaws
> The young green leaflet's harrier, sworn
> To strew the garden, strip the shaws,
> And show our Spring with banner torn.
> Was ever such virago morn?
> The wind has teeth, the wind has claws.
> All the wind's wolves through woods are loose,
> The wild wind's falconry aloft. (401)

That opening leads us to the counsel to accept the fierce moods of nature as the means of giving us "edgeing keen" for "The sharpened life commands its course." It is a secular version of the faith that God tests and tempers the soul by trial, here implicitly linked to the acceptance of the rigor of evolutionary advance. Man is chided in "Earth and Man" for questioning that evolution proceeds by selection of the fittest: "He deems her cherishing of her best-endowed / A wanton's choice." Rather, Meredith endorses the process:

> She winnows, winnows roughly; sifts,
> To dip her chosen in her source:
> Contention is the vital force,
> Whence pluck they brain, her prize of gifts,
> Sky of the senses! (403)

The doctrine is as stern as bracing, requiring the subjugation not only of egoism but self. Unfortunately not only does Meredith demand more than poor humankind can offer, but he at times confuses the general with the individual case. "Never is the earth misread by brain" writes Meredith in "Hard Weather," a dogma no more true than Wordsworth's "Nature never did betray / The heart that loved her," and equally likely to ring with mocking irony: Wordsworth must have rued the lines after his sister Dorothy's mental break in 1834.

The fact is that when Meredith focuses his attention on earth, beauties and pleasures dominate; when he focuses on human experience, pain and death come to the fore. There is great significance in the two titles, *Poems of the Joy of Earth* and *Poems of Tragic Life*. Though one can argue—as does Meredith on occasion—that the melancholy and tragedy of life result from a failure in our reading of earth, it is nevertheless hard not to feel a radical discontinuity between the poet's views as he faces now toward nature and now toward men. In some poems Meredith explains the unpleasant, painful, and evil as necessary to create individual strength and to drive toward the evolutionary improvement of the species. This view is repeated in "Outer and Inner" which finds in nature the lesson of the shaping of the world by pain as well as pleasure.

> sure reward
> We have whom knowledge crowns;
> Who see in mould the rose unfold,
> The soul through blood and tears.   (426)

At other times evil is seen not so much as a shaping evolutionary force as an inevitability magnified by egoism. The mixture of delight in the pleasures of earth and stoic acceptance of pain, the same forgetfulness of self in the service of evolutionary advance is the counsel of "The Thrush in February." Meredith's thrush implies no higher harmony nor concealed promise: it simply reminds us that we continue to remember the song after the singer has departed. The individual bird, flower, or person contributes a song, spot of color, or personality to a world which depends on such collectively for its charm and beauty while remaining heedless of the individual.

> We fall or view our treasures fall,
> Unclouded, as beholds her flowers
>
> Earth, from a night of frosty wreck,
> Enrobed in morning's mounted fire,
> When lowly, with a broken neck,
> The crocus lays her cheek to mire.   (414)

It is an effective image for an attitude which has considerable intellectual appeal but small power to comfort.

Meredith surely recognized that many readers would find his reading of earth gracelessly unpalatable, and therefore that such a reading, anchored neither scientifically nor philosophically, must be put forth through a variety of poetic appeals. "Change in Recurrence" accomplishes through the implications of two dozen lines of description a kind of ironical distancing of human tragedy and loss much more convincing than the some 560 discursive, rhetorical, and sentimental lines of "A Faith on Trial" in the same volume. The "Hymn to Colour" develops one figure—an expansion of the traditional identifications of light with life and of darkness with death to include that of love with color; the result is a Rossetti-like dance of abstractions arguing that love, life, and death illuminate and imply one another just as fully as do color, light, and dark. The existence of love not only demands both life and death but ought to reconcile man to death and lead him to shape life toward a higher, that is, less egoistic, level.

It is of course much easier to give intellectual assent to such a formula than to live by it. Meredith disarmingly recognizes this in the irony of certain poems. The strategy works well in "The Question Whither" where double and at times outrageous rhymes have the effect of assuring us that the speaker wryly recognizes the difficulty of constant allegiance to evolutionary goals beyond our experience.

> We follow many, more we lead,
> And you who sadly turf us,
> Believe not that all living seed
> Must flower above the surface.   (424)

Similarly successful is the combination of intellectual strenuousness and playfulness in "Woodman and Echo." Taking advantage of irony-suggesting, ambiguously toned four-beat lines interspersed in a relatively short irregularly rhymed poem, Meredith is serious without being solemn as he sets the seemingly impossible goal of applauding the necessity of our own demise and finding joy in echoing a harmony which requires our destruction.

> For all shall fall,
> As one has done,
> The tree of me,
> Of thee the tree;
> . . . .
> We tower to flower,
> We spread the shade,

> We drop for crop,
> At length are laid;   (456)

The self-parodying statement of the obvious undercuts its own banality.

While Meredith's treatments of evolution and egoism tend to prolixity, the simple assertion of necessity and peace of submerging egoism in an acceptance of earth's cycle is succinctly captured in "Dirge in Woods" and "Woodman and Echo" and even more briefly summed up in the description of dead leaves which is "The Year's Sheddings" (1888):

> The varied colours are a fitful heap:
> They pass in constant service though they sleep;
> The self gone out of them, therewith the pain:
> Read that, who still to spell our earth remain. (462)

Those four lines may serve as the summary, not simply of the creed Meredith again and again would urge on us, but the ultimate reduction of the Romantic desire to find strength, guidance, joy, and inspiration in nature.

III

It may be the contemporary preference for restless irony over triumphant resolution and for painful dubiety over strenuous assertions of faith that causes us to prefer the vision of life in *Modern Love* to that in Meredith's nature poems. It may be that *Modern Love* seems to claim a higher level of art because it sprang from Meredith's deepest sense of life, or that the unique control exhibited in the poem makes us feel that there is less of theory, more of true feeling here than in the poems of earth. In any case while the latter are fascinating in their dogged yet varied insistence on an end-of-the-century redaction of the Wordsworthian nature-worship, *Modern Love* fascinates by the exploitation of language in the service of a complex and powerful interweaving of thought and feeling which is the sufficient and final justification for poetry.

The curious and somewhat awkward fact is that Meredith's one supreme poetic success came relatively early in his career as poet. In an excellent analytical essay on *Modern Love,* Norman Friedman has written, "it is Merdith's best poem for the same reason it is a complex

132

one: it is the record of the man he was in the process of becoming, so to speak, the man he is."[6] Rather, I think, it is the record of the man Meredith could only briefly confess. Wrung from the tragedy of his marriage with Mary Peacock, the sonnet sequence insists on a complexity which Meredith elsewhere seems to have felt that he must simplify and a human perversity which he elsewhere insists can be controlled. The poems of earth offer a foil against which *Modern Love* stands more vividly; in turn we may measure the intensity of Meredith's struggle to achieve, maintain, and persuasively state his reading of earth by the painful richness of *Modern Love* which it repudiates. The "faint thin line" of the final sonnet has proved so difficult to interpret precisely because it is so tenuous a counterpoise to the tragic vision which informs the total poem. Meredith spent the rest of his life as a public poet attempting to validate the hope so tentatively imaged in that closing sonnet.

Despite the distaste expressed by the initial reviewers, recognition of the power of *Modern Love* began well before the end of the century. Richard Le Gallienne's 1900 study, which contributed significantly to Meredith's reputation, judged it "Mr. Meredith's one great poem of tragic life. It is, moreover, Mr. Meredith's one great achievement in poetic art."[7] That valuation has held; John Lucas's excellent 1971 essay on Meredith's poetry concludes by affirming that *Modern Love* "is not equalled elsewhere in his work and . . . only very occasionally is it approached."[8] It is hard to know which of the virtues of this magnificently unique sonnet sequence is pre-eminent. It is equally hard to remember that it appeared as early as 1862. Many of the sonnets of Rossetti's *House of Life* were being written at the time Meredith was writing *Modern Love,* and much in each set of sonnets is wrung from similarly anguishing personal relationships. But Meredith's is the much more modern treatment of sexual love: the demotion of abstractions like Love, Desire, Life, and Hope, the representation of a realistically detailed situation, the tracing of the twists and turns of the tortured mind; these make Meredith's poem seem much more modern in attitude than Rossetti's or any other nineteenth-century sequence. To nineteenth-century readers the sixteen-line form of these sonnets must have seemed the least radical of their departures from tradition.

Happily the sonnet form brought into play Meredith's strengths as a poet while cancelling his major weaknesses. In the first place Meredith seems to have required the pressures of briefer forms to make his language truly economical rather than eccentrically truncated and elliptical. The forced concentration of effort seems also to have sharpened his use of rhyme. Too often the infelicities and extraneous excursions in his poetry result from the apparent need to find rhyming pairs; such instances rarely occur in *Modern Love*. And Meredith's penchant for images taken from outside the poetic tradition—often combined with quite traditional imagery—works well here where the emotions and thoughts of the narrator range from the common to the vulgar to the idealistic to the hypocritical.

Le Gallienne and others have been criticized for their rashness in comparing Meredith's sonnets to Shakespeare's, but nevertheless there is at least significant similarity in the packed effectiveness of the imagery and the economy of individual word choices. The opening sonnet has been too much dissected to require, perhaps even to admit, a further detailed analysis, but its richness admirably demonstrates the specifically poetic pleasures to be discovered by a careful reading of the whole fifty. The description of the wife's sobs strangled like little snakes suggests the sound, the violence of emotion in the quiet bed, and the husband's fascinated revulsion. The sobs, which will prove venomous whether strangled or not, introduce serpent imagery which runs through the sequence. The modifier "stone-still" prepares for the image of sculptured effigies which closes this sonnet while the "pale drug of silence" anticipates the ultimate tragedy when it will be found that "Lethe has passed those lips." The sword imagined lying between the husband and wife is both the sword of the warrior traditionally included on tomb sculpture and an ironic reference to the sword symbolically placed between chaste lovers sharing a bed in medieval romances; the "sword that severs all" is not only death but "that fatal knife / Deep questioning" of the final sonnet.

Imagery which links sonnet to sonnet, and figures which intrigue with multiplicity of suggestion at times combine with splendidly evocative images. Though "each sucked a secret" is a simple enough clause, the verb suggests a thought turned over in the mind like a lozenge in the mouth, surreptitiously tasted, held invisible, and yet perhaps betraying itself by almost involuntary movements of the facial muscles. To these poetic qualities the addition of the novelist's touch is apparent in the pacing of the story and the careful and conscientious exploration of the mind tossed on waves of sexual, social, moral, and egoistic impulse. These virtues combine strikingly, for instance, in Sonnet XVII. Surface hypocrisy is effectively evoked but at the same time melded with the imagery of a game—and games, one knows, have a way of engaging more than the surface of one's mind and personality. The reference to a game prepares for the "greater wonder." Having begun the game in hypocrisy, pain, and perversity, the husband and wife increasingly admire each other's skill until the warmth of their looks contains as much genuineness as pretense. Images of light qualify the apparent superficiality of the couple's conduct: after all, light glinting, gleaming, and sparkling off surfaces is pleasing. The reference to buoyancy similarly qualifies our pejorative judgment of superficial and manipulated conversation. Not only the complexity of the interrelationship between the husband and wife but the mixed pretense and sincerity of all social intercourse emerge. "They see no ghost" works both as metaphor and as an allusion to Banquo at Macbeth's banquet. As in Macbeth's castle, host and hostess are well aware of the specter invisible to the guests, and the couple's skill is emphasized by the implied comparison to the disarray of the thane of Cawdor and his lady after the murder of Duncan.

In addition to the poetic virtues of construction and phrasing, the power of *Modern Love* derives largely from its dramatization of the complex way human thought and emotion are interwoven; such interweaving challenges Meredith's explicit philosophy as found in the poems of earth. Sonnet XIII states much of Meredith's usual point of view: As in "The Thrush in February," nature is pictured as dispassionate: "Upon her dying rose / She drops a look of fondness, and goes by, / Scarce any retrospection in her eye." But the whole of *Modern Love* is at war with such stoicism. It is not to be expected that men or women will "Lose calmly Love's great bliss."

Modern Love has been accorded the contemporary compliment of being read as an ironical poem with an unreliable narrator whose posturings, insensitivities, and intellectual dishonesties we are to see through. Such a reading is inevitable in these days, and that offered us by John Lucas is well argued indeed.[9] But I do not think it will finally do. Ironical the poem indeed is, but the kind of irony Lucas sees puts it too much into the camp of satire. Such a reading earns Meredith praise for greater subtlety at the expense of overlooking his full and painful recognition of irreconcilable impulses and perversely destructive attitudes which are like petards a yard below the philosophy he elsewhere espouses. The "earth" poems state an ideal conception of life which is almost impossible to translate into daily commerce with the world which *Modern Love* paints. We may call for "more brain" indeed; but will it come when we do call?

I commented earlier on the curious opposition between the joy of earth and the tragedy of human life in Meredith. This disjunction is partially obscured by the fact that the poems of "tragic life," those which appear in the volume of that title and elsewhere, are not finally as successful as the best of those which speak the joy of earth. They tend, moreover, to be much less personal, treating old legends and historically distanced subjects rather than the poet's response to his immediate experience. *Modern Love* is the great exception: the human tragedy here made vivid is contemporary, deeply felt, and by implication typical of almost unavoidable human follies.

If it is true that the prevailing melancholy of Matthew Arnold's poetry is a necessary balance to the cheerful urbanity of that writer's essays, it is also true that *Modern Love* is a revealing counterweight to the philosophy of Meredith's earthloving poems. Indeed the closing lines of the final sonnet of *Modern Love* and the closing lines of Matthew Arnold's best-known poem, "Dover Beach," are revealing companions. Arnold's speaker calls upon the loved one to be true as a last, dubious defense in a world envisioned as a battle-ground; Meredith suggests that rare achievement of evolutionary advance as the individually cheerless justification of an otherwise victoryless struggle.

> And we are here as on a darkling plain
> Swept with confused alarms of struggle and flight,
> Where ignorant armies clash by night.

and

> In tragic hints here see what evermore
> Moves dark as yonder midnight ocean's force,
> Thundering like ramping hosts of warrior horse,
> To throw that faint thin line upon the shore!

These images of dark battle manifest themselves on the shores of similar mental seas.

We are not required to assume that because none of Meredith's poems of affirmation ever achieved the power of *Modern Love,* the poet was somehow living out his own version of the Victorian Compromise for the 47 years between 1862 and his death in 1909. There is nothing of sophistry in the "earth" poems: the old Romantic argument—as it survives after severe mauling in the latter half of the century—is made honestly, so honestly that there is no possibility of smuggling in a last bit of transcendental sentimentalism to help it go down. One accepts it with heroic gust or not at all. From the beginning Meredith is a conscientious craftsman; I have tried to recognize those poems in which craftsmanship is raised to a higher power by happy inspiration. The old figure of a capricious, fickle, and fastidious muse is still serviceable after all; to have enjoyed her company even so often as Meredith did is rare good fortune.

NOTES

1. *Meredith: The Critical Heritage,* ed. Ioan Williams (New York: Barnes and Noble, 1971) offers the convenience and editorial care in gathering contemporary reviews and articles that one has come to expect from this series.

2. Trevelyan, *The Poetry and Philosophy of George Meredith* (London: A. Constable, 1906), pp. 4–5, 69.

3. Trevelyan devoted much of the chapter "The Singer of Strange Songs" to listing the causes of Meredith's obscurity, as does M. Ridley in his essay on Meredith's poetry in *Second Thoughts* (London: Dent, 1965).

4. *The Poems of George Meredith,* ed. Phyllis B. Bartlett, 2 vols. (New Haven and London: Yale University Press, 1978). My parenthetical page references for Meredith's poetry are to Volume I of this edition.

5. Volume II contains "Poems Published But Not Collected by Meredith," "Posthumously Published Poems and Trivia," and "Unpublished Poems and Fragments." Of great interest to the scholar, and offering more pleasure and interest to the general reader than one expects of such gatherings of occasional poems and bits of material from a poet's workshop, this volume brings forth no previously unknown gem.

6. Friedman, "The Jangled Harp: Symbolic Structure in Modern Love," *Modern Language Quarterly,* XVIII (March, 1957), 10.

7. LeGallienne, *George Meredith: Some Characteristics* (London: John Lane, 1905), p. 112.

8. Lucas, "Meredith as Poet" in *Meredith Today,* ed. Ian Fletcher (New York: Barnes and Noble, 1971), p. 32.

9. See note 8.

SWINBURNE: A PERSONAL ESSAY AND A POLEMIC

ROBERT PETERS

To say that Swinburne's flamboyance attracted me would be easy. He gesticulated
wildly and screeched at the top of his voice—to the amazement (and
the amusement) of George Meredith and the Rossetti brothers. He
was a shameless algolagniac. He loved sliding down banisters naked.
He was a passionate swimmer, and seemed to regard the English
channel as his own bathtub; on one occasion he nearly drowned but
washed up on the beach still alive. He was splendidly irreverent: at
a meeting with Tennyson he removed himself from the Bard's presence to an antechamber where he declaimed his own verses. One of
my mentors at the University of Wisconsin loved to deride Swinburne,
and not very imaginatively, by pitching forth the commonplace that
Swinburne's poetry ("verse," he called it) was nothing but a "fuzz of
words" (a shameless steal from Browning) who sang, mellifluously it
is true, but with something of a songbird's musical diarrhea. I owe
that professor a good deal—he made me suspect that there was considerably more to Swinburne than the professor had allowed. He later
moved full-time into University administration, a change possibly
managed by Swinburne's laughing shade.

In those days, the late forties, I was something of an esthete, wrote
my dissertation (under the supportive eye of Jerome Buckley) on the
poets of the 1890s and the several arts. I cultivated Bohemian types.
I was increasingly fascinated by late Victorian aesthetics, and particularly with the writers and artists of the so-called Decadence— Wilde,

138

Beardsley, Symons, Symonds, Pater, Solomon, Dowson, Gray, and Johnson. Once I had received the PhD. and was settled into teaching, I began to see Swinburne as an almost archetypal figure looming just ahead of, and inspiring, the late Victorian art for art's sake movement. Since I enjoyed his poetry greatly, on its own terms, I wanted somehow to convey my enthusiasm to students as exactly as I could. Obviously, to appear before a class and chant selections from *Poems and Ballads; First Series* for fifty minutes, no matter how adept one is, is a bore—and the students who would respond to that treatment would respond at a skin-deep level. I sought to be more analytical about Swinburne. Behind his much noted plethora of words, his impressive, largely ignored verse techniques anticipated later movements in English poetry, including the much admired sprung-rhythms of Gerard Manley Hopkins.[1] His ideas on religion and society, though derivative of Aeschylus, Shelley, Hugo, and Blake, were nonetheless sufficiently his own in their iconoclasm. He was much more than a pale imitation of other writers, or the facile singer of mindless anapestic feet.

I desired (and still desire) that my students perceive Swinburne as a magnificently vital writer, relevant to our times, stirring for both his music and his humanitarianism. If they are to look closely they will find an amazing verse craftsmanship based on the best traditional poets from the ancient Greeks forward. He demands so much more of the attentive reader than a sensuous passivity. Even his abstractions, skillfully employed, possess vitality and magic. One problem is, of course, that Swinburne is a poet who shows little development throughout a long career. This in itself makes writing about him difficult for interpreters and critics, and is responsible for the usual complaint that since there was no growth, and since he wrote for so many years, he succeeded mainly in producing a dulling monotony of ideas and effects. I know of no other poet so proficient in his art in the early stages of his career as he was during later ones. To assume that such a poet is inferior and mediocre because of this is a mistake. What Swinburne requires is something other than the usual critical treatment, where a critic proceeds from volume one and works through volume ten charting all the changes of thought and technique. Swinburne's methods and ideas can be examined in representative poems from any point in his long career. A sequential study, volume by volume, would be repetitious.

139

Obviously Swinburne is something of a cause for me, despite the fact that my interests for the past few years have been devoted to my own poetry. I remain surprised that so little has been written on him, compared with other figures of his age. But what has been produced is nearly always first-rate. If we were to invent a quality-thermometer for gauging the worth of books on famous poets, my guess is that studies of Swinburne would register considerably higher in relation to the numbers of those books than those for more fashionable poets. The most recent study is Donald Thomas' *Swinburne: The Poet in His World* (1979). Important earlier excellent studies are Philip Henderson's *Swinburne: The Portrait of a Poet* (1974), Jerome J. McGann's *Swinburne: An Experiment in Criticism* (1972), Clyde K. Hyder's *Swinburne: The Critical Heritage* (New York, 1970), Jean Overton Fuller's *Swinburne: A Critical Biography* (1968), John D. Rosenberg's "Introduction" to the selected poetry and prose (1968), Cecil Y. Lang's six volume edition of the letters (1959–1962), W. R. Rutland, *Swinburne: A Nineteenth Century Hellene* (1931), George Lafourcade's *La Jeunesse de Swinburne* (1928) and *Swinburne: A Literary Biography* (1932), T. Early Welby's *A Study of Swinburne* (1926), and Harold Nicolson's *Swinburne* (1926).

1.

As a young professor at Wayne State University, I began gathering notes towards a lengthy study of Swinburne's poetry. Before long I realized that if I were to understand this vast body of work, knowing something about his theories of poetry would be essential. I turned to his criticism, finding there an incredible array of pieces on a vast assembling of writers, ranging throughout English and Continental literature. Reading him was a joy—even at his most crabbed and tortured there seemed a design; he often parodied the pompous critics of the age (he mocked Arnold in particular). He struck me as a civilized and urbane Carlylean figure, but one devoting his iconoclastic energies to literature and art rather than to overtly metaphysical and social themes, as Carlyle had done. And although he later turned vituperative towards Carlyle, calling him *Thomas Cloacinus,* one doesn't read far in Swinburne's criticism before one senses his vast debts to Carlyle—the rambunctious humor, the devastating ironies, the imitation of voices for purposes of parody, the complex Germanic sentence structures, the ruthless independence of mind and feeling, the name-calling and energetic blastings of assorted human pretensions.

Swinburne's criticism constitutes a body of work unique in its range and style. It is a sheer pleasure to read; and it made fearless pronouncements unpopular in their time: Swinburne extolled Charlotte Brontë over George Eliot, Byron over the other Romantic poets, Chapman over other Elizabethan poets, Browning over Matthew Arnold. His work on the Elizabethans, incidentally, and on William Blake, stimulated fresh assessments of these hitherto neglected writers. His contributions to Elizabethan studies remain seminal.

The result of my interest in Swinburne's criticism was *The Crowns of Apollo: Swinburne's Principles of Literature and Art.*[2] Realizing that Impressionist criticism was greatly out of fashion and generally ridiculed by New Critics and others in the early sixties, I decided to systematize Swinburne's thinking about other poets, dramatists, novelists, and about art and aesthetics in general. I discovered in those vast pages of the monumental Bonchurch edition of the *Works* that there was indeed something of a single whole arranged around the most strenuous principles. Swinburne's vivid sense of tradition going back to the ancients impressed me. I had no idea I would find so much substance and so much connecting tissue.

A few comments, then, by way of pointing directions: Swinburne pioneered in realizing the enormous power of synesthesia as a device both for poetry and for criticism. He managed to incorporate in a single telling image or metaphor, nervous in its evocations, a remarkable blending of sense impressions, anticipating what the French symbolists were later to do. These are exactly the qualities John D. Rosenberg, in his excellent essay on Swinburne's poetry, describes as "Swinburne's love of mixed effects," giving to the work a "Turnerian quality." The poetry, Rosenberg says, "is charged with the tension of delicately poised opposites: shadows thinned by light, lights broken by shade, sunset passing into moonrise, sea merging with sky. He is obsessed by the moment when one thing shades off into its opposite, or when contraries fuse. . . ." Rosenberg continues by noting Swinburne's "superb senses, each of which must have transmitted a peculiar counterpoint. This basic, polarizing rhythm," Rosenberg continues, "runs through his being and manifests itself in his compulsive use of alliterating antitheses in prose and verse." His recurring synthetic images are the result of Swinburne's perceptions experienced as "paradoxes."[3]

Swinburne provided a seminal corrective to the Victorian writer's obsession with exuberant detail. While he himself early shared some of the Pre-Raphaelite enthusiasm for such exuberance, he insisted that such detail must be subordinated to a principle he derived from his thinking about William Blake, that each detail, well-employed, must contribute to an idea of "gathering form." Swinburne was an organicist in his theories, believing in something like a Platonic ladder of cognition—aesthetic effects ring higher and higher until finally they are spun into that exalted, transcendent realm of Beauty so prized by Shelley and the Romantics. *Passion* was Swinburne's word for the excitement we feel experiencing art. And there are varieties of *passion*, he insisted, on a scale moving from lower to higher. His theories were always dynamic—as his principle of "gathering form" shows. A fine work of art exudes *energy*, and, like one of Swinburne's ubiquitous ocean waves, accumulates force and "form" as it drives towards the shore. As it nears land, its energies gather into a stunning visual impressionist whole. As a critic, and by example as a poet, Swinburne was a major countervoice to the didacticism and moralizing so prevalent in Victorian writing. He proclaimed that the first business of the poet is to write fine verses and not to "redeem the age and remould society." Didacticism in art he lambasted as "the frantic and flatulent assumptions of quasi-secular clericalism." Inspired by Blake's example again, he insisted that art can never be the "handmaid of religion, exponent of duty, servant of fact, pioneer of morality."[4] And he supplied this warning for the trimmers: Those "who try to clip or melt themselves down to the standard of current feeling, to sauce and spice their natural fruits of mind with such condiments as may take the palate of common opinion, deserve to disgust themselves and others alike" ("Blake" 248). In the mid 1860s when these pronouncements (and a host of others like them) appeared, Swinburne's was indeed a minority voice, one to be echoed shortly by James McNeill Whistler and Oscar Wilde.

Another of Swinburne's virtues as a critic was his amazing ability to enter chameleon-like into a piece of literature.[5] He is, I think, the finest of Impressionist critics. At his best he renders in generally stunning prose an equivalent for what he has read and perceived. He explained his method in one of his pieces on Victor Hugo:

> This style of Victor Hugo's is not easy to catch and reproduce effectively. To find fault with it, lay a finger on the flaws and knots of it, set a mark against this or that phrase—even to seize on some salient point and hold it up in the way of parody—these are the easy things to do. It has singular alternations of fluent power and sharp condensed angular thought; moves now softly and freely, now with a sort of abrupt military step, a tight-laced, short-breathed kind of march, as it were; a style broken and split up into bright, hard fragments of spar, that have a painful sparkle in them, and rough, jagged notches and angles; then, again, it shifts into quite another likeness, becomes flexible, soft, sinuous, as the over-growth of trees or grass; with a passionate eager beauty in it that dilates every word and sentence to the full; a feverish excess of blood, a tremulous intensity of life. It is hard at times to keep up with the pace of it; the very written words seem to have a conscience and a vitality in them, to heave and beat with the fever of excited thought, to quiver with actual sensuous passion. Moreover, the style expands and opens up into vast paragraphs, coherent, indeed, but only as water coheres; "tumbling, weltering spaces of sea with no good anchorage for miles," that drift the reader breathless out of reach of rope or spar. Evidently, however, this matter, too, is best as it is; these are the forms into which the great thought and purpose of the writer naturally cast themselves, they fall and lap of their own accord into those folds and creases, and so the meaning of the book gets clothed and set out as suits it best.[6]

The critical approaches we have valued in our own time have been more analytical, more attentive to poems and plays as "verbal constructs," more self-consciously scientific and, I think, boring to read. A poem is not an intricately jewelled watch in which every part functions as moving cogs and wheels; there must be space in art for the flawed work, for passages of decreasing intensity, pauses for the reader to catch his breath before he is spun on towards the heights. Here, obviously, Swinburne shares with Ruskin and Carlyle, and most of the Victorian poets, the idea of the flawed work, characteristic of most long poems with their passages of quiet alternating with passages of intensity. The Victorians seemed to feel that such imperfections or modified orchestrations in works of art remind us mortals that we too fall short of perfection. The achievement is in the striving; or, as Browning wrote, "A man's reach should exceed his grasp, or what's a Heaven for?"

Swinburne seemed to have twentieth-century critics in mind when he warned: "If we insist on having hard ground under foot all the way we shall not get far."[7] Freedom rather than rigidity, flexibility rather than a stereotyped approach, he felt, best provide critics with opportunities for success.

2.

Obviously Swinburne's poetry no less than his criticism requires some detailing of its unique qualities. He has been badly read and too easily dismissed. And Swinburne is a difficult poet to be specific about. He is intellectually complex and fond of paradox. He is as complex a technician and craftsman as any other poet of his age. Today's students, by reading and sensing him carefully, can touch the wellsprings of earlier poetry better than they can by reading most other Victorian poets—Swinburne was indeed conscious of a classical tradition of art preceding him.. It is a truism to say that his *Atalanta in Calydon* is the finest Greek verse drama written in the nineteenth century. And young poets, drenched today in free verse techniques and projective verse journalese, anxious to learn their craft, would profit, I think, by immersing themselves in Swinburne's poetry.

Another much-heard truism about Swinburne is that once he has bitten you (he might have preferred *fanged* or *whipped*), you become a passionate aficionado. So my apologies for being an enthusiast. I sincerely hope, however, that what I have to say about his poetry will stimulate a few readers to read him with more care than they might otherwise have done.

First, I shall briefly examine Swinburne's facility for subordinating to an informing artistic effect observations made from nature. Second, I shall examine some instances of his use of synesthesia. Third, I shall comment on his impressionism and shall hope, however briefly, to describe his Impressionist verse style. I realize, of course, that I am excluding other valuable topics from my discussion: Swinburne's sexuality, his passion for liberty, his humor present in his self-parodies and in his parodies of other poets, his virtues as a novelist, his verse dramas. To a degree, I suppose, his sexuality and his humanitarianism are implied throughout my discussion, as is his detachment from his chaotic times, so enamored of evolutionary theories, science, and commerce. His insistence on the fixed, all-encompassing attributes of art can still enrich our own troubled spirits in an ill-centered, threatening age. For he asserts the profoundest of human values—those of the human spirit free from constricting religious, social, and political ties. He breathes a kind of anarchism of enlightened souls, inspirited by the transcendent, aesthetic feelings generated by art.

Swinburne had his say about the verbal decoration proliferating in much Victorian poetry—an important phenomenon since tortuous lines and sentence patterns and complicated sceneries—gingerbread—constitute a major Victorian verse style. There are Browning's elaborate catalogues of Renaissance lumber rooms, of natural settings with their eft-things, *pompion-plants, Oak-worts,* gourd-fruits, honeycombs, and finches; Tennyson's landscape and medieval sceneries, his massive, highly complicated verse paragraphs twisting and turning in folds innumerable (see the description of Arthur's throne in "Lancelot and Elaine," ll. 430–442); William Morris' luxuriously described towers and turret-roofs, Philip J. Bailey's and Sydney Dobell's verbal foliage; George Meredith's complex nature description and genre-bits; Rossetti's Willowwood settings; and Francis Thompson's involved gingerbread verse—"Corymbus for Autumn," for example, which is nearly swamped by excessive metaphors and a diction *fleshed out* from various verbal storehouses, past and present.

In these matters, as in nearly all others, Swinburne was his own man. Apart from his brief dalliance with the Pre-Raphaelites, reflected best in sections of "Laus Veneris," "The Sundew," the slaughter of the boar passage in *Atalanta in Calydon,* and the battle scenes of *Erectheus,* Swinburne's work reflects little of this gingerbread style. He himself complained of the "fretted" traceries he found in Tennyson's verse, and in the work of Tennyson's followers. He preferred poets—like Arnold of *New Poems* and much of Walter Savage Landor—who didn't assault us with visual exactitudes. In these poets "nothing is thrust or pressed upon our eyes." These poets have a "Greek spirit." Readers "breathe and move" through their landscapes, and are not "tripped up and caught at in passing by intrusive and singular and exceptional beauties which break up and distract the simple charm of general and single beauty, the large and musical unity of things."[8]

Swinburne's own transformations of poetic materials are as much intellectual and abstract as they are feverish and passionate. At their purest, his symbols attach themselves to objects at few points—sometimes at none, as in the following couplet from *Songs Before Sunrise* (1871) where Love as a vaguely rendered sky bends over a lover without touching her:

> Love, like a clear sky spread
> Bends over thy loved head.

Or, from *Bothwell:*

> Her soul is as a flame insatiable
> And subtle as thin water. (1. 46)

The success of such imagery depends upon our willingness to suspend disbelief in the heightened and transformed qualities of such lucent metaphors. Swinburne's imagination seemed to work best in a Watteau-like haze shimmering somewhere in a special zone between the physical and the transcendent, developing penumbras of meaning. He preferred to dissolve the solid and the visible; at his most characteristic engaging the reader in a play of light and shadow of an almost purely aesthetic-intellectual kind. Even when he is most erotic, the trappings of his poems are apt to be generalized rather than specific. A passage from "Hesperia" describing a femme fatale in her bower, contains thorns, leaves, snakes, gleaming eyes, hissing tongues, foam, desert dew, and lips. All of these are curiously inexact. While there are gleams, there is little or no color. When Dolores' lip-foam blends with the "cold foul foam of the snakes" winding round her, we are still dealing with abstractions. The action itself, repellent to most nonsnake lovers, remains conceptual—we construct a scene of particular intensity, of a woman's incredible lust projected via her manipulation of the snakes; she is a creature vastly larger than life—a symbol, if you will.

Another poem, "In the Bay," a panegyric to Marlowe and Shelley, envisions the souls of these earlier poets projected against a sunset. Although Swinburne gives the illusion of a real locale—"here, where light and darkness reconciled/hold earth between them as a weanling child"—the setting is merely an illusion. Nature makes way for some artificial personifications: light and darkness are parents and earth the "weanling child" who in Marlow's times held a promise lost in Swinburne's.

Swinburne preferred poems then in which natural details are kept subordinate to some developing figure. He introduced thematic motifs and then improvised in a somewhat circular fashion rather than in a swift but logical flow from image to image and sound to sound. He resembled a composer developing materials for a sonata. His ideal paralleled one he discerned in Shelley—Shelley, Swinburne said, sought "to render the effect of a thing rather than the thing itself; the soul and spirit of life rather than the living form, the growth rather than the thing grown."[9] Swinburne's figures and his visual details acquire a conceptual acuteness, what Paul de Reul,[10] called "the coloring of an idea" in Swinburne. What de Reul saw was that Swinburne's best symbols, based in reality, strive to escape the limitations of the actual. Nature seemed inadequate for Swinburne, and, again according to de Reul, it is this disdain for the concrete, the known, and the familiar that most estranges Swinburne from readers.

Swinburne's treatment of the landscape of "At Eleusis" is revealing. The countryside is a human body in distress, sterilized by Demeter. Images of doors, iron locks, and plows imposed on sexually charged references to *womb, seed,* and *mate,* deprive the poem of the realism in details we might find in Tennyson, Robert Browning, or Rossetti. Even the lines in which raping men "widen the sealed lips" of the land, with their Miltonic overtones, are intellectualized and artful. The ploughed fields ache as a body aches, the wind personified is frustrated, the burnt fields lie helpless.

Swinburne would have found Tennyson's defense of the following passage from *Maud* thoroughly uncongenial:

> I know the way she went
>> Home with her maiden posy.
> For her feet have touch'd the meadows
>> And left the daisies rosey.   (11.432–35)

When a critic complained of the facility of this verse, Tennyson defended himself by explaining that when one's feet disturb a patch of white daisies one does indeed expose their rosy undersides—a botanical fact!

Swinburne's method of simplifying natural details for an allegorical or symbolic effect is particularly clear in a passage from "At Eleusis" describing Persephone's rape by Hades. The passage is a kind of play of Whistlerian whiteness—the flowers are not named—except that we are told after the event transpires that they are white or purple "waifs . . . of the pasturage." Hardly very specific. The event itself is mythical and is, therefore, at a remove from the passions of real human beings. Hades' passion is stylized and conceptualized.

As Persephone reclines in her bed of wild flowers, chill water slides over her reddening feet, killing "the throbs in their soft blood." Birds

—we are told neither genus nor number—perch by her elbow, peck at her hair, and stretch their necks "more to see her than even to sing." The actual abduction is presented in an elaborately constructed verse sentence, distanced by the intrusion of the speaker proclaiming her own reverence for Persephone's body. The reporting is curiously decorative, abstract, and bloodless. Here is the passage:

> For Hades holding both *white* wrists of hers
> UNLOOSED the girdle and with *knot* by *knot*
> *Bound* her between his wheels upon the *seat,*
> BOUND her pure body, holiest yet and dear
> To me and God as always, clothed *about*
> With BLOSSOMS LOOSENED as her knees *went* DOWN
> *Let* fall as she let go of this and this
> By tens and twenties, tumbled to her *feet,*
> *White* waifs or purple of the PASTURAGE.

The sentence is a model of balanced stylistic effects: alliteration and repetitions of key words, confined mainly to the left side of the passage, and masculine rhymes and half-rhymes, arranged for the most part on the right side, developing around *seat* and *feet.* Obviously, as my italics show, Swinburne's longitudinal division of his verse sentence is only approximate; his effects are intertwined and cross over. The crisp qualities of the monosyllabic *bound* echo similar properties in a majority of the masculine end-words on the opposite right-hand side of the sentence. Moreover, *bound* pairs with *down,* connecting both sides and underscoring the tying-up motif—*knot, unloosened, loosened, bound.* Also, *let,* appearing twice in line 7, helps to interweave the halves. The stylistic effect produced, nicely complements the transpiring action, as reported by Demeter. The illusion of reportage is maintained, if somewhat artificially, through curiously flattened prepositional phrases: in line 1 an ordinary possessive is expanded in a Rossettian fashion—"white wrists of hers"; in line 3, the pair of linked adverbial phrases, "between his wheels upon the seat" are splayed out foreshadowing some of the colloquial woodenness of "holiest yet and dear/To me and God as always" and the flat vagueness of "of this and this."

By allowing bare natural metaphors to stand for themselves without much adornment, and by rendering these metaphors as abstractions rather than as palpable, definable, classifiable objects in the

148

physical universe, Swinburne achieves a classical tone. Art, he insisted, is not life: realms of the spirit are distinct from the insane, confusing varieties of forms in actual life—to abstract these forms is a technical means of creating art: the flowers, animals, birds, and trees of such poems need never pass as definitions for the botanist or the geologist.

Intimately related to Swinburne's transformations of natural detail is his pioneering use of synesthesia. His model was certainly in part Baudelaire and his famous theory of *correspondences,* where the universe becomes a forest of symbols, and where a conjoining *or* blending of metaphors of the senses clusters around a single image. Also, quite apart from Baudelaire's influence, Swinburne's own intensities of mind and feeling led him to such images—to cluster sense responses was to artificialize, to naturalize, image behind that metaphor.

Several examples appear in his early masterpiece "Laus Veneris," his treatment of the Venus and Tannhäuser story written in fiery quatrains inspired by Fitzgerald's *Rubaiyat of Omar Khayyam.* One of the most elaborate of his synesthetic passages occurs early in the poem. Tannhäuser who has sapped Venus sexually—she is asleep beside him—hallucinates and imagines Love (Amor/Cupid) standing near Venus's head. The knight confuses Cupid with Christ—the love god wears a crown of thorns. His lusting flesh is on fire. Initially, then, Swinburne's image is complex—is the image Christian or is it pagan? Obviously, in the Christian Knight's psyche it is both. Suddenly, however, there are other fascinating accretions. Love, "wan," suddenly becomes sea spume "blown up the salt burnt sands":

> Hot as the brackish waifs of yellow spume
> That shift and steam—loose clots of acrid fume
> From the sea's panting mouth of dry desire. . . .

Sight, touch, taste, sound commingle in a rich texture of effects. We *see* "wan" Love, we *see* foam blowing onto the hot sands, we *see* yellow spume, we *see* clots of fume. We *touch,* in a sense, the burned sands, and *feel* the hot spume. We *taste* the brackish spume. We hear the sea's panting mouth. The sea becomes an enormous leviathan of lust. What an evocation of fires! The passage resembles the traditional epic simile, in that the forward motion of the poem seems to delay itself in order to allow the poet to embroider his theme. Swinburne's

149

passage, however, goes far beyond the generally simple contributions of the ordinary epic simile; his blending of sense effects is an artful attempt to induce us to *sense* lust as it overwhelms Tannhäuser's mind. Yes, Swinburne here is partially literal, or true to nature; we do see, almost as if we are observing a stylized etching of the beach, the foam reaching the heated sands. But Swinburne's genius refuses to allow us to linger long over such an easily fabricated picture; for he suddenly personifies the sea, in an incredible image of a huge sea-monster, a leviathan of lust. We have moved a considerable distance from the rather straightforward image of the Cupid/Christ wearing his gilt thorns—a blend of Christian and pagan myths. Swinburne wins us over by his skillful blending of sense impressions. His art here triumphs over what another poet, say a William Morris, would have handled in a straightforwardly literal, decorative fashion. It seems to me that the incredible image of the panting sea anticipates what Symbolist poets were to do a generation or so after Swinburne.

One more image, among several equally useful, from "Laus Veneris," will demonstrate that Swinburne's use of synesthesia was a consciously developed technique, and not simply a rare, chance occurrence. Tannhäuser's account of a battle fought to wrest the Holy Land away from the pagans is realized in a tissue of sensory images. The Knight's recall of the battle involves his senses of smell, sound (shriek of spears and bows snapping, the breathing of the battle itself), and sight. The whole recalling becomes a stunning visual object, rendered finally almost as a Beardsleyesque graphic design of serpentine line— as the opposing ranks of "beautiful mailed men" move into combat, the pure lines of those ranks slip into a snake's sinuous movement. Swinburne renders a visual pattern in cool, almost detached terms, as it transpires in the Knight's psyche. For a moment the recollection frees Tannhäuser from his lustful obsession with Venus—but not for long. In an instant, and with a stroke of genius, Tannhäuser moves the metaphor of the snake as it images the battle lines over into his obsession with Venus as his femme fatale. The transition is entirely credible in terms of Swinburne's central theme of lust Venusian. This is, I feel, an exceptional moment in Victorian poetry. Swinburne's reference in developing his stunning visual motifs here, as nearly always, is art and not verifiable reality. To see that charged moment just before the hosts of mailed men engage in battle as a sinuous line of light (and sound) means that one must in a sense time-stop vision.

The warriors remain inactive until the perceiver has *seen* the image of light, has made an engraving or a painting in his mind, and, guided by Swinburne, lets go and senses the motion as a gradual slipping of lines into a vision of chaotic battle. Even here, however, the reader is suddenly returned to the Venus theme; it is Venus now that he sees, Venus as serpent. Art, for Swinburne, seemed to provide the distance he required between raw events and their presence in his imagination. In his fashioning of such splendid images he is in the company of painters.

Impressionism is a term that literary critics have borrowed from painting. To simplify, in painting, impressionism refers to the juxtaposition of minute strokes of color, to be combined by the perceiver's eye and blent into tones the painter desired. For example, in a canvas by Monet (or by Renoir, Degas, or Pissarro) we perceive green by visually fusing juxtaposed small strokes of yellow and blue. The effect produced is of an atmospheric shimmer of greens produced without our losing the properties of the tints constituting the greens. The impressionist painter captures the play of sunlight over surfaces, fragmenting objects into tints and hues, infusing the atmosphere with colors absorbed from those objects. In Monet's *Sunflowers,* the air around the vase is as alive with color as the vase itself and the scrap of Persian carpet on which it rests.

In applying *impressionism* to poetry, it is easy to sidestep the issue of verse technique and record instead some quivering, hesitant emotion, or describe passages flickering with sunlight. But such recordings will not suffice. We must look, as Pater said, to "the literary architecture" of the poems in question, to see whether that architecture "involves not only foresight of the end in the beginning, but also development or growth of design in the process of execution," leading to some "unity of the whole."[11] We have already seen something of the nervousness behind Swinburne's particular creation of symbols and moods. Nervousness, obviously, implies flickering and evanescence. Speed and motion are among Swinburne's chief characteristics —the Apollonian dance, derived from Apollo, god of poetry, himself, spins, whirls, and moves through Swinburne's poetry. The swift anapestic line generates much of the kineticism we associate with Swinburne. At its best, the poetry has an impressive architecture, in Pater's sense. Towards understanding how his verse impressionism works, as words play against words, and lines against lines, I shall examine two passages from his late masterpiece "By the North Sea." The whole poem is an elaborate metaphor for the act of Apollonian creation and the dominance of art over all transiency.[12]

The first stanza of "By the North Sea," part of the dedication, presents a trio of characteristic Swinburnian images—*sea, wind,* and *sun* (or, *sound, breath,* and *light*) symbolizing the free creative spirit of man. Death, a shadow cast by life upon fate, symbolizes life's ironic triumph over fate. The passage sustains two predominant sounds: *th* and *t.* There is a remarkable absence of sharp imagery and detail. The first stanza is an *abba abba* pattern: the rhymes or near-rhymes are *breath, create, passionate, faith, safe, great, fate,* and *death:*

> Sea, wind, and sun, with light and sound and breath
> The spirit of man fulfilling—these create
> That joy wherewith man's life grown passionate
> Gains heart to hear and sense to read and faith
> To know the secret word our Mother saith
> In silence, and to see, though doubt wax great,
> Death as the shadow cast by life on fate,
> Passing, whose shade we call the shadow of death.

If one divides this stanza more or less medially (possible because of the disposition of the caesurae and the natural pauses), one sees that end rhymes indigenously allow the right portion to carry richer sounds than the left. The images, pallid and bare, call little attention to themselves and evoke quietly penetrating relationships. In the total music of the passage, separate words are subordinated to an overriding effect of blent senses in combination. In general, masculine rhymes *(create, great, fate)* occur at the ends of lines where the reader pauses to absorb the metaphysical content. Swinburne involves us in complex, intellectual abstractions. Faster soft-rhyme echoes *(breath, faith, death)* carry us swiftly into the succeeding lines where they halt, usually at a caesura placed skillfully midway through.

This oscillation between soft and harsh effects, between *th* sounds and explosives, produces a verbal shimmer, ubiquitous in "By the North Sea." This effect can be compared to the Impressionist painter's practice of juxtaposing small nervous strokes of color. To alternate *breath* and *create* as key sounds attracting individual echoes is not of course unusual. What is unusual is the exclusive dependence on such controls within this tightly knit stanza. Note, for example, the several internal effects echoing *breath* and *create* in one form or another: *spirit, heart, secret, doubt; wherewith, however, though,* and *death* are the more obvious examples.

In grasping Swinburne's nuances, we enjoy a complex Impressionist art. His sound patterns, so full of shadings, are an exercise in impressionism by association. Nervous on-going designs assemble around key words ... *death* is an example. In this instance feminine words dominate: *boundless, endless, blossoms, fruitless, powerless.* Flickering white swallows and fluttering grass, though seemingly precise are, in fact, vague; yet they serve as nervous images flashing through the dusky, cloudlit skies. The landscape itself is desolate— a more expanded version of the sterile site he celebrates in "A Foresaken Garden." The vast landscape is shot through with swiftly moving negative energies. In an impressionist, restless, flickering way, we juggle his positives and negatives, motifs of pleasure and pain. The birds' songs "fall," the image borrowing impact from the visual detail of frightened wings seen as "lightnings that flee." Swinburne manages to create a complex tissue of mental and auditory effects implying their opposites, a quality unique in his poetry and particularly successful in "By the North Sea."

Delicate impressionist rhymes based on certain key polysyllabic feminine words *(hunger, passion, hunger, winter)* culminate (stanza 6) in a potent image of storm and floundering ships, symbolizing the rage of the sea. Destructive and ravenous, the sea is no longer the life-giver. This oscillation between roles requires a certain alertness from the reader, a shift of mind, a counterpart to the quick fluctuations of sight and sound everywhere in the poem. As Swinburne presents his swiftly rendered symbols, transitions are minimal. Verse sentences pile upon one another, their solidity arising from an assemblage of various impressionist effects and not from any solid rational progression of thought and feeling. As lines race forward, clustered with paradoxical meanings and actions, images assume symbolic force. The attention they require of us is not dissimilar to some of the effects found in the work of Baudelaire, Verlaine, Rimbaud, Laforgue, and Mallarmé; in this sense, developing his own style, Swinburne anticipates these writers.

Midway in "By the North Sea," our view moves leisurely from land out to the sea's yellow edge which devours the land and beyond, to flickering clouds and more birds. Here, all human problems dissolve into the earth, where they "sink under /Deep as deep in water sinks a stone." Impressionist seeing creates a special joy in freedom:

> Tall the plumage of the rush-flower tosses,
>   Sharp and soft in many a curve and line
> Gleam and glow the sea-coloured marsh-mosses
>   Salt and splendid from the circling brine.
> Streak on streak of glimmering seashine crosses
>   All the land sea-saturate as with wine.

The passage is fresh and buoyant, glimmering as it does with streaks of sea-shine. Curves and lines suggested by broad expanses of marsh vegetation abound, always generally rather than specifically seen. Tossing rush-flowers produce ample, rounding curves; there is a massed single impression of beauty. All hues are carefully controlled, in the manner of Whistlerian merged tones. Only the generalized billowing contours of the flowers divide these massed forms from the sea—which sheds a metallic light and assumes various tints of blue. Earlier in the poem the sea was wan, grey, and sunless. Sensations of touch and taste weave through visual and kinetic ones. Lines describing natural forms are both sharp and soft. The marsh mosses are salty. Combined, these motifs produce a single effect, a beautiful climax for the stanza—the land is "sea-saturate as with wine." The whole landscape is stained with color, without distinctive configurations. Accompanying the various plays of sunlight, a surface impressionism, are verbal and thematic motions playing throughout, enhancing the visual effects. The whole landscape is stained with color, without distinctive configurations. The allusion to *wine* carries, of course, connotations of color and taste and, in addition, possesses ceremonial or ritualistic overtones and evokes an epic past. In summary, while these lines produce a surface impressionism of sunlight as it transforms a landscape and breaks up the precise contours of individual objects, they do a good deal more. A verbal and thematic motion plays throughout, enhancing the visual effects.

The interplay of contrasting, swiftly moving sets of rhymes characterizes Swinburne's verse impressionism at its best. *Tosses, mosses,* and *crosses* relaxed, on-going, and soft, are checked and drawn in by clipped, long-vowelled monosyllables *(line, brine, wine).* In addition to managing such skillful interweavings of sense images and alternating end rhymes with their positive auditory effects, Swinburne characteristically treats the stanza as a unit more or less divided medially, a sort of form with a vertebra. The compound subjects of lines 3–5, and the streaks of line 6, show this. Contributing also is the weight provided by the rhymes *tall, salt,* and *all* of lines 1, 4, and 6. These tight rhymes comprise part of the frame for the section (aided also by the assonance of *gleam* and *streak* of lines 3 and 5) and are in tensile balance with those softer feminine end rhymes which seem to dissolve in the distance.

We move next to a muted view featuring a "low grey sky" cloven by "clear grey steeples," a Whistlerian motif of grey on grey with the heavier grey pricked out by spires. The latter symbolize human fear-lessness before the "blast of days and nights that die" and prepare for the final irony, the crumbling of graveyard and church into the sea. Unfortunately the stanza is loose and uninspired. Grey is the hue of a man's troubled face and of clouds troubling the land. The transfer-ences happen too easily. The "towers and tombs" watching "stern and sweet" over the lonely dunes lack symbolic power. Interwoven *in* sounds constitute the best technical feature here. Stanzas 6–8 blend these sounds: *thinned, sinned,* and *wind* as end rhymes in stanza 6; *wander, squander,* and *yonder* in 7; *olden, golden,* and *beholden* in 8.

The vision of Odysseus materializes slowly, as the poet laments that only in pre-Homeric times did the present landscape bear signs of life and death. In the present, this sterile waste is more a symbol of death than a real locale: "Here is Hades, manifest, beholden,/Surely, surely here, if aught be sure." The place is "the border-line" between life and death. Life's wild motions, its "lightning joys and woes," occur here only to expire. This is the same Hades, the speaker says, where Hercu-les met Anticleia's spirit and found proof that souls after death love even more intensely than in life. In this symbolic underworld love "lives and stands up re-created."

But Hercules suffers since he, the only mortal allowed to cross death's threshold and live, is unable to grasp his mother's shade. The brief meeting is painfully but delicately described, concluding the vision and returning the speaker to the present "all dispeopled here of visions" and "forlorn of shadows": "Ghostless, all its gulfs and creeks and reaches/Sky, and shore, and cloud, and waste, and sea."

These final symbols, elemental and abstract, recall Shelley's and Whitman's similar handling of broad motifs: procreant large forces of nature and the universe stilled and colored by the poet's mood. For Swinburne they are consciously pallid. There is perhaps more of a hunger for the past in Swinburne than in the other poets; nor does Swinburne embrace the disparate natural and social forces of a vivid present, as one finds them in "Song of Myself"; nor does he absorb much of Shelley's remarkable power to transform classical material into a symbolic equivalent for a vital, apocalyptic social and ethical vision transpiring in a graspable future (see *Prometheus Unbound,* particularly the final act). Swinburne here joins the ranks, if he is not, indeed, the leader, of those writers (Arnold, Pater, John Addington Symonds, Oscar Wilde, and Arthur Symons among them) who contrasted their hunger for a romanticized past with a desperate Philistine present. Swinburne's label for the latter was "the new Gaza where we live." It is in such passages as these that Swinburne is most purely the early Victorian aesthete.

In this brief essay I have stressed three aspects of Swinburne's poetry—his subordination of literal detail to broad artistic effects, his employment of synesthesia as a means for subordinating detail by means of an exalted interplay of nerves and *passion,* and his cultivation of a verse impressionism, advanced in his day, for conveying shimmers of both visual and conceptual effects. The business of the artist is to transform the physical world around him through the alembic of his own heightened senses, controlled, into works Apollo himself would bless. Paramount among human experiences, art alone, according to Swinburne, enables the human spirit to transcend the finite and the flawed and touch eternal Beauty. While the general contours of his thinking may strike us as too Romantic, his faith in the role of the artist in a chaotic, centerless, threatening time retains its force. His great technical prowess, recalling Chaucer's concept of the poet as "maker," is still a considerable model for poets today wandering through the mazes of free verse forms. He sought a harmony between both the sensuous and the meditative elements of poetry. An energetic *form*—his phrase for it was "gathering form"— was the means for the synthesis he craved.

I conclude with a plea for more perceptive, unbiased studies of Swinburne both inside and outside the classroom. In many ways he incorporates various concerns held by other poets and artists of the age: a high seriousness of theme, a practiced craftsmanship— with something of a guild-maker's attention to his fashionings, and a faith in the iconoclastic creative temperament as a source for broad human truths. No other poet of his age, except for Tennyson perhaps, was so purely the artist—which makes for enormous problems in teaching him. Delving into the interior of an ambitious poem is not easy. And yet it seems to me that the only way finally to comprehend a poem is to locate, examine, and describe elusive facets of style. We must move past the humorous accounts, then, of Swinburne's odd physical demeanor, past his outrageous mannerisms of voice and person, and past his obsessions with sadomasochism, to the enormous body of his work itself, including the dramas, the fictions, and the criticisms. I could easily continue this polemic, but before I expose myself to complaints of special pleading, I shall merely declare that my early graduate school enthusiasms, and my discoveries on first teaching Swinburne, remain undimmed. He is indeed a splendid feast.

NOTES

1. See Elisabeth W. Schneider, "Sprung Rhythm: A Chapter in the Evolution of Nineteenth Century Verse," *PMLA,* LXXX (1965), 237–53.
2. Wayne State University Press, Hilberry Publication Prize, 1965.
3. "Swinburne," *Victorian Studies,* XI:2 (1967), 149–150; later reprinted as the Introduction for *Swinburne: Selected Poetry and Prose* (New York, 1968).
4. These statements appear in the Bonchurch Edition of Swinburne's *Works,* "William Blake," XVI, 139. See *The Complete Works of Algernon Charles Swinburne,* ed. E. Gosse and T.J. Wise (20 vols., London 1925–27), hereafter cited as *Works.*
5. "Swinburne as a Critic," *The Sewanee Review,* XXXII (1924), 407. Newton Arvin, in his pioneering essay, remarked on Swinburne's uncanny ability "for *feeling himself* into a piece of literature . . . and in reproducing the experience for another."
6. *Works,* XIII, 169–170.
7. *Works,* XVI, 125.
8. *Works,* XV, 77–78.
9. *Works,* XV, 380.
10. *L'Oeuvre de Swinburne* (London and Paris, 1922), 58, 62.
11. "Style," *Appreciations,* Library Edition, pp. 22–23.
12. Another celebration of the Apollonian artist figure is the forty-part "In the Bay," *Poems and Ballads: Second Series.*

READING ONESELF INTO HOPKINS

WENDELL STACY JOHNSON

For people who both read poetry and teach it there is always a mildly schizoid tension between personal enjoyment and pedagogical communication of sense. The tension is embodied in our usual admonition to students: respond to the sound and the feeling of the poem, but avoid substituting the response for a verifiable meaning; give your reaction to the words, but do not simply "read yourself into" them. Are we in effect always contradicting ourselves? Are we trying, *our* selves, to have it both ways?

The answer of a transactional critic concerned with the psychological bridge between a subjective experience and a verbal icon, but emphasizing the experience, may be to allow individual association so much leeway that a student has to stray very far indeed—and with some poems the student can hardly go too far—before producing a skeptical, limiting reaction, "Look at the words." Professional critics and teachers putting their own transactions on paper have often appeared to think that they require little if any self-limiting. No poem provides a better example, as an object of criticism, than Gerard Manley Hopkins's "Windhover" sonnet: from the time it was published until now, commentators have been reading their own meanings into it as interpretations. Elisabeth W. Schneider puts the matter bluntly. "*The Windhover* conveys one logically and poetically possible central meaning, and only one, in which all the parts of the poem and all the images find a place. Belt buckles and buckles in armor are not a part of it; they belong to some other poem, by some other poet."[1]

158

This animadversion may at first strike one as stringent to the point of rigidity, but other writers on the poem have been so self-indulgent, fixing on eccentric or over-emphatic significations for single words like the verb *buckle* and the noun *morning* in disregard of context or logic, that they have in effect been the other poets writing other poems. (Some have not even bothered to take their cues from Hopkins's own words.) Either that or, like the earliest Hopkins critics of this century, they have substituted fanciful biographies and amateur psychoanalyses of Hopkins the man for responsive reading.

To some degree a result of certain current fads, the praise for misreading and the license given a creative or poetical critic to fabricate his or her own "vision," there is something disturbingly off the point about a good deal of such recent interpretation, the kind of mystical-magical interpretation to which "The Windhover" and the rest of Hopkins have been subjected. There is communicable value in good poetry, and Hopkins is a more valuable poet, with richer and deeper meaning to communicate, than his academic critics are in their criticism.

At the same time, there can no doubt be some danger in a too strict or literal-minded authoritarian reading that pretends to objectify a poem and translate its meaning whole and pure, as no paraphrase or interpretation ever does. In fact, the great danger is that a critic will combine highly personal associations with the categorical imperative, so that almost pure subjectivity is transformed into some specious objectivity: the poem then becomes hermetic scripture and the critic a self-illuminated authority, a commentator as prophet. The more extreme a reader's independence of text, the more extravagant a critic's claim of luminary insight into an essence beyond textual trivialities of verbal coherence. Thus the poet's own voice is unheard and the variety, the partial unpredictability, that results from discourse upon a text is missing.

Whether combined or separate, the two modes—that of free association and that of impersonal, dogmatic, and apparently logical analysis—represent ways of the Hopkins critic's substituting something else for the real object, which is or should be, after all, the poetic art of Gerard Manley Hopkins.

Hopkins invites us to consider the relationship between an utterly personal subjectivity—his own "queerness"—and a false, impossible objectivity in reading because that relationship, that problem, is at the

159

core of this art. It is one version, a reader might say, of his authentic internal tension. "Reading oneself into" an experience is the very act that each poem demands of us; that is why his can often be personally meaningful poetry rather than soulless artifact. But reading oneself into it, incorporating one's own emotion and intellect into the real body of the poem, both entering and being entered by its incarnate essence, is not at all the same as subordinating the art of Hopkins to our purposes. There are different senses of "reading in"; the sense in which that act is necessary is quite unlike what we ordinarily intend when we use the phrase, which is really "reading out" and away from the poem, or expressing ourselves not in it but rather in spite of it.

The idea of reading and the very word *oneself*—or *self*—are especially significant in Hopkins. Both suggest to him a given quality along with a personal response. For Ruskin, one of the poet's two great masters, the live mind is always reading—that is, seeing nature, pictures, buildings, as well as reading words, and constantly interpreting what is seen, heard, felt. For Newman, that other great master, the authority of what is read—in particular, the scriptures and sermons, dogmas and documents of church history—must constantly be tested and applied by a receptive intelligence. For Hopkins, to read is to understand sounds and references by actively interpreting, by finding meaning within oneself that truly corresponds to external meaning. Complete meaning exists, then, not only in things but in the relating of things to a mind. This is true, first of all, of the meaning within sound and rhythm, the essential meaning of the spoken word—the word spoken or chanted or sung as in song, incantation, and prayer.

Reading of poetry should always, of course, be reading aloud; but for Hopkins the saying and hearing are crucial because his is a poetry that relies for meaning on the sounds of the pulse, the bell, the echo, the mouth uttering words. Hopkins's words are normally monologues or dialogues, very often given the specific form of dialogue that is called prayer. A prayer may seem to be the attempt only, the overture to a dialogue that is not completed. So Hopkins complains:

> My prayers must meet a brazen heaven
> And fail or scatter all away.

And, again,

> my lament
> Is cries countless, cries like dead letters sent
> To dearest him that lives alas! away.

160

But if such prayers do appear often to go "away," they still must be spoken or sung.[2] The poet must sing, ring, echo God's "mouthing" of Himself. This is his burden in *The Wreck of the Deutschland.*

> How a lush-kept plush-capped sloe
> Will, mouthed to flesh-burst,
>   Gush!

The poet "mouths" both by biting sacred fruit and by giving it voice, the sound of his mouth; sound is first imagined within the hearing heart, then uttered—and then, at last, echoed in the ear and the responsive mouthing of the reader. Although a visual image is evoked here and the idea of Word is involved in all of this (the idea of Logos theology), the foremost transaction is a serial one moving from verbalized vision to poet's voicing to reader's responsive explosion in speech. The poem as the mouthing of an echo can exist only as it is read or exclaimed aloud.

At its most effective, then, the voice of Hopkins makes one echo or sing or pray whether one has meant to or not, just as the stressful mouthing of God has made Hopkins do. Reading aloud, we utter the Word and we become the poet himself.

The *Wreck of the Deutschland,* although inconsistent, does in large part represent Hopkins's poetry at its most effective. The work can be described as an ode or as a hymn; Schneider finds it to be, at last, a prayer—a prayer for England to be converted as the poet himself has been converted. According to any definition, the *Deutschland* must be taken to represent a very personal answer within an answer, the poet's own echoing of the tall nun's response to disaster as she utters the word *Christ,* and a personal answer that elicits in turn the reader's answering voice of feeling as he or she reads words aloud in the singing, ringing rhythm that the words as if by their own volition constitute. A reader who professes to have little knowledge as to what the poet is "about" can hear and utter the rhythm, the sound, the vitality of this poetic process. Metrical effect, here, is not anything imposed upon the subject. It *is* the subject. It is the poem. Here Hopkins gives us not in technical language that might be needlessly difficult (much as he can dwell on such language in his notes and letters) but in the very sound of stress or tension, his idea and his experience of stress.

For this singing poetry is, precisely, "about" the poetic and personal mystery of stress. It is concerned not so much with *inscape,* in and of itself—the natural shape or form of the creation, Hopkins's frequent subject matter—as with the *in*stress that helps to define the psychology, the religion of a historically realized being or a life made incarnate.

> His mystery must be instressed, stressed;
> For I greet him the days I meet him, and bless when I
> understand.

To "understand" is not only intellectual: it is a matter of hearing and repeating. The reading aloud of the poem, from this point on (the speaker having waved his hand in farewell for the moment to a more pictorial inscape or nature within the stressed creation) becomes essential. Heart and history, sound and song become one, as the stress springing not from natural bliss but from living a sacrificed and sacrificing utterance "dates from a day" and "rides time like rising a river"—moves through time, that is, as the poem does.

Throughout the poem, sound effects and intense rhythms carry a reading, a meaning. The alliteration is repeated: instress itself begins as the river of time at a source, the source

> Of his going in Galilee;
> Warm-laid grave of a womb-life grey;
> Manger, maiden's knee;
> The dense and the driven Passion, and frightful sweat;
> Thence the discharge of it, there its dwelling to be,
> Though felt before, though in high flood yet—
> What none would have known of it, only the heart, being
> hard at bay.

And,

> Thou art lightning and love, I found it, a winter
> and warm;
> Father and fondler of heart thou hast wrung:
> Hast thy dark descending and most art merciful then.

In the sixteenth stanza,

> One stirred from the rigging to save
> The wild woman-kind below,
> With a rope's end round the man, handy and brave—
> He was pitched to his death at a blow,
> For all his dreadnought breast and braids of thew;

162

> They could tell him for hours, dandled the to and fro—

and so on, throughout the poem. We hear echo as well as the repeated and overwhelmingly intense alliteration in such internal rhyming as *none-known* and *heart-hard,* as in other examples of slant or imperfect rhyme. Some of these, occurring within the circular pattern of terminal rhymes—ababbcba—are *Bremen, women, them in* (stanza 12), *leeward, drew her, endured* (stanza 14), the potentially comic *knew in them, ruin them, astrew in them,* (stanza 21), the serious rhyming *Francis, lance, his, glances* (stanza 23), and the ultimate and deeply serious rhymes *door, reward, Lord* (stanza 35).

Again the poem leads up to climax, hesitates, then moves onward —all of this is effected through sound—to form a river that is an echoing song. The process is set up by stanza 18, the speaker's address to himself that becomes a reader's address to *him*self:

> Ah, touched in your bower of bone,
> Are you! turned for an exquisite smart,
> Have you! make words break from me here all alone,
> Do you!—mother of being in me, heart,
> O unteachably after evil, but uttering truth,
> Why, tears! is it? tears; such a melting, a madrigal
> start!
> Never-eldering revel and river of youth,
> What can it be, this glee? the good you have there of
> your own?

A "glee" or "madrigal" is a song—a song that utters, wending and wording itself so that it absorbs all into the music. Storm, passion, and prayer can be heard by a reader who cannot fully explicate the poetry, and this only by the passionate musical action of reading or virtually chanting aloud words that do seem to utter themselves.

The reading aloud may accommodate many highly personal senses of the music, the prayer moving through time, no one of which we can call completely wrong—if the reading aloud gives voice to the rhythms, sounds, and overwhelming emotions of the common language made available here. *The Wreck of the Deutschland* is, of course, a Christian poem with specific historical references written by a deeply religious and quasi-mystic poet. But even its Christian message can be taken as a metaphorical vehicle that is capable of carrying varying individual references so long as the musical metaphor remains and is sounded clearly in a reader's ear and voice.

Is the matter very different for a sonnet like "The Windhover" or for the terrible late poems? In some of Hopkins, the lines are to be heard as vital sound, but is any personal, idiosyncratic sense of the poems about instressed inscape—rather than about dramatic instress —allowable in place of religious or psychological explication?

There are apparent differences as well as an underlying relationship between the two kinds of verse, that primarily of stress and that primarily of inscape.[3] The latter kind, where meaning often derives from images rather than Swinburnean sound and energy, takes individuality, the paradoxical nature of the self, as its subject. And surely one self is distinct from another—Christ from Satan, devotee from debauchee, sacred oblate from secularist, Gerard Manley Hopkins priest and poet from the reader (critic, professor, graduate, or undergraduate student). Can one in any fair sense read oneself into the self of the artist who writes about the most intimate experience in the most idiosyncratic language? Must one not instead take Ruskin, Newman, or, say, Carlyle—*and* Hopkins—as the master, the authoritative voice whose greatness consists in his challenging us to interpret him?

Hopkins, who does not write vatic poetry in the manner of such Victorian prose masters, might reply that he is trying to "read himself into" a Master's inner being. And he might, after all, add the questioning comment, can a poet or a critic read himself or herself into the scape of a bird?

No, in a way. In a way, for a momentary vision and for a poem, yes.

The poet and speaker, the reader and speaker, are trying in the poetry of scape—landscape, seascape, treescape, birdscape—to achieve not the vatic but the authentic. Hopkins calls it the "authentic cadence." To be authentic is to write with a person's own hand, to be that which is truly oneself; it is also to be genuine, to be credible by being responsive to truth.

It is to be common—that is, to communicate—by being original. Poetry, for Hopkins, repeatedly conceives what one thing has in common with another, what for instance the poet and reader have in common with a bird. This is a truth, a poem. So what one truly sees in the bird, both what can actually be defined of its riding or flying

164

upon the wind and how one visually perceives the phenomenon, makes up a response aesthetic and moral. It is the response that Ruskin would define as uniting truth to nature with true nobility of style—which is a fineness of seeing, perceiving, in effect of being. In spite of the poet's detractors, this authentic response is meant to be commonly available and is opposed to affectation, to perverse inventiveness.

Ruskin's doctrine of truth to sacred nature does not, fully understood, mean passive representation. Truth-seeing and truth-telling cannot be passive for a serious Victorian poet like Tennyson or Browning. Nor can it for Hopkins. The principle of inscape is, like that of instress, an active principle: to see is to act.

"I caught," at the beginning of "The Windhover," puts reaction and action into one verb; in the moment of catching, the poet echoes a natural chord so that this self is for this moment identified with this subject. The subject (not only the object or topic) is a bird, and birds are often for Hopkins bright images—or dark—of selfhood.

One self can have in common with another its limitation, its mortality. "The Nightingale," for Hopkins, is a voice in a harsh world, singing to and singing of a mortal self. Its mode is minor, dark, like that of the *Deutschland.* Like the greater poem, this verse tells the story of a shipwreck through the acute senses of a person "at home," not in the heart of the wrecking world—yet aware of the terrible mortal music of that world. Poet and reader are listeners, only echoes, and not singers here.

These are lines, then, about apparently passive being. So are the lines of "The Caged Skylark," which evoke the shape of selfhood in an image that seems uncompromisingly fixed. The mortal image of embodiment does not dissolve into music; it is hard fact—the fact that a poetic skylark (not Shelley's, not pure spirit) may sound lovely but is in a prison. And although Hopkins uses Blake's rhyme of *cage* and *rage*—

> A Robin Red breast in a cage
> Puts all Heaven in a rage—

this fact is truly inescapable, without escape, for Hopkins is not a latter-day Romantic advocating the need for and possibility of total human freedom. There is, he concludes, no freedom from the self. The imprisoning body is as much a part of the human scheme as of the rhyme scheme in this poem: the echoing of *cage* and *rage* in the words *stage* and *age*—this last the basis and essence of the rhymes—is an augury not only of aging and dying but also of reviving, of the body after death that is to be somehow both formed and liberated.[4]

A difficult dwelling upon self—reader's, poet's, every person's—is complemented by verse in a dominant mode, with its bright images, lyrics on the circling bird and the king-fisher, lyrics of a mortal self's immortal song which all but dissolve the mortality in the timeless music.

In "Let me be to thee as the circling bird," the image of that first line is merged with the "music" of the "common word" that makes "authentic cadence" of a prayerful song which is also a flight.

The verse of the "circling bird," written when Hopkins was still an Anglican, seems temporarily untroubled; it is all about self singing. The authenticity of this hymn is in its common word *love,* meaning both the nominal—"God is Love"—and the verbal—"to love." Its verbal music links subject, singer or poet, to object, God, and because the word is common to all nature it links all who hear and speak— to one another and to all objects of hearing and speech. Again, what Hopkins calls selving is not to be observed but to be commonly engaged in: it is to be communicated. And the religious lyrics of Hopkins are, as we may well conclude, in several senses that amount to one meaning, communion hymns.

The most fully lyric sound of self is realized in other hymn-like lines, "As kingfishers catch fire, dragonflies draw flame." This is a poem entirely about active, not suffering and merely mortal, self:

> Each mortal thing does one thing and the same:
>   Deals out that being indoors each one dwells;
>   Selves—goes itself; *myself* it speaks and spells,
> Crying *What I do is me: for that I came.*

So we return to speaking, sounding; and this becomes the function of even a bird that knows mortality, knows bodily imprisonment. Bird is identified with man, as his image suggests what, through Christ, Creator has in common with creature, person in common with thing, and poet in common with reader.

> I say more: the just man justices;
>   Keeps grace: that keeps all his goings graces;
>   Acts in God's eye what in God's eye he is—

Christ. For Christ plays in ten thousand places,
Lovely in limbs, and lovely in eyes not his
To the Father through the features of men's faces.

"As kingfishers catch," "I caught." That second phrase (again) is the starting point of "The Windhover." In this sonnet Hopkins merges dominant and minor modes, the various birdscapes, the several sets of images, to produce perhaps his most intense version of how self can be read into nature and thus into the most natural, true, or authentic singing which is original—and at the same time common—poetry.

Once more, what the poet has caught is fire: the fiery light of natural skies at first and, finally, an inner light or fire of feather, furrow, ember. First, there is the fire of landscape, then the more particular light of inscape. Once more, too, inscape is both shape and shaping. It is acting, a performance to be seen and sung, echoed by an audience —if only an audience of one. The audience must "draw" out inner meaning and make it by reading it, authentic.

I caught this morning morning's minion, king-
dom of daylight's dauphin, dapple-dawn-drawn Falcon,
in his riding
Of the rolling level underneath him steady air,
and striding
High There, how he rung upon the rein of a
wimpling wing
In his ecstasy!

All of this is communication as much by voice—breathless, excited —as by visual imagery; but eye and heart respond as well:

then off, off forth on swing,
As a skate's heel sweeps smooth on a bow-bend:
the hurl and gliding
Rebuffed the big wind. My heart in hiding
Stirred for a bird,—the achieve of, the mastery
of the thing!

There may be an echo here of the phrase "Let me be to thee as the circling bird"; if so, the speaker's hidden heart not only stirs for but is identified already with his falcon, and the bird's mastery of the wind

167

is analogous to a singer's mastery of the vocal elements, the singer's or actor's breathing problems that these lines seem to embody.

Certainly, the break between octave and sestet gives a performer of the poem his best chance to catch his breath, to pause as there is a pause in the development of theme.

The development proceeds, after the hesitation, from inscaped music inspired by a vision to instressed reflection upon that vision, its forming element. The octave is music of praise for God in nature, in a daylight's kingdom—the king-dom of Christ the King or Prince of creation—with its airs and magnificently graceful movements—like the skate's swinging—of natural things. The octave is a breaking down gracefully as the natural thing is told to bend itself or buckle to an only seemingly external pressure—at the moment it does buckle —so that pride is broken to be prouder yet, the airy shown to be authentically vulnerable and thus, in yet more graceful air, more brilliant. Failing to read the poem more or less this way, even without adding the formula bird=Christ=poet=reader=humankind, is failing to catch not only its theology but its rhythm (its punctuation and its mounting breathless and then hard, often monosyllabic, sound) *and* its self-proclaimed logic.

> Brute beauty and valour and act, oh, air, pride,
> plume, here
> Buckle! AND the fire that breaks from thee then,
> a billion
> Times told lovelier, more dangerous, O my chevalier!
>
> No wonder of it: sheer plod makes plough down
> sillion
> Shine, and blue-bleak embers, ah my dear,
> Fall, gall themselves, and gash gold-vermillion.

Truth, finally, is seen with the eye of the mind, of reflective memory: the memory that by seeing them again (after the speaker has seen the bird) interprets buckled sillion and blue embers, their inner fire waiting to be scaped—or shaped, or shown—by stress.

If all of this seems like reading a single meaning into "The Windhover," at least that meaning should be large enough to accommodate all of the words of the poem, the images and the rhythms; any such reading should be not eccentric but concentric and at last in-centered, finding the reader's own sense of self through consistency with—in fact, finding it within—those images and rhythms that constitute the poem's self.

Self as a deliberately chosen subject appears repeatedly in Hopkins, in these poems about birds, in "The Lantern Out of Doors" and "The Candle Indoors" about self hidden or revealed, and in such verses as "Henry Purcell" about peculiar selfhood in the highly individual style or visually parallel manner (again, a bird's plumage becomes the sign of self). Selfscape instressed at its lowest pitch, farthest from any communion with God and others, is the darkest and most dreadful reality; instressed at highest pitch in song, self is the brightest and most glorious realization.

The dark poems dwell on mortal self without buckling or echoing; the brilliant ones reflect, resound with, celebrate a paradoxically eternal fire and choir of singing.

Even the darkest and supposedly most difficult of the verses can be available to the relatively uninformed student. It takes little knowledge of religious experience to hear the rhythms of depression, the language of despairing self. These universal plaints are modern, too.

It might be said that the sequence of dark sonnets both begins and ends with this profound sense of despairing self: the self's despairing or almost doing so because of its being self. Is there no way, modern faithless readers and writers ask, to escape from ego? And Hopkins asks, too, only to answer that there is a way but that it is the way not of escape but of living through self; "Carrion Comfort" refuses the carrion expedient of feeding on the dead self, saying, instead,

these last strands of man
[I'll "not untwist," not] cry *I can no more.* I can;
Can something, hope, wish day come, not choose not to be.

His exhausting journey into the darkest depths of depression ends just short of giving himself up. The end of these lines on refusal to despair is, still, wrestling:

That night, that year
Of now done darkness I wretch lay wrestling with (my God!) my God.

The poet cannot choose not to be. He is. The poem is. The reader is. And all because some source *is* that all beings reflect, echo, reiterate. This, after all, not depression or withdrawal pure and simple, is the burden of such lines as even "No worst, there is none"—a sonnet the extravagance of which is actually contradicted by the lines of poems that follow it.

Not only is it true to say, as the ending of "No worst" says, that "all/ Life death does end and each day dies with sleep." It is also true to say, as in "I wake and feel the fell of dark, not day," that there are worse and worst: the worst of all, depression beneath this mortal depression, is spelled out in an ultimate curse. Adam's lesser curse is to be himself separated from God, and this is the fallen ego, the source of mortality (as in "Spring and Fall"); the full and worst curse is to be lost not in the sibyl's mixture of dark and bright but in the damned self utterly and after death an alien from its Creator.

> I am gall, I am heartburn. God's most deep decree
> Bitter would have me taste: my taste was me;
> Bones built in me, flesh filled, blood brimmed the
>   curse.
>
> Selfyeast of spirit a dull dough sours. I see
> The lost are like this, and their scourge to be
> As I am mine, their sweating selves; but worse.

The phrase "I am gall" echoes one in the last line of "The Windhover," [embers] "Fall, gall themselves"; but that line goes on to "gash gold-vermilion," to inner light.[5] Hopkins introduces in his sestet, too, a past tense that echoes the time words of both *The Deutschland* and "The Windhover": "my taste was me." A period has ended, as the instressing necessary to elucidate brilliance—the period of pressure and depression—has ended, and through suffering in selfhood the speaker has come to vision so that he *can* speak. Utter selfhood is sickening and terrible, but that absolute state is never quite reached in human time (or all persons would be Godless, lost), although the deepest spirit most itself and thus most stressed may seem dangerously close to it. Still, it is the state, the stasis, only of the dead and damned.

Utter selfhood for the Carlylean Romantic is Godhead, ultimate Heroism, the apotheosis of Ego. Utter selflessness for the Keatsian Romantic is Bliss, ultimate Unity, the absorption of ego into a divine Universe. Neither way is possible in Hopkins, for whom total Heroism would be diabolical (as well as mad) and total self-abnegation sacrilegious (as well as suicidal). But a modern reader does not require the literary references or even theological notes to grasp what here the poet's voice declares: that it is a bore and dreary to be always oneself, that it is a secret glory and an inescapable pride to be always oneself.

The speaker's or the reader's self is caught as the windhover is caught. One has to be rebuffed, buffed, to shine triumphantly; self has to know self's darkness to know the bright light of self.

So the last of the darkest poems says: "My own heart let me more have pity on"—

> let
> Me live to my sad self hereafter kind,
> Charitable.

This extraordinary poem is a prayer for grace to love oneself, a necessary grace if only—as we need no new psychology to tell us—those who cannot love themselves cannot love others. Those for whom subject and object are separate, not kind or kindred, are incapable of all the moral graces that take root in a sense of authentic being.

The sestet of "My own heart" is an instructive conclusion.

> Soul, self; come, poor Jackself, I do advise
> You, jaded, let be; call off thoughts awhile
> Elsewhere; leave comfort root-room; let joy size
>
> At God knows when to God knows what; whose smile
> 'S not wrung, see you; unforeseen times rather—as skies
> Betweenpie mountains—lights a lovely mile.

The reference to "poor Jackself" picks up one of the poet's favorite pieces of slanging. In "The Candle Indoors" a common person is "Jessy or Jack," and at the end of the "Heraclitean Fire" the poet himself will be just Jack (a "joke" and "poor"). Jack is the ordinary self, common and—having life and love in common with all others—the extraordinarily true realization of self. It is only superficial, false selfhood by which one is jaded, bored. (This boredom, however, is serious: it comes of the "jading and jar of the cart," in the *Deutschland,* from "Time's tasking," which is that dull measuring out of stress, that monotonous workaday life leading slowly to a desperate need for peace, for death.) If "root-room" is left, some moments of peace and quiet, authentic self that is joy can grow—God knows how, when, and to what end.

The reading cannot be flippant here or casual. God does know, the poem says.

Now the key Romantic word of "joy" which is life in itself has come to mean my life in God's as well as my self. Such joy is not after all to be "wrung" from Him by wrestling, any more than the bell's sound or glee can be really rung by human will (surely some punning is meant here) or foreseen as the moment of bright sky—pied or dappled, with sun beaming through the mountains or darkness—might be foreseen in a weather prediction.

With his "joy" Hopkins reminds us of affinities with the great Romantic poets: the Coleridge who suffers dejection (and disillusionment about the source of joy), the Keats whose intensity of passion costs an intensity of torment, but also the Wordsworth whose sense of ennobling joy in self-realization has been reinforced and transformed for Hopkins by his teacher Ruskin. "The shepherd's brow," a marvelous late poem long incorrectly put among the poet's fragments and unfinished works, is his most explicit response to Romantic sensibility. In it he is, like other major Victorians, both the inheritor and the critic of Romantic tradition. One has only to hear some Blake, some Shelley, and some Carlyle, and then pronounce these words, to catch the dappled action and reaction, freed energy and drawing back, voiced now as latter-day and negative Romanticism.

> The shepherd's brow, fronting forked lightning, owns
> The horror and the havoc and the glory
> Of it. Angels fall, they are towers, from heaven—
>   a story
> Of just, majestical, and giant groans.
> But man—we, scaffold of score brittle bones;
> Who breathe, from groundlong babyhood to hoary
> Age gasp; whose breath is our *momento mori*—
> What bass is *our* viol for tragic tones?

The rhythms and abstractions are Romantic, the references biblical: shepherds, angels, and heaven. If Milton seems proud in his Nativity Ode, wanting to rival the Wise Men, then Hopkins too seems proud and shockingly so, in his dissatisfaction with being a mere shepherd-onlooker as angels fall, as God's own glory is made manifest. The complaint sounds Calvinistic: how far I am from Heaven! Even Milton's paganizing of the Christian myth into a cosmic tragedy—or at least an epic with some tragic characteristics—can hardly help. We are human beings, lowly as the shepherds, and our bodies of numbered, fragile bones are scaffolds or signs of mortality, our breathing is gasping and not the tragic sound of a noble instrument; we eat "hand to mouth" like all animals, like them eliminate. Worse—worst of all—we do it with "shame." Yet, again, the worst points to the best: it is just this human shame at being animal that implies a human aspiration to some glory. Still, shame is good and bad. For a true Romantic it may be the indication of divine potentiality, this virtually "divine discontent." For Hopkins, shame is part of pride, of the deadly danger implicit in selfhood, even while it shows the human self's Christlike potential, a limited potential that, in order to be realized, has to be disciplined, held in, or stressed—so that the self remains the common self, common and not communal, and does not as a Faustian echo try to absorb the universe of otherness into its ultimately peculiar selfhood.

Men and women are individuals with individual names.

> And, blazoned in however bold the name,
> Man Jack the man is, just; his mate a hussy.
> And I that die these deaths, that feed this flame,
> That . . . in smooth spoons spy life's masque mirrored: tame
> My tempests there, my fire and fever fussy.

One who is "just" a man is properly a just man; a "hussy" is a housewife, good in her house or in herself. Neither is very passionately Romantic. Both belong, I belong, in the world of spoons and mirrors, not that of royal masques and conflagrations. Romantic tempests themselves are, after all, to be tamed, fiery spirits to be controlled as well as recognized. Otherwise, egoists do make fusses—and become crotchety, silly. The last line reveals Hopkins's sense of humor, dark humor perhaps but the kind that can smile at itself as it can revel in and now and then revile itself.

Again, Jackself, "Jack the man," means the peculiar ordinary creature. Yet he echoes the Creator, as his poems do, and he reflects in his hard-pressed self the creative and eternal life, as diamonds do. "The Leaden Echo" and "The Golden Echo" use the imagery of hard things and the sound of dull or musical repetition to reinforce this sense of self. So does the last of Hopkins's major works, "That Nature is a Heraclitean fire and of the comfort of the Resurrection."

If one teaches Hopkins primarily through sound, the two Echoes may provide the best poetry for reading aloud. The poem, or set of poems, breathes, gasps, races, and of course echoes and re-echoes its sense: that breathing life can be monotonous, the repetition of a living-dying cycle with its petty and repeated moments, or can be a single line of melody and in the very temporal rhythms of its utterance a time-transcending music. Hopkins commented that he "never did anything more musical."[6] As in music, the echoing chords are everywhere, from "be beginning" to "Despair, despair, despair, despair" and then the new beginning in the echo "Spare!"

"Spare!" means "spare yourself" (self, have more pity, give yourself space yet for joy) and perhaps also "thin" (the chance of Heaven must seem thin or slight). In renouncing despair, once more, the self can relax enough to find room for music, even joy—or at least the hope for all that beauty to be re-found, retained, "yonder."

"The Leaden Echo" and "The Golden Echo," which can be overwhelming if well chanted, hardly require in themselves more explication. Reading them aloud expressively is explicating them.

But, finally, we may have to say more about the lines that make up —as much as any—a final testament. (At least, a nearly final nearly public testament: "To R. B." serves, perhaps, as a more personal last defense of "my muse," an "explanation" of the "carol" of "creation" for Hopkins's beloved Bridges.) "That Nature is a Heraclitean Fire and of the comfort of the Resurrection" is, like its very title, complex. The title announces a proposition and goes on to suggest an essay. This poem is logically carried by verbal imagery from stage to stage, to turn only at a clarion call, to flash in sound "at a trumpet crash" its verbal and explosive truth.

The three stages in its logic are, first, the celebration of a constant nature, ending with the end of the eighth line; second, the elegy on mortal nature, ending with the fifteenth line and with the falling syllables of *dejection;* third, the asserting of the supernatural that informs all created nature and redeems, sustains, the otherwise mortal creature who is the fiery "manshape," humanly inscaped self.[7]

Although a redeeming voice is heard only in the third stage, with a sound that alters vision, Hopkins's imagery of light and shining is sustained throughout. Vision presents an inscaped light, a light that can be deeply realized, finally, through an instressing and a voicing sound: "the Resurrection."

So the poem gives voice at first to a vision of landscape, of light-filled bonfire sky and earth, with clouds and shiny ooze reflecting nature's source; and then reflects on fullest inscape, manshape, which again, a star, mirrors that source but also like all natural marks soon dies; and then at last reflects more comprehensively on the "Jackself" that—as in "the shepherd's brow"—must "feed this flame," to find

174

and speak in that instressed essential Jackself not only sky, pool, star, but harder, hardest substance of reflection, the diamond. This substance, self, is soft fuel transformed by the pressure most intense on earth. The hard-stressed image of the gem becomes a reflector, a vision, but also—paradoxically—an echo or a voicing, and, at one and the same time a present—what "I am"—and a past—"he was"—as it is at once the self and the Christ:

> In a flash, at a trumpet crash,
> I am all at once what Christ is, since he was what
> I am, and
> This Jack, joke, poor potsherd, patch, matchwood, immortal diamond,
>   Is immortal diamond.

One critic has pointed out the tendency of Hopkins's verse to shift in focus, from the earlier to the later, from inscape in the natural order to human inscape in general (or in others) to the inscape of the poet's own being.[8] A parallel tendency is the movement from representation of natural land-, sky-, and sea-scape, first in external groups and then in particular figures, to a profoundly personal experience of moral and psychological shape ("the shape I am in," so to speak), through an intensifying of the conviction that inscape can be defined only as the result or embodiment of instress. This movement occurs not only from poem to poem, from the *Deutschland* to the "Heraclitean Fire," but also, by either implication or the verse's own explication, within the evolving shape of each poem. It is associated with the movement from vision to voice, from the imagined or real vision of a scene and the visual celebration of natural and literally reflective or light-suffused imagery to a creative voice giving the viewer's response and thus poetically shaping, forming, in words and sound what is observed.

This is why, for Hopkins's poetry, reading is the imperative mode —reading aloud to hear the sound, hear the shape—and reading oneself (in the sounds) is the final subject.

Now to take our bearings in this dark forest. The poetry of Hopkins can be read as immediate, personal experience, and given a great many different, highly individual responses, as long as it is carefully and truly read aloud. The theology that forms it can be transformed by a largely uninformed reader. But that is possible only if the reader

175

hears the breathing life of the poem and repeats it, and if the reader perceives that self—his self as well as the poet's—is identified both *with* a vital force and *as* the object of that force. It is, in a sense, asking little of the reader, the student. In this sense, the poetry of Hopkins is easier to read than the poetry of Arnold, Tennyson, or Browning —or, possibly, that of Swinburne. One must, however, add a *caveat:* the responsive student must, to "catch" Hopkins, relax and feel the rhythm. The unmusically rigid, schematic intellect can push too hard and go astray, as it has in so much Hopkins criticism.

NOTES

1. See *The Dragon in the Gate: Studies in the Poetry of G. M. Hopkins* (Berkeley, 1968), especially the chapter on "Three Baroque Sonnets." Schneider's chapters on the *Deutschland* and sprung rhythm appeared earlier in *PMLA.* This volume of criticism, the best in print on the poetry of Hopkins, is not over-dogmatic, even though the passage quoted here might suggest such a tone: Schneider represents, in fact, that rarity among Hopkins critics, one who is able to say of a line or a passage that she is not certain about its meaning.

2. In "Nondum," as well, to cite only one other example, there is "no answering voice" to "our psalm." The concern with fervent prayer's not being answered occurs elsewhere in Victorian poetry, especially in Tennyson—not only within the lyrics of *In Memoriam* but also with "The Vision of Sin" and its perplexed seeking for the meaning of an answer given, if at all, in a language that no man can understand.

Citations from Hopkins's poetry refer to the text of W. H. Gardner and N. H. MacKenzie, in the (fourth) Oxford edition (London, 1967).

3. The two words *inscape* and *instress* have provided matter for extended critical discussions and disagreements (as much as the phrase "sprung rhythm," on which Schneider is as clear as others are opaque). Hopkins himself, whose love of word play could lead him to play games in the prose forms of solemn discourse, does not always help: he contradicts himself in his several nice definitions. The easiest, and the best, way to understand these terms is to observe how Hopkins uses them in his poetry; there he is consistent.

Inscape is modelled, apparently, on the word *landscape,* and it certainly takes the moral as well as the aesthetic sense that Ruskin gives that word. *Scape* and *shape* are, of course, two forms of one term (like *skirt* and *shirt*). The prefix *in* is meant to emphasize the fact that organic shape as in vistas and pictures, in out-of-doors or in human nature, has an inner principle expressed by outer appearance. The inscape of a tree or bird is the shape of the thing perceived as expressing its living principle, an identity that is both unique—as each creature differs from every other—and generic —as each bird or tree has recognizable formality in common with every other bird or tree. The inscape of a human being is the external shape, including physical appearance, gesture, voice, and so on (the whole "signature"), that shows forth a unique inner nature or soul. Poetry of inscape can be nature poetry or moral poetry, for as the good thing is true to its purpose by revealing its Creator's beauty, so the good person is true to his created nature by acting out the Creator's fuller Nature; it is likely to be both.

Stress is the creative force that forms or shapes, even bends and nearly breaks—that is, makes finite shapes as the forces of air, earth, and gravity do—and it is completely realized to become *in*stress when the formed being, the shape or scape in nature, accepts its finite existence, its own definition. *Instress,* too, is a natural, a physical, fact; but it is also a condition with moral implications, especially for human beings. To accept his finitude, both his divine origin and his reflective or dependent nature, is for a man to be instressed (often, this means suffering): not striving to be god or independent self, nor accepting passively like an automaton without a will, but assenting inwardly. This is the person's shape of selfhood: to be fully oneself as an assenting soul, an *in*stressed *in*scape.

4. This is one of the points at which we must, after all, bring in external and special information to interpret the poem. "The Caged Skylark" is specifically about a church doctrine, the Resurrection of the Body. It becomes crucial to explain this mysterious idea that the spiritual body is to be, at the end of time, identified with the carnal (but perfected) body; otherwise the poem makes no sense. Modern thinking is so alienated from orthodox religious tradition that one has to explain not only here but also in other places: in discussing the *Deutschland,* that the Feast of the Immaculate Conception celebrates the virgin birth of Mary, not Jesus; in discussing "Spring and Fall," that the Fall of Man does not in general Christian or biblical interpretation mean simply the loss of sexual innocence (in spite of the Augustinian, Calvinist, and Miltonic distortions) and indeed that such an aspect of the myth is virtually irrelevant to the great mystics, most of the great Christian poets, and, certainly, to Hopkins as a Catholic.

Although W. H. Gardner, John Pick, the Jesuit scholars, and Paul Mariani are mostly reliable on such matters, a surprising number of Hopkins critics are not; many "fable and miss."

5. The verbal and thematic combination "fall-gall," "gash-flash" represents one of Hopkins's favorite echoes. Another version of it occurs in the lines on "St. Alphonsus Rodriguez":

> Honour is flashed off exploit, so we say;
> And those strokes once that gashed flesh or
> galled shield
> Should tongue that time now, trumpet now that
> field,
> And, on the fighter, forge his glorious day.

6. See, in the Gardner and MacKenzie edition, p. 282.

7. Among all of Hopkins's variations on the sonnet form, this is the most difficult to reconcile with a basic pattern, even though the poet calls it a "sonnet with two codas," including "many outrides and hurried feet." (See page 293 in the fourth edition.) It seems to have twenty-two lines, some broken and the first very long, rhyming aab-baabcdcdcdcccfffggg.

8. Bell B. Chevigny, "Instress and Devotion in the Poetry of Gerard Manley Hopkins," *VS,* 9 (1965), esp. 145. See, for a close analysis of one poem from the point of view of this scheme, emphasizing a human inscape, William B. Thesing, " 'Tom's Garland' and Hopkins' Inscapes of Humanity," *VP,* 15 (1977), 37–48.

THOMAS HARDY—POET

PAUL ZIETLOW

In becoming a poet, Thomas Hardy made himself into something that he seemed destined never to be. Born in 1840, the son of a rural Dorset stonemason, he had largely to educate himself in languages and literature, and his professional training, received in his youth in Dorchester, was in architecture. He set off for London in the 1860s, a young man from the provinces, to pursue a promising career as an architect; but a hankering after literature kept breaking to the surface, first in poems that were not to editors' tastes, and then in fiction, the publication of which came more easily. He continued to write verse intermittently throughout his long and successful career as a novelist, until in the 1890s he gave up fiction, focused his best energies on poetry (which he maintained had always been his first love), and worked on poems almost daily up to the date of his death in 1928. For Hardy poetry was, like nothing else, an exclusively self-willed activity, not something done to please an audience or put bread on the table. As a poet Hardy experienced the freedom to make his own tastes and interests his exclusive standards, to perceive things in his own distinctive way and express his perceptions in his own distinctive terms. He defined and completed his humanity through poetry by asserting his independent identity against the tendencies of things, against the forces of social circumstance and convention, against uncongenial literary traditions and received taste, against established opinion, against personal doubts and fears as well as the contingencies of daily life, against change, chance, and oblivion. The assertion of independent vision

178

against the Forces—in this lies the enduring relevance of Hardy's poetry.

Hardy introduced himself formally as a poet with "The Temporary the All," the first poem in his first collection, *Wessex Poems* (1898). In it the speaker laments that short-term expediencies have come to define the totality of his being. "Change and chancefulness" put him in juxtaposition with a friend, a lover, and a dwelling, all of which he accepted even though they fell short of his high ideals. His life's occupation was also the result of temporizing:

> "Then high handiwork will I make my life-deed,
> Truth and Light outshow; but the ripe time pending,
> Intermissive aim at the thing sufficeth."
> Thus I. . . . But lo, me!

Now he realizes that he has nothing more to show for himself than the series of compromises: "Sole the showance those of my onward earth-track—/ Never transcended!"[1] I have suggested elsewhere that Hardy may have begun his first collection of verse with this poem because it can be seen to imply a turn in his career, from the compromise of fiction to the high ideal of poetry, and to offer his credentials as a poet familiar with diverse literary traditions by employing diction with an Anglo-Saxon ring ("life-deed," "onward earth-track") and a classical (Sapphic) meter. Whether or not this is the case, the poem, placed as it is, expresses the disappointment and frustration of a life surrendered to chance and change in a way that invites biographical speculation.

The destiny recorded in "The Temporary the All" may seem all too commonplace, but the language is jarringly strange, so idiosyncratic that for many readers it probably impairs the force of the poem. It could be argued, for example, that the awkwardly prosaic phrase "high handiwork" reflects a significant inarticulateness, a limitation of imaginative power, a deficiency of vision; the speaker's problem could be said to be not that he was willing to settle temporarily for less, but that he lacked the ability to define for himself a more. One tends to think of poetic language as an imaginative heightening; here, Hardy seems to insist on prosaic lowering. At the end of *The Prelude*, Wordsworth, in a state of inspiration, exploits the resources of eloquence to exalt the imagination, celebrating

179

> how the mind of man becomes
> A thousand times more beautiful than the earth
> On which he dwells, above this frame of things
> . . . . .
> In beauty exalted, as it is itself
> Of quality and fabric more divine.

For Hardy, in contrast, the mind is curious, unaccountable, interesting, anomalously human—not beautiful, not divine. Typically, the speakers in his poems, in a moment of clarity, select from a sprawling country marketplace of language—one that includes an antique shop and a second-hand bookstall as well as vegetable stands and cattle pens—words that redefine downwards, that re-establish relationships within the frame of things. Transcendent achievement is "high handiwork," work of the hands above the ordinary in the sense that it does not conform to expediency, that it is willed by the worker and persisted in even when the time is not ripe, that it expresses resistance to the pressures of the world in which the work is done. It is no more than that, but what an achievement if it is at least that much!

To get a feel for Hardy's poetry, one must become sensitive to the guarded wisdom in this tendency to redefine downwards, a tendency evident in his characterization of himself as a poet. The traditions of literary criticism familiar to Hardy were rich with elevated definitions of poetry and poets. Shelley, an extreme example but appropriate because he was a favorite of Hardy's, defined poetry (in "A Defence of Poetry") as "the record of the best and happiest moments of the happiest and best minds," and characterized poets in a series of rhapsodic metaphors as "the hierophants of an unapprehended inspiration; the mirrors of the gigantic shadows which futurity casts upon the present; the words which express what they understand not; the trumpets which sing to battle, and feel not what they inspire; the influence which is moved not, but moves." Hardy honored Shelley's "Ecstatic heights in thought and rhyme" ("Shelley's Skylark," *CP*, p. 101), but his own feet seldom left the ground, and he saw himself in more self-consciously cautious and humble terms. Hardy is more in tune with Wordsworth's conception of the poet in the Preface to *Lyrical Ballads* as "a man speaking to men"; and he quotes approvingly Wordsworth's definition of poetry as "the breath and finer spirit of all knowledge; ... the impassioned expression which is in the countenance of all science." Yet Hardy shrank from Wordsworth's kind of faith in poetry's transcendent utility: "[The poet] is the rock of defense of human nature," wrote Wordsworth; "an upholder and preserver, carrying everywhere with him relationship and love. . . . the poet binds together by passion and knowledge the vast empire of human society, as it is spread over the whole earth, and over all time." Hardy comes closest to this sort of optimism when he acknowledges in his Apology to *Late Lyrics and Earlier* (where he quotes Wordsworth) the possibility that, "by means of the interfusing effect of poetry," religion and rationality could be reconciled, which must happen "unless the world is to perish." But will this happen? "I forlornly hope so. . . . But one dares not prophesy" (*CP,* p. 562).

Hardy resists seeing himself as a prophet, a visionary, or an elevated sage. Wordsworth claimed for the poet, in distinction to other human beings, "a greater readiness and power in expressing what he thinks and feels, and especially those thoughts and feelings which, by his own choice, or from the structure of his own mind, arise in him without immediate external excitement." As a poet, Hardy is bound more directly to the randomness of immediate stimulation. He may respond more promptly than other people, and be more persistent in expressing himself, but what he responds to is the casualness of circumstance, circumstance which includes the unforeseen workings of his own consciousness. As a poet, Hardy presents himself as an attentive man with a long memory who is roused to speech by what he notices and what he remembers. Memory is not so much a means for recollecting emotion in tranquility as it is a haunting, chiding, irrepressible background to the present, the existence of which produces a present experience, usually an awareness of disparity, pain, and loss, seldom of growth, development, or progress. In his brief Preface to *Poems of the Past and the Present,* Hardy describes his personal poems (as opposed to narratives and dramatic impersonations) as "a series of feelings and fancies written down in widely differing moods and circumstances, and at various dates . . . [possessing] little cohesion of thought or harmony of colouring. I do not greatly regret this. Unadjusted impressions have their value, and the road to a true philosophy of life seems to lie in humbly recording diverse readings of its phenomena as they are forced upon us by chance and change" (*CP,* p. 84). Records of experiences forced upon him by circumstance, seen for a moment in a personal, distinctive way, and presented in their immediacy, without adjustment—these are what Hardy conceived his poems to be. As for the truth they offer—it lies in aggregated insight, not heightened vision. One could hardly find a more cautiously humble way of putting it.

There is a certain disingenuousness in Hardy's rather self-effacing statement, resulting in part from a desire to forestall criticism. Anticipating the charge of unrelenting pessimism, Hardy characterizes his poems as offhand comments on life as it passes. Hardy, like Robert Frost, often assumed the self-protective mask of humble simplicity. Yet the statement provides many clues to Hardy's performance as a poet. His poems frequently resemble "records," direct accounts of something witnessed. As in "The Reminder," the poems often begin with the speaker's noticing something, frequently as if by chance:

> While I watch the Christmas blaze
> Paint the room with ruddy rays,
> Something makes my vision glide
> To the frosty scene outside.

He then describes what he sees:

> There, to reach a rotting berry,
> Toils a thrush,—constrained to very
> Dregs of food by sharp distress,
> Taking such with thankfulness.

Finally, he records his reaction, in this case by questioning the chance cause of his re-awakened awareness of suffering:

> Why, O starving bird, when I
> One day's joy would justify,
> And put misery out of view,
> Do you make me notice you! (*CP*, pp. 268–69)

There is a sense here of poetry stripped down to its most humble essentials: an event, and a participant to record it. Hardy has numerous poems describing apparently trivial incidents in which circumstance and witness converge, sometimes as if by design, to produce a movement of the mind toward new or renewed understanding. In one of the most quietly powerful, "An August Midnight," one gets the sense of chance as a stage-manager, setting the scene for insight:

> I
>
> A shaded lamp and a waving blind,
> And the beat of a clock from a distant floor:
> On this scene enter—winged, horned, and spined—

A longlegs, a moth, and a dumbledore;
While 'mid my page there idly stands
A sleepy fly, that rubs its hands. . . .

II

Thus meet we five, in this still place,
At this point of time, at this point in space.
—My guests besmear my new-penned line,
Or bang at the lamp and fall supine.
"God's humblest, they!" I muse. Yet why?
They know Earth-secrets that know not I. (*CP,* pp. 146–47)

The poet presents himself here not as an image of the mind in beauty exalted above the frame of things, but as an attentive witness to chance circumstance humbly acknowledging his limitations in relationship to the things of the earth on which he dwells, "At this point of time, at this point in space."

Both these poems of trivial circumstance affirm a community of consciousness among living things: birds feel pain and insects possess earth-secrets just as human beings feel and know and interpret what they see. For Hardy, the existence of consciousness is in itself a chance circumstance—indeed, the governing chance circumstance of cosmic history—and side-by-side with the poems of response to momentary incidents there are "diverse readings" of the all-encompassing event. What strange fate introduced consciousness—the power to feel, to desire, to form a purpose, to imagine, to hope, to judge, to know—in the midst of an utterly indifferent, sometimes apparently hostile arena of change and chance? In answer to this question the humble recorder becomes boldly playful. One version sounds like science fiction:

I thought a germ of Consciousness
Escaped on an aërolite
  Aions ago. . . .
  . . . . .
And that this stray, exotic germ
Fell wanderingly upon our sphere . . . (*CP,* 769)

In another, a god created, but then forgot:

—"The Earth, sayest thou? The Human race?
By Me created? Sad its lot?
Nay: I have no remembrance of such place . . . " (*CP,* p. 123)

183

Often Hardy credits human beings with an ethic superior to that of their creator, and in some of his most delightfully sardonic poems he has his imagined divinities express puzzlement over the unforeseen results of their acts of creation:

> "Strange that ephemeral creatures who
>   By my own ordering are,
> Should see the shortness of my view,
> Use ethic tests I never knew,
>   Or made provision for!" (*CP*, p. 278)

Here Hardy is the comic master, exerting the consciousness with which he was endowed to imagine the perplexity of his creator: God's humblest have mind-secrets, heart-secrets of their own. Yet consciousness is no laughing matter, and its workings are irritatingly refractory. Hardy's eyes tell him that chance circumstance, having enabled human beings to experience consciously, also causes suffering to be the most common experience. Yet he cannot suppress gestures of hope, for by nature he, like all humanity, is "Unreasoning, sanguine, visionary," terms he uses in "To An Unborn Pauper Child"; there, after wishing passionately that the child would never be born, he turns back against the bleakness of his realistic expectations:

> And such are we—
> Unreasoning, sanguine, visionary—
>   That I can hope
>   Health, love, friends, scope
> In full for thee; can dream thou'lt find
> Joys seldom yet attained by humankind! (*CP*, p. 128)

One might say that here the movement of the speaker's mind is the cause for perplexity. His dreaming heart refuses to be governed by knowledge.

"Diverse readings of [life's] phenomena"—the phrase insists that there is something "out there" to be "read" if poetry is to come into being. A distinctive feature of Hardy's poems is the sense they give of an external world to which the speakers respond, a world filled in from the worms of the sod to the farthest seen stars, and rich with an endless diversity of human happenings. Many of the great poems of the nineteenth century are explorations of the self, workings out of inner conflict or spiritual division, even when, as in *In Memoriam*, the personal struggle is presented as a private type of a public cultural crisis. Others are imaginative recreations of the distant or mythic past, Renaissance Italy, for example, or Arthurian legend, and often evoke a sense of superior color, energy, and vitality in the ancient and remote, as opposed to the drab mechanisms of Victorian England, even when, as in *Idylls of the King* or *The Ring and the Book,* the human issues involved have direct contemporary relevance. Other of the great poems of the nineteenth century appear to be complex images of the poet's consciousness, exterior projections of the inner self, even when the exterior projections are recognizable land- and sea-scapes, as sometimes in Swinburne, rather than metaphors, symbols, and mythic evocations, as usually in Rossetti; the poets seem often to dwell in the realm of imagination, of myth, of art. As a poet, Hardy dwells on this earth. The past in his poetry is primarily what he remembers from personal experience, or what he has heard from the elders, or what he can infer from the relics and buildings and burial places left behind by generations now dead. In some of Hardy's poems there is re-examination of the self, but most of these are concretely domestic, prompted by a sadly commonplace human experience, the death on November 27, 1912, of his first wife, Emma.

It is not that Hardy is unusually gifted at rendering poetically the textures and energies of experience itself. Gerard Manley Hopkins works in this way, possessing through the vital distinctiveness of language and structure the vital distinctiveness of the inspiring experience, so that reading the poem produces the thrill of concrete immediacy. By the by Hardy sometimes achieves this effect, but it is not peculiarly his, nor one at which he aims. He records, describes, names what is "out there"; he does not capture and render it incarnate in the poem. His poems inventory a world of things: hillsides, trees, tombstones, buildings, fires in the hearth, old furniture, coffins, the stars; and they populate that world with a diverse humanity: country folk and townspeople, husbands and wives, parents and children, noble dames and trampwomen, soldiers and the sweethearts who await news of their fate. Chief among the people, of course, is Hardy himself, who records what he notices as well as his own personal destiny, focused in his love affair and subsequent life with Emma, a drama played out on the same landscapes that appear in the less personal poems, and amidst the same buildings and graveyards and relics of the past. In Hardy's poems one gets the sense of a whole society of which the poet is a participating member, a whole culture and the earth on which it dwells. He tells the story of this culture, one of long decline made up of a multiplicity of individual subplots, among them the tale of the poet's love. This sense in Hardy's poetry of a full and complete world, and the poet describing it from within in an ongoing series of unadjusted impressions, is the aspect of Hardy's poetry that unites it to the novels. This sense can be realized only by reading Hardy's poems in number, not as discrete anthology pieces. As a poet, Hardy is not primarily an imaginative singer—although he is sometimes that—but a chronicler of the world.

I have chosen the word "chronicler" because of its root association with time. For Hardy, the All is temporal. The experiencer changes in time, making his "readings" in "widely differing moods and circumstances," and what he sees is in flux, "phenomena as they are forced upon us by chance and change." Hardy cannot rise above the world, but moment by moment he can record how things look "At this point of time, at this point in space." He professes to leave the records of the moments in "unadjusted" form, refusing to deny the experiential validity of any clear formulation of how any given phenomenon appears to him at any given time. I have suggested elsewhere that Hardy may have turned exclusively to poetry in part because in brief lyrics he could be more faithful to the everchanging nature of experience than he could in the novel, which required a more sustained coherency of vision. Whether or not Hardy had this conscious motive, his poems are remarkably various, seeming to ebb and flow with the tides of chance and change. He offers a multitude of diverse responses, many of which, for example the quasi-mythological fables or the poems about Emma, can be grouped together as variations on a theme. Each variation is a moment of clarity and formal control; each has a tentative truth of its own, and their accumulation is "the road to a true philosophy of life." The poet is limited by the quality of his alertness, and by how much he can see (Hardy, like the speaker in his poem "A Sign-Seeker," often expressed a desire to see ghosts, visions—more than the natural world had to offer). The more he can see, the more experience he can absorb, the fuller will be the house of his soul. In "The House of Silence," a child sees a quiet, shaded dwelling, a place, apparently, of no movement, no life; the speaker corrects him:

> "Morning, noon, and night,
> Mid those funereal shades that seem
> The uncanny scenery of a dream,

> Figures dance to a mind with sight,
> And music and laughter like floods of light
>   Make all the precincts gleam.
>
> "It is a poet's bower,
> Through which there pass, in fleet arrays,
> Long teams of all the years and days,
> Of joys and sorrows, of earth and heaven,
> That meet mankind in its ages seven,
>   An aion in an hour." (*CP,* p. 474)

There is vision in this, not the vision of transcendence or inspired insight, but the vision of comprehensive awareness.

Experience is also temporal in the sense that both phenomenon and observer have a past and a future. The two converge for a moment, but Hardy's records of the convergence frequently include an awareness of a larger temporal frame. To experience something fully is to encounter it with an apprehension of what it appeared to be before or of what previously happened to it or of where it came from, and sometimes also with forebodings of its inevitably being lost or laid to rest:

> I set every tree in my June time,
>   And now they obscure the sky.
>
> And the children who ramble through here,
>   Conceive that there never has been
> A time when no tall trees grew here,
>   That none will in time be seen. (*CP,* p. 334)

By implication in this poem, "At Day-Close in November," the state of childhood is an innocence of memory and foreboding; the poet, blessed, and burdened, is at the other extreme.

Again and again Hardy's poems portray the importunity of memory. He can hardly look at something in the present without recalling something in the past, and often recollection is the form of his response to the things that he notices:

> Nine drops of water bead the jessamine,
> And nine-and-ninety smear the stones and tiles:
> —'Twas not so in that August ... (*CP,* p. 578)
>
> The twigs of the birch imprint the December sky
>   Like branching veins upon a thin old hand;
> I think of summer-time, yes of last July ... (*CP,* p. 770)

187

> A bird sings the selfsame song,
> With never a fault in its flow,
> That we listened to here those long
> Long years ago . . . (*CP,* p. 598)

Sometimes Hardy honors what he recollects:

> Joy-jaunts, impassioned flings,
> Love, and its ecstasy,
> Will always have been great things,
> Great things to me! (*CP,* p. 475)

Often he expresses a sense of loss:

> —But it's not the selfsame bird.—
> No: Perished to dust is he. . . .
> As also are those who heard
> That song with me. (*CP,* p. 598)

And frequently memory is more painfully complex.

While the overt contrast in "At Day-Close in November" is between the poet and the children, there is a more subtle contrast between the poet then and now. He planted the trees in his youth with a clear design and hopeful intentions; but the darkly ominous language that he chooses to describe the fulfillment suggests a new awareness of ironic, unintended consequences: "now they obscure the sky." The germ of consciousness has unaccountably flowered in memory, and memory also unaccountably bears strange and bitter fruit for Hardy; what he, not chance, initiated in the past, now has developed according to a logic of its own to perplex his life. The poems of memory associated with Emma, among which "At Day-Close in November" might well be numbered, are fraught with bafflement and pain. Emma died in November; as the poem "Everything Comes" makes explicit, Hardy had planted trees to enclose and shade the home they had built together; now that the trees are mature, Emma lies entombed in eternal shade, and the trees obscure his vision. The trees can be taken as an image of the relationship, one that began in hopeful love and ended in irony and obstruction. Sifting through his memories, he comes to see that it was he and she, and not the sort of blinded natural force that he had described earlier in "The Lacking Sense," who had "all unwittingly . . . wounded where [they] love[d]" (*CP,* p. 116). Looking at a graveyard on a day "When Oats Were

Reaped" in August 1913, Hardy reaps a barren harvest: "I wounded one who's there, and now know well I wounded her;/ But, ah, she does not know that she wounded me!" (*CP*, p. 772). In their later years, he and Emma were like forgetful gods, missing the opportunity for exploiting memory to revive the love of their youth:

> Why, then, latterly did we not speak,
> Did we not think of those days long dead,
> And ere your vanishing strive to seek
> That time's renewal? (*CP*, p. 339)

Now that she is dead, memory forces "Penance" upon him; he draws near a keyboard from which in the past he callously withdrew while she played ("I would not join. I would not stay"), but it is too late:

> "and the chill old keys
> Like a skull's brown teeth
> Loose in their sheath,
> Freeze my touch; yes, freeze." (*CP*, p. 631)

Memory is now out of control, sometimes making the world look empty:

> Till in darkening dankness
> The yawning blankness
> Of the perspective sickens me! (*CP*, p. 338)

Sometimes it invades the mind, an uninvited intruder:

> O the regrettings infinite
> When the night-processions flit
> Through the mind! (*CP*, p. 464)

Hardy's poems insist on faithfulness to the unadjusted, jagged edges of memory that chance and change force through the surface of his consciousness. Now grown old, he realizes that he was, after all, made in the image of his fancied creators, that, like the unconsciously weaving forces of nature, he danced in a self-enclosed dream, likewise unconscious of the meaning of the moment:

> Childlike, I danced in a dream;
> Blessings emblazoned that day;
> Everything glowed with a gleam;
> Yet we were looking away! (*CP*, p. 167)

189

For Hardy, the ultimate danger is to be "looking away" when the occasion for perception and thought presents itself, and the act of writing poetry became for him his means of maintaining, to the extent humanly possible, an attentive watchfulness.

These various themes—the humble assertion of human perceptivity against the random movements of the world, the sense of a world "out there" in which the poet participates, the power of memory—provide an illuminating background to Hardy's penchant for strictly regular external forms in his poems. Culture, Hardy thought, was in a state of dissolution, and formal experimentation gave poetry a "structureless and conglomerate character."[2] Hardy insisted on regularities and repetitions of form; almost all of his poems rhyme, and most are written in repeating stanzas. External form is the manifestation of the human will, a shape given to the moment of perception forced upon the poet, a self-consciously human gesture of order. Life almost never rhymes, but the lines in which Hardy records his perceptions of it almost always do, and he went so far as to construct empty "verse skeletons" to be used as the prosodic patterns for the records of subsequent perceptions (*Life,* p. 301). Many of the forms Hardy uses are relics of his country origins, the bones of a way of life from which the flesh was falling away. His is the countryman's love of song, hymn, and rhymed tale, of chiming words that release one momentarily from moods of guilt and sorrow:

> Rhyme, Ballad-rhymer, start a country song;
> Make me forget that she whom I loved well
> Swore she would love me dearly, love me long,
> Then—what I cannot tell! (*CP,* p. 239)

Hardy, too, writes as a country singer, making countless verses in the rhyme schemes and stanza forms of the songs he heard as a child and thereafter in Dorset, and of the hymns he sang in church, sometimes to the accompaniment of his father's violin. He also wrote numerous rhymed tales recounting the woes, superstitions, and odd happenings of country folk, many of them based on local traditions, and some on written history. As a personal poet, he recorded his ever-changing perceptions of the world and the self; as a poet of the countryside, he sang songs and told tales. Ideally the songs and tales were to be played and sung at country dances, to be heard in a moment of leisure by a family gathered around a hearth. But the dances and family gatherings as he knew them were fading into the past, victims of economic chance and change. As a country singer, he, too, is a relic of the past, an anachronism enduring in a changed present. He could not arrest time to preserve the culture that survived in his dimming memory; but in the traditional forms of its art he could record one man's personal vision of its passing:

> It looms a far-off skeleton
> And not a comrade nigh,
> A fitful far-off skeleton
> Dimming as days draw by. (*CP*, p. 309)

II

While in Hardy's poetry there is a powerful sense of a world "out there," there is an equally powerful sense that odd and distinctive principles of selectivity govern what the poet notices and responds to in that world. For Hardy, the art lay in the principles of selectivity: "Art is a changing of the actual proportions and order of things, so as to bring out more forcibly than might otherwise be done that feature in them which appeals most strongly to the idiosyncrasy of the artist" (*Life*, p. 228). The poet does not create in the sense that he makes a new imaginative fusion, a new reality with the materials of the commonplace; Hardy seldom celebrates the imagination or any kind of creative power in the manner, for example, of Wordsworth or Coleridge. Rather, he calls attention to what appeals distinctively to him: "in life the seer should watch that pattern among general things which his idiosyncrasy moves him to observe, and describe that alone. This is, quite accurately, a going to Nature; yet the result is no mere photograph, but purely the product of the writer's own mind" (*Life*, p. 153). The matter of art is ordinary life ("actual proportions and order of things," "Nature") but what art reveals is not this common-place matter—it is there for all people to see with their own eyes—but a new and distinctive way of seeing it: "Art consists in so depicting the common events of life as to bring out the features which illustrate the author's idiosyncratic mode of regard; making old incidents and things seem as new" (*Life*, p. 225). The tendencies of things seem determined, or, if not determined, at least unalterable; the artist resists the tendencies by seeing them in his own idiosyncratic way.

It was Hardy's idiosyncrasy to see and describe the patterns of hope blighted, aims thwarted, achievement frustrated, realization, when finally arrived at, arrived at too late. Whether this idiosyncrasy was shaped by the peasant fatalism of the country folk among whom he was reared, by the works of nineteenth-century philosophical pessimism read in his youth and adulthood, by the thwartings and disappointments of his personal life, or by some hereditary blight of the soul, Hardy tended to define life downwards. The themes of life offering only to deny, of chance and change preventing the fulfillment of the heart's longings, of iron necessity's strict and remorseless limiting of the boundless possibilities that hopeful and vulnerable humanity can conceive for itself—these themes appear in a multitude of forms, ranging from a shaking of the fist at the cosmos, through a quiet questioning of the ironies of fate, to protective withdrawal to a safe place from which to view the futile welter of human doings. These themes and forms are so broadly pervasive as to lead some readers to perceive ironic pessimism as the only note heard in Hardy's poetry. One early poem describes a winter landscape in "neutral tones" of white and gray, where long ago lovers parted after bandying words on the dispiriting subject of "which lost the more by our love" (*CP,* p. 12). Another poem questions the meaning of a similarly diminished landscape, "dawning, pool,/ Field, flock, and lonely tree," offering among other answers that it might be the "live remains/ Of Godhead dying downwards," and ending in bleak uncertainty: "No answerer I. . . ." (*CP,* pp. 66–67). A late poem recalls a childhood experience of seeking shelter from the rain in a bower of ferns where, despite the drops that trickle through, the child made "pretence I was not rained upon," and asked the foresightful question, " 'Why should I have to grow to man's estate,/ And this afar-noised World perambulate?' " (*CP,* p. 864). Another late poem describes how an early poetic thought sprang up with "the lightness of a lark . . . then leapt all over the land," only to return "maimed and mangled": "Yea, verily, since its birth Time's tongue had tossed to him/ Such travesties that his old thought was lost to him" (*CP,* p. 865). In still another late poem of old age, he expresses his impotence to fill the dead silences of an empty house with the sounds of vitality from the past: "It seems no power on earth can waken it/ Or rouse its rooms" (*CP,* p. 866).

The sustaining power of love, the joy in communion with nature, the affirmation of something transcending the limitations of human beings, the renewed vitality to be gained from examining one's growth and development, the capacity of the creative imagination to fill the silences with song, the ability of poetry to inspire human sensitivity

—these are among the great themes of English verse. Hardy thrilled to such themes, but they did not accord with the way things looked to him. He often quite consciously subverted them, sometimes with a twinge of guilt at the futility of doing so, as in "He Resolves to Say No More":

> Why load men's minds with more to bear
> That bear already ails to spare?
> From now alway
> Till my last day
> What I discern I will not say.

In the last stanza of this poem Hardy suggests the terms of his self-defense: the truth, no matter how unpalatable, is liberating. Yet, all things considered, it might be better for liberated seers to remain silent:

> And if my vision range beyond
> The blinkered sight of souls in bond,
> —By truth made free—
> I'll let all be,
> And show to no man what I see. (*CP,* pp. 929–30)

For Hardy the choice was between describing things as he saw them and remaining silent; there was no middle way. In much Victorian literature an effort was made to find a middle way, to reconcile traditional values to a changed world, to see a transcendent nobility in suffering and in modes of acceptance and renunciation, to console and ameliorate. Matthew Arnold is a case in point. He himself wrote poetry of diminished vision (in his most familiar poem the world is said to have "really neither joy, nor love, nor light,/ Nor certitude, nor peace, nor help for pain"), but he felt profoundly uncomfortable with verse that merely exposed desperate truths. He found sustenance and inspiration in the literature of the past, and he applied to the present, standards derived from a tradition of poetic consolation and stay. In the decade before Hardy wrote some of his most militantly bleak poems, Arnold suppressed his *Empedocles on Etna*—a poem about the loss of faith and vitality that ends with the hero's suicide —explaining in words applicable to much of Hardy's poetry that he deplored works "in which the suffering finds no vent in action; in which a continuous state of mental distress is prolonged, unrelieved by incident, hope, or resistance; in which there is everything to be endured, nothing to be done"; and he defined a "poetical" representation as one that will "inspirit and rejoice the reader ... convey a charm, and infuse delight." Arnold here is speaking of drama, not of lyric, but it is no wonder that, having associated poeticalness with inspiration, joy, charm, and delight, qualities infrequent in his own verse, he should have gone on to abandon the poetry of diminished vision and taken up an educational mission, the central theme of which was the sustaining power of culture: how knowledge of "the best that is known and thought" can help one define and develop the "best" in oneself. Arnold returned to lyric expression when he had developed the confidence that he could see "the morning break," as he does in "Obermann Once More"—when, catching the echo of his father's voice dispelling "Panic, despair," he could cry out, "On, to the bound of the waste,/ On, to the City of God," as he does in "Rugby Chapel"—when he could find consolation and stay in the personal and cultural past, as he does in "Thyrsis":

> The light we sought is shining still.
> Dost thou ask proof? Our tree yet crowns the hill,
> Our Scholar travels yet the loved hill-side.

Arnold, in asserting that poetry should offer vitalizing sustenance and nurture to the reader, speaks for a prevailing Victorian critical taste, for a great poetic tradition, and for an eternal human longing. For Hardy, the yearning for positive vision, which, as a human being, he shared, was a curious and painful anomaly of existence, a trick of the cosmos. The critics' desire for a literature of hopefulness in a culture whose advanced thinkers seemed to be defining out of existence most of the bases for hope, was, for Hardy, ossified conventionality. What appealed to Hardy in the Greek tragedies was not catharsis, but the sense of grim inevitability; and the iconoclasm in writers like Shelley and Swinburne was the element of the great tradition that he found most fully congenial. He abandoned novels of vast, fatalistic melodrama (some of them, it should be noted, many readers have felt to be tragically "poetical" in Arnold's sense of the word) for poetry of diminished vision, not because he associated poetry with inspiration, joy, charm, and delight, but because it meant for him freedom, freedom to counter prevailing views, freedom to describe the truth as he saw it: "Poetry. Perhaps I can express more fully in verse ideas and emotions which run counter to the inert crystallized opinion—hard as a rock—which the vast body of men have vested interests in supporting. To cry out in a passionate poem that (for instance) the Supreme Mover or Movers, the Prime Force or Forces, must be either limited in power, unknowing, or cruel— which is obvious enough, and has been for centuries—will cause them merely a shake of the head . . . If Galileo had said in verse that the world moved, the Inquisition might have let him alone" (*Life,* pp. 284–85).

Hardy will always have an appeal as a man speaking out with quiet force against the establishment. He presents himself as a clear-eyed seer who unflinchingly denies pacifying illusions. He does not resist belief as a matter of choice:

> Why thus my soul should be consigned
> To infelicity,
> Why always I must feel as blind
> To sights my brethren see,
> Why joys they've found I cannot find,
> Abides a mystery.

One would think that the believers would at least have tolerance for their benighted fellow—"My lack might move their sympathies/ And Christian charity!"—but instead they "charge that blessed things/ I'd liefer not have be" (*CP,* pp. 67–68). Hardy associates the bustle of blind optimism with the times, with mainstream Victorian opinion:

> The stout upstanders say, All's well with us: ruers have nought to rue!
> And what the potent say so oft, can it fail to be somewhat true?
> Breezily go they, breezily come; their dust smokes around their career,
> Till I think I am one born out of due time, who has no calling here.

In this poem Hardy resists "the potent," who charge that the man taking "a full look at the Worst . . . disturbs the order here" (*CP,* p. 168). In his poetry Hardy contrasts the certified powers with the humble few, the well-bred with the lowly born, urban sophisticates with untutored provincials. In "Mute Opinion," the established authorities speak out "Through pulpit, press, and song," but the "large-eyed few, and dumb,/ Who thought not as those thought there" see the truth; things turn out "Not as the loud had spoken,/ But as the mute had thought" (*CP,* p. 127).

I have said that Hardy resists seeing himself as a prophet or visionary or elevated sage, and that he instead presents himself as a humble recorder of a world seen personally, idiosyncratically. There is a sense, however, in which he is a spokesman, giving voice to the mute, expressing the vision of the "large-eyed few." The toilers of the countryside, the humble provincials and lowly born whom life offered little and denied much, the disappointed in love, the bereft, the betrayed, the rejected—even the abused birds and beasts of the fields and woodlands—it was these among whom Hardy counted himself, these whose experiences compelled his attention. He could do little to console them or ameliorate their lot, but he could make them be seen and heard. Underlying Hardy's bleak vision is compassion, a terrible identification with unmerited suffering. The powers proclaim; the dynasts quarrel; the sages and prophets offer sophisticated rationalizations; the poets dream fanciful visions. Through Hardy, the humble cry out: "Our aims have been thwarted; we are perplexed; *we are in pain!*" In his poetry, one of their number resists the potent and disturbs the order, seeing things in his own way, and putting things in his own terms.

And how strange his own terms could be! Several years ago, when I was teaching a graduate seminar on Hardy's poetry, I walked into class one day and found written on the board, " 'Pits, where peonies once did dwell'— *YUCH!!!*" The line comes from "The Revisitation," a narrative written in an improbable stanza form, in which a middle-aged soldier revisits the scene of a youthful courtship late at night, and finds that his former lover has been mysteriously drawn to the same place. The two fall asleep, and when they awake in the daylight, the soldier, seeing the ravages of time in the woman's features, recoils involuntarily. She notes his response, the two quarrel, and then they part in bitterness just as they had done years before. The speaker concludes, "Love is lame at fifty years." The stanza in which the offending line appears reads, in part:

> Time's transforming chisel
> Had been tooling night and day for twenty years, and tooled too well,
> In its rendering of crease where curve was, where was raven, grizzle—
> Pits, where peonies once did dwell. (*CP,* p. 194)

Already at that time the poem had become one of my favorites of Hardy's, partly for its strange combination of romantic yearning and bitter fatalism, but also for the bulldog tenacity of its unpoetically idiosyncratic language. But the students didn't like it.

The students' response to Hardy's style is a common one. One often finds something like it in the academic criticism as well as in the early reviews: if not rejection, scornful resistance, and if not these, condescension. The stanza quoted above, said the students, was fumbling, inept, a failing attempt at something better. To the argument that Hardy may well have intended exactly the experienced effects, the reply was that he then had no poetic taste, that he did not understand what poetry really is. "O Willer masked and dumb!" Hardy cries out to one of his fancied deities, accusing it of "labouring all-unknowingly,/ Like one whom reveries numb" (*CP,* p. 186). It is not unnatural to recoil in numbed astonishment from lines like these, and to assume that the "Willer" who created this poem also labored unknowingly.

Many English poets have employed language that is harsh, grating, labored, bizarre, or prosaic; and we have been taught to seek out an organic expressiveness, an appropriateness of the language to the matter of the poem. Certainly this is sometimes possible in Hardy. The labored, prosaic diction in "To An Unborn Pauper Child" could be said to fit the wasteland world of the poem:

> Hopes dwindle; yea,
> Faiths waste away,
> Affections and enthusiasms numb;
> Thou canst not mend these things if thou dost come. (*CP,* p. 128)

The metered prose of the conclusion to "The Impercipient" seems appropriate for a speaker who is unable to join the "bright believing band": "Enough. As yet disquiet clings/ About us. Rest shall we" (*CP,* p. 68). The contorted last lines of "Hap" seem to hiss grotesquely with the defiance of one who lacks even the comfort of knowing that some "vengeful god" had intended his suffering:

> —Crass Casualty obstructs the sun and rain,
> And dicing Time for gladness casts a moan. . . .
> These purblind Doomsters had as readily strown
> Blisses about my pilgrimage as pain. (*CP,* p. 9)

And there is certainly effective onomatopoeia in the description of an artillery burst made by the old soldier who speaks in "Valenciënes": "A shell was slent to shards anighst my ears" (*CP,* p. 20).

197

Yet in situations in which only the greatest strainings of critical ingenuity could define an organic appropriateness, Hardy again and again startles and challenges the reader with the bizarre word, the contorted phrase, the labored circumlocution, the grating sound. In a lyric recollecting early romance, he describes the play of sunlight on the waves with the odd phrase, "purples prinked the main" (*CP*, p. 351). Sometimes there appears to be unintentional comedy: "—People frisked hither and thither"; "the worms waggle under the grass" (*CP*, pp. 686, 765). In one of his most widely admired poems, Hardy expresses the disparity in the relationship between his past and present self with labored circumlocution and obscure imagery:

Down there I seem to be false to myself, my simple self that was,
And is not now, and I see him watching, wondering what crass cause
Can have merged him into such a strange continuator as this,
Who yet has something in common with himself, my chrysalis. (*CP*, p. 319)

Elsewhere he describes his childhood illusion of his mother's omnipotence with lugubriously ponderous solemnity: "Deeming her matchless in might and with measureless scope enbued" (*CP*, p. 169). One often gets the sense even of haste, carelessness, or ineptitude:

But I saw not, and he saw not
What shining life-tides flowed
To me-ward from his casual jot
Of service on that road. (*CP*, p. 684)

"To me-ward"! This is a favored construction of Hardy's, found also in "To An Unborn Pauper Child":

Vain vow! No hint of mine may hence
To theeward fly: to thy locked sense
Explain none can
Life's pending plan ... (*CP*, p. 128)

Prosaic flatness, skewed syntax, grating sound, bizarre diction, odd coinages—these are so prevalent in Hardy's poetry as to characterize his voice as a poet, as to be personal idiom.

It is claimed in the *Life* that the apparent inartistries of Hardy's style were intended, a product of "the art of concealing art." As for irregularities in rhythm and meter, "He knew that in architecture cunning irregularity is of enormous worth, and it is obvious that he carried on into his verse, perhaps in part unconsciously, the Gothic art-principle . . . resulting in the 'unforeseen' (as it has been called) character of his metres and stanzas, that of stress rather than of syllable, poetic texture rather than poetic veneer; the latter kind of thing, under the name of 'constructed ornament', being what he, in common with every Gothic student, had been taught to avoid as the plague" (*Life,* p. 301). Hardy thought that the more emotional and passionate the poetry, the less poetic the diction. In the Preface to *Lyrical Ballads,* Wordsworth "should have put the matter somewhat like this: In works of *passion and sentiment* (not "imagination and sentiment") the language of verse is the language of prose. In works of *fancy* (or *imagination*), 'poetic diction' (of the real kind) is proper, and even necessary" (*Life,* p. 306). For Hardy, the imagination—the power to create fanciful visions (which, of course, was not what Wordsworth meant)—produces a poetry that requires a special kind of language to sustain its effects. In contrast, when the poet expresses the passion felt in response to perceived, not imagined, reality (when he wants passionately to explain why a pauper child should never be born), he speaks the language of prose ("Affections and enthusiasms numb"); this language, thus employed, has a music of its own: "Poetry. There is a latent music in the sincere utterance of deep emotion, however expressed, which fills the place of the actual word-music in rhythmic phraseology on thinner emotive subjects, or on subjects with next to none at all." Hardy sees this idea to be "the only one which explains all cases, including those instances of verse that apparently infringe all rules, and yet bring unreasoned convictions that they are poetry" (*Life,* p. 311). Hardy seems to posit two kinds of poetry making two kinds of music: on the one hand the poetry of veneer, of constructed ornamentation, of mere imagination, of rhythmic phraseology; on the other, the poetry of cunning irregularity, of texture, of passion, of sincere utterance, of rule-infringement. The first category is self-evidently poetry, the kind of thing that we are used to; the second, of which Hardy's is one of countless possibilities, appears to be something else, but it brings the unreasoned conviction that it is, after all, poetry.

An unreasoned conviction of a poetry in unpoeticalness—this is a central experience that grows upon the attentive and persistent reader of Hardy's poems. For me, Hardy's theorizing about rhythm and diction seems rather facile, evidence mainly of his consciously resisting a tradition of high poetic eloquence. The language of his poetry is just plain idiosyncratic, and there is no way to provide a rational basis for accepting and even loving it. Discussing Wagner and Turner, Hardy once applied his idea of idiosyncrasy to aspiration and style. He prefers the late phases of both artists, he wrote, "the idiosyncrasies of each master being more strongly shown in these strains. When a man not contented with the grounds of his success goes on and on, and tries to achieve the impossible, then he gets profoundly interesting to me. To-day it was early Wagner for the most part: fine music, but not so particularly his—no spectacle of the inside of a brain at work like the inside of a hive" (*Life,* p. 329). What Hardy strives for in the style of his poetry, it seems to me, is a language that is "particularly his," that brings him into existence as a unique seer and speaker, that is appropriate not to what it describes or even to the speaker's emotions, but to his own voice, its distinctive tones and inflections. It is impossible fully to achieve this task, for language, to be useful at all, cannot be unique, but must be communally understood; yet the effort is "profoundly interesting," not beautiful, not inspiring, not uplifting, necessarily, but interesting. Although Hardy was morbidly sensitive to criticism, he risked being scoffed at for his efforts, for he was confident that the hostile critics were narrowly conventional, unwilling to adjust to work that did not meet their expectations: "It is *the unwilling mind* that stultifies the contemporary criticism of poetry" (*Life,* p. 383). Attacking the romantic notion that great poets die young, he insisted that "the glory of poetry lies in its largeness, admitting among its creators men of infinite variety" (*Life,* p. 384). Hardy's relevance in part lies in his unflinching effort to enlarge the boundaries of poetry by presenting the reader with the buzzing idiosyncrasies of a unique voice. "Pits, where peonies once did dwell" —unreasonable as it may seem, precisely to the extent that this line in its repellent oddness fails the test of all conceivable touchstones, it is profoundly interesting.

III

As a poet, Hardy has been difficult for scholars to place in terms of literary history. Should his poems appear in anthologies of nineteenth- or twentieth-century literature? Should they be taught in Victorian or in modern courses? To be sure, he was born in 1840, and most of his ideas and poetic tastes and techniques were shaped in the mid-Victorian period. Yet his poems did not begin to be published in quantity until 1898, and most of them were written in the first quarter of the twentieth century. The studied formal qualities of the verses as well as the use of simple song and unembellished rural tale seemed, in an age when considerable formal experimentation occurred, to hearken back to a past that the poems often depict with controlled longing, even nostalgia. Yet the bleakness of vision and the sense of crushing irony seemed to reflect home truths for readers, old as well as young, who lived through the First World War. Hardy is not quite in tune with Tennyson, Browning, or Arnold, nor with Yeats, Pound, or Eliot. He seems to share more affinities with American poets like Edwin Arlington Robinson, Edgar Lee Masters, and Robert Frost than with most of his countrymen, and with the youthful British poets struck down or blighted by the war like Wilfred Owen, Rupert Brooke, and Siegfried Sasson than with most of his own generation. Often he is presented as an anomalous lingerer from one period, or as a curious forerunner of another. Somehow he does not quite fit in.

Hardy's long life certainly helped shape the distinctive character of his poetry. He seemed to have lived beyond his time, and in many of his poems he speaks with the voice of a ghost, a phantom, a spectre from the past—as a person not fully present. He writes as one who has experienced the diminishment of physical power, who has seen the creeds of his childhood shattered by the progress of thought, who has witnessed the passing of the customs and values of the country society in which he was born and nurtured, who has suffered the deaths of his parents, siblings, wife, and old friends, who has watched the faith in the future of a thriving age dashed in a cataclysmic slaughter. Yet for Hardy the sense of not quite fitting into one's time is typical of the human condition: everyone seems somehow to be in the wrong place at the wrong time because everyone is unaccountably endowed with the ability, almost always thwarted, to live in the heart and the imagination beyond the contingencies of circumstance. The old person's feeling of valued things lost is the converse of the young person's hopeful illusion that things can be bettered, change and chance transcended. The rhythms of circumstance jar against the rhythms of the heart:

> I look into my glass,
> And view my wasting skin,
> And say, "Would God it came to pass
> My heart had shrunk as thin!"
> . . . . .

> But Time, to make me grieve,
> Part steals, lets part abide;
> And shakes this fragile frame at eve
> With throbbings of noontide. (*CP,* p. 81)

Hardy is a Victorian at odds with the Victorian mainstream, a modern at odds with the onrush of events. It is always possible to surrender—to drift with the stream, to rush on with events—and remain mute. This would be denial of life and self, and Hardy refused to surrender. He felt the power of circumstance to be crushing, but it could not blind his eyes, it could not stop his heart, it could not obliterate his memory, it could not arrest his pen. What is central to Hardy's poetry is not the fact of old age or any circumstantial condition of his existence in the realm of change and chance, but the throbbing heart, the unblinkered vision, the vivid memory, the moving pen. These endure, and survive the disappointment, the diminishment, the failure, the loss. What makes Hardy's poetry so interestingly sustaining is his refusal to be quieted, his insistence on having his say as a way of asserting his identity and dignity against the drift of things. Even something within himself called for silence, as he cries out in "He Resolves to Say No More": "O my soul, keep the rest unknown!" All praise to the forgetful god who allowed Hardy to delay this resolution and postpone its expression until the close of his last, posthumously published collection of poems!

NOTES

1. *The Complete Poems of Thomas Hardy,* ed. James Gibson (New York: Macmillan, 1976), p. 7. Hereafter abbreviated *CP.*
2. Florence Emily Hardy, *The Life of Thomas Hardy, 1840–1928* (London: Macmillan, 1962), p. 363. Hereafter abbreviated *Life.* This edition combines *The Early Life of Thomas Hardy* (1928) and *The Later Years of Thomas Hardy* (1930), both published by Macmillan in London. The *Life* is actually an autobiography written in the third person by Hardy with the assistance of his second wife.